BRIEF GARLAND

By the Author:

Brief Garland
Komantcia
Rifles for Watie
Sports and Games

BRIEF GARLAND

●

By Harold Keith

Thomas Y. Crowell Company / New York

Published in the United States of America
By Eakin Press
A Division of Sunbelt Media, Inc.
P.O. Box 90159
Austin, TX 78709
email: eakinpub@sig.net
www.eakinpress.com

2 3 4 5 6 7 8 9

1-57168-334-8

L.C. Card 73-140644

for
my granddaughter
Cynthia Marie Hollinger
who in fourteen more years will be
old enough to play girls high school
basketball.

Author's Note

●

In researching this story, I leaned heavily on my nephew Jim Keith, former girls' basketball coach at the Sayre, Oklahoma, and Elk City, Oklahoma, high schools and president of the Oklahoma High School Girls Basketball Coaches Association. His philosophy of the sport, knowledge of its strategy, and sympathetic understanding of its girl players were invaluable.

Two other outstanding girls basketball coaches who gave assistance in personal interviews were Charles Heatly, coach of state championship teams at Lindsay, Oklahoma, and Chuck Neubauer, athletic director of Valley High School of West Des Moines, Iowa, who coached state championship girls teams at Gladbrook, Iowa, High School. Iowa is also a hotbed of the girls high school game and I wanted that perspective, too.

Two former players at Sayre, Oklahoma, High School—Mrs. Donna Ryan of Lorenzo, Texas, and Mrs. Jerry Ann Bibb of

Liberal, Kansas—graciously gave me help from the player's viewpoint.

My appreciation goes also to Bruce Drake, former University of Oklahoma and United States Olympic assistant coach; to Chet Bryan, who formerly coached basketball at Norman High School; to Ray Thurmond, University of Oklahoma freshman coach, and to Aaron and Louise Fischer, publishers of the *Waynoka,* Oklahoma, *News.*

To Robert L. Pendarvis, Norman attorney, I am indebted for advice concerning the story's legal aspects. Prudence Little, assistant to the attorney general of the state of Oklahoma, kindly found for me the little-known Oklahoma statutes forbidding the disbarment of married students from attending high school or participating in extracurricular activities. Suzanne Samson contributed valuable editorial advice.

Others who gave information were my mother, Mrs. Arlyn Keith; Dr. Don Robinson; Ken Rawlinson; W. E. Blackwood; Jim Rutherford; the late J. Don Garrison; Bert L. Corr, Jr.; Mrs. Gin McLean; Maury White; Dr. Gene Braught; Leo Higbie; Wayne Cooley; and the late Lance Ewbank.

Foster Harris, director of the University of Oklahoma professional writing school, read the story in manuscript. So did four Norman High School students—Frankie Robinson, Loppy Robinson, Sherri Berthrong, and Earl Singh—and Lynn Dickinson, who attended Norman Central Junior High School. I am grateful to them all.

Harold Keith

Contents

A Note from Coach Jim

This book is written about a coach and a team in Oklahoma when schools played a very popular six player game of basketball. In this version, the court was divided in half. The three guards played defense when the opposition forwards had the ball. The guards went on offense when they gained possession of the ball. Then they advanced the ball to the forwards, who attempted to score. The forwards played defense when the opposing guards gained possession of the ball. Neither guards nor forwards were allowed to cross the center line. It created two three-on-three half-court presses at each end of the floor.

In the 1980s the rules were changed. Girls, as well as boys, would play the five player game on the full court. Girls across America quickly adapted to the traditional game.

The two games are alike in many areas. The strategy is similar. The five player game is one of power and running. The six player game is one of finesse, requires less physical prowess, and has more room to operate.

The role of the coach is the same in each game: The relationship with the players; the team discipline; the teaching of fundamentals; the conditioning; the public relations between parents and fans; and being the chief promoter of girls' basketball in the school and community are the responsibilities common to coaches in both games.

This book is about the six player game in Oklahoma, because it was the only basketball for girls at the time. This in a great story about girls' basketball, and its climb to respectability with other sports.

This is the special situation of a man who had been forced to coach a girls' athletic team. He found the girls to be great competitors and students of the game. He loves it and never wants to coach boys' athletics again.

This book was originally written with the rise of girls' athletics in America. Due to the tremendous growth in all female sports, especially girls' basketball, it was decided to reprint this "classic."

It will bring back many memories to those who played the game and will inspire the younger players of today.

Coach Jim Keith, retired

BRIEF GARLAND

Chapter 1

●

Oral Agreement

Middleton was a different sort of town, and as he drove into it in late August, Lee Driskill had no warning of the trouble that awaited him there.

He braked at a stop sign and marveled at the power of the wind. A large cardboard box skipped end over end across two yards, clumping noisily. A cluster of small elms, bent and buffeted by the gale, leaned crazily toward the road, looking as if they were about to tiptoe across it. The courthouse's water sprinkler, rotating slowly, threw a feeble spray toward the parched lawn, but the water seemed to disintegrate in the savage gusts and be blown all over the landscape.

"The shortgrass country," Lee Driskill mused. "Where men gasp for air every time the wind drops to less than forty-five miles per hour." His voice, curiously penetrating despite its light tenor quality, carried well against the blast.

His wife, Jean, laughed. She was a wiry girl whose brunette hair lifted in the breeze. "That's the first word you've spoken in half an hour," she said. "You're the quietest basketball coach I've ever seen. You're not this quiet when you're wearing that red baseball cap and blowing that whistle down on the court."

The corners of Lee Driskill's mouth crinkled good-humoredly but he did not reply. A level-eyed young man of twenty-six, he wore a well-cut blue shirt, striped tie, and gray slacks, indicating that despite his modest salary he liked to dress well. The long, straight line of his chin suggested that he expected discipline on his teams and would enforce it firmly.

In every mile of their trip they had seen the grayish shortgrass that resembled an immense golfing green. Lee was a history teacher, as well as a coach, and he knew all about this curly sward that grew so close to the ground that a rancher from another state hunting for pasturage would have passed it by. Yet it afforded the finest year-round grazing of all. When trampled upon, it stood up again as curly as before. Even in time of drought cattle fattened on it, just as had the buffalo herds hundreds of years earlier when the only inhabitants of the land were the wild Comanche Indians and their implacable enemies, the helmet-crested Spanish horsemen.

Jean turned around, facing the back seat. "Alice,

he's sure high and mighty since he got this Middleton job. He won't even talk to us now that he's making eight hundred dollars more salary money. He's so delirious with joy that he'll probably forget himself and get up early every morning to cook our breakfast while you and I sleep."

The big gray setter in the back of the three-year-old sedan raised her head and whined, her feathered tail brushing back and forth across the vinyl seat covers. The Driskills had wanted children but were unable to have any, so the dog enjoyed many privileges and lived in the house like one of the family.

Pressing his toe against the throttle, Lee Driskill pulled across the intersection. Jean's teasing, he knew, stemmed from her pride in him. She gloried with him in the position he had earned. He was eager to meet the boys who would play for him on the Middleton High School basketball team. His captain, a sunburned kid named Scott Wells, he had already met and liked. After five years as an assistant coach it felt good to have his own team at last. It felt good to have a head job and to know that he could handle it.

Through the dust he saw the high school building of native limestone which he had visited in July when he had come to talk to John Bannister, the superintendent, and to rent the four-room brick house where they had already unloaded their furniture.

He parked in the shade and got out. "You want to come up with me, Jean? It might be cooler up there. I'm going to find Mr. Bannister."

"I believe not. I'll take Alice home and leave her in the house. Then I'll drive downtown and shop for groceries. I have my key. You go ahead and do whatever you have to."

Lee headed up the stairs. There was no air conditioning and the halls were stifling, but the place hummed with activity. Teachers, most of them women, hurried from room to room, preparing everything for tomorrow's enrolment and the coming of the students. On the second story, Lee found the superintendent's office.

But the man seated behind the desk was not Bannister. A big, squat stranger, with a face like an automobile wreck before all the broken glass had been swept up, was barking orders and dominating everything. Who is he? Lee wondered. Where was the superintendent? Lee saw that the stranger had particularly intimidated Miss Rogers, the superintendent's secretary, a kindly, older woman who wore silver spectacles. Nervous and discomposed, she fluttered about, trying to please him. Three other teachers, also waiting to see him, were cowering against the wall.

Lee waited two whole minutes and saw that the stranger was deliberately refusing to take notice of him. Finally he walked behind the railing and thrust out his hand. "Excuse me, I'm Lee Driskill, boys basketball coach," he said. "Where's Mr. Bannister?"

The big stranger turned around slowly. His eyes, beady and black and vigilant, flicked insolently up and down the coach's slight frame, scrutinizing him from head to heels. He ignored Lee's hand.

"I don't care who you are, sir. You're going to take your turn. Stand back of that railing." His hair and eyebrows were shaggy and streaked with gray. His voice snapped like a bullwhip.

Astonished, Lee stepped back.

When the man turned and walked away with a weaving sideways motion, his large head and huge misshapen shoulders reminded Lee of a cobra's hood. On the other side of the room his voice was still abusive. "Miss Rogers! Miss Rogers! Where are you?"

Fear in her face, the secretary hurried in from a nearby storage closet where she had gone to find a pencil. "Yes, sir?"

"Miss Rogers, would it be asking too much around here for you to stay on the premises long enough for me to dictate some letters? When I need you, you're always gadding about somewhere else. Get your pad."

While Miss Rogers jumped to find it, the man turned again to face Lee. "And you're not the boys basketball coach."

The words stung Lee Driskill. He stiffened with shock and felt something hot, savage, and altogether violent rising in him. Staring at the man, Lee saw a triumphant leer come over his face as if Lee's emotional agitation had fed and satisfied some sadistic hunger within him. Instantly the man's mood changed. He smiled with charming sweetness, and Lee felt the goose bumps rising on his arms.

"We've switched you," he purred, his voice suddenly gone soft and silky. "You're still coaching. But not boys basketball. We have somebody else to coach our boys."

For a moment, his little eyes continued to dart over

Lee, wringing every possible shred of enjoyment from the scene. Then he turned, and with one hand rolled the superintendent's swivel chair under him, spun it around so that the back was in front, straddled it, and eased his bulk into it. Ignoring Lee Driskill, he began to dictate to the distraught Miss Rogers.

Lee walked out of the office and down the hall.

"Lee! Lee Driskill!" Hugh Morgan, the principal, strode toward him. Lee had met the principal during his previous visit. Morgan was tall, balding, jovial. He wore a white shirt and bow tie. "It's good to see you, Lee, boy! When did you get in?"

Lee gestured over his shoulder toward the office he had just left. "Who's he? The big, insulting guy back there."

"That's Gus Brawley. President of the school board. Glad you're here, boy! Get moved in all right?"

"What's going on here? He just told me I wasn't the coach." Lee waited for an explanation.

Morgan's neck began to crimson. He looked embarrassed. "You're still coach. But not of the boys team."

"That's what he said. If I'm not coaching the boys team, what am I coaching?"

The principal dropped his eyes unhappily. "You're coaching the girls team."

Lee's mouth popped open. "I'm what?" He wouldn't be caught dead coaching any girls team. They had released the girls coach back at Fairfield, where Lee had been coaching, because he couldn't handle girls. Girls weren't serious about basketball. Girls were high-strung. The only thing those Fairfield girls wanted was to travel on the team bus with their friends on the boys team.

"I'm sorry, Lee. I know how badly you wanted to coach boys."

Lee was still thinking about those Fairfield girls. They didn't want to learn basketball. Worst of all, they didn't want to win. They just wanted to wear shorts before a crowd. The Fairfield superintendent had begged Lee to take the job, promising him a raise. "Just unlock the gym before practice and throw the ball up. Just keep order," he had pleaded. Lee had turned him down flat.

Lee frowned, determined to have the reason. "Mr. Bannister hired me to coach your boys team. Where's Mr. Bannister?"

Morgan wiped his hands across the hips of his slacks. "Lee, Mr. Bannister had a heart attack yesterday—a bad one. He's in the hospital. They aren't letting visitors come within a mile of him. If he pulls through, he's going to be laid up for a long, long time."

The news staggered Lee Driskill. The superintendent, a thin man, had looked healthy. "I'm sorry," Lee said. "He seemed like a good man. I was looking forward to working under him."

Morgan dropped his eyes again, then raised them frankly. "I'm going to level with you, Lee. Most school boards consist of one voice and four echoes. It's that way here. Gus Brawley is the voice of our board. He gave the land on which this school stands, so he runs the school board and hires and fires the teachers. He gave the land on which the Methodist church stands, so he runs the church and picks the pastor. He runs the whole town. He owns much of it. He's mixed up in farming, ranching, and oil. He's in the bank. He controls everything through his loans and influence.

He hired Bannister. Now that Bannister is ill, he's taken over the school himself. He was a superintendent someplace in Texas twenty years ago."

Lee continued to stare and frown. "Who's he putting in my job as boys coach?"

"Bill Hooper, the university's star player last year. You've read about Hooper, all-state, all-conference, all-everything. He's George Brand's nephew. George Brand is president of Brawley's bank. He's also on the school board."

Lee blew out his breath in one long weary exhalation. The picture was clearing. "Looks like that lets me out. Everything's all cut and dried. I can't go back to Fairfield because they've filled my job there. I'm all moved in here, and I find out I don't have the job I was promised. But I'm not about to coach anybody's girls team. I'm going home and make some phone calls. I'll get another job."

Morgan looked almost stricken. "Hold on now, Lee. Everybody here likes you. Everybody was impressed with you when you visited here last month."

"I'll say they were. They were so impressed with me that they gave my job to someone else before the bell rang for the first class."

"Things might work out yet. Hang on a while. Don't be sore."

Lee turned to go. "I am sore. Sore as the devil. But I'll get over it, I guess. So long."

As he walked downstairs, he dreaded having to tell Jean. She liked their new home. An automatic washer and an electric oven came with the house. Jean had looked forward to the new conveniences. She had earned them. And now, this.

Lee walked home. When he sank into the big chair in the living room, angry and discouraged, something cold and damp thrust its way between his hands, and a shaggy head lay in his lap. The dog's brown eyes looked at him devotedly. Lee pulled her ears affectionately. Alice always seemed to know intuitively when he needed mothering.

I must rouse myself, he thought. There's so little time left. Then he thought of one thing he'd have time to check before Jean came home.

Taking the dog, he walked to the hospital, a white frame structure standing on a hill in a grove of black locusts. Lee hoped to see Mrs. Bannister for a moment. He thought she might volunteer some explanation for the board's strange action.

He found her sitting huddled in a rocking chair in an upstairs lobby, a frightened little woman in a black sweater. She looked so different from when he'd met her in July, so shaken and depressed, that he decided to say nothing about his job. With her sat their two children, a boy eleven and a girl nine. Fear darkened their young faces, too.

As Lee bent over her, the creaking and sighing of the tree boughs outside seemed almost a lament. "Mrs. Bannister, I'm Lee Driskill, the new basketball coach. I met you last July when I came over to talk with Mr. Bannister about my new job, remember?"

She seemed touched and pleased that he had come. Her low voice barely discernible above the gale, she said, "Of course, I remember you, Mr. Driskill. How is Mrs. Driskill? You rented the Hogsett house, didn't you? Are you all moved in?"

"Yes, we've moved. Mrs. Driskill is fine. I just found out about Mr. Bannister. I'm awfully sorry for you. If there is anything Jean and I can do—anything at all—please let us know." He looked at the two youngsters. "How about the children? Why don't you let me take them home with me for dinner? Why don't you come too? We'd like very much to have you all."

"Thank you, Mr. Driskill, but they've eaten. We all want to stay right here together—in case we're needed." She peered up at him, her face filled with fear.

He lingered for a moment, visiting with them. As he walked away, he was haunted by the resigned, stricken look in their faces as they sat there helplessly, listening to the moaning of the wind, waiting for the tragedy that might strike at any moment.

At home that night, Jean took the bad news calmly. While she browned the salmon cakes and dished up the cole slaw, Lee settled himself at the small telephone table and wore out the long distance. The results were discouraging. Everyone sympathized with him, but all the jobs were filled. There was no shortage of advice, a lot of it inflammatory.

"Don't let them get away with it, Lee! They're working you like creamery butter."

"Talk to the other school board members."

"I'd go get me a lawyer and take 'em to court."

Lee thanked each of them and stayed on the telephone. He finally reached the man he had tried to call first of all but who had been involved in a night staff meeting.

Joe Brody, principal at Varney, one hundred miles southeast, had been football coach at Fairfield, where Lee had been basketball assistant. Lee knew that Varney, like Fairfield, was so small that if you drove through it real fast on Monday you couldn't see the town because of the wash on the lines. But he didn't care. The smaller the town, the more important basketball was. He'd coach anywhere.

"Hey, Long Knock! Don't let 'em tie that anvil round your neck," Joe exclaimed. He had nicknamed Lee "Long Knock" after Lee had once hit a golf ball three hundred yards with the wind in a match between them. "I coached a girls team back at Doxey. That's why I got out of basketball. The girls' fathers tried to run my team. Especially the fathers of the worst players. They resented a coach who couldn't win with *their* girl playing when he had won with somebody else's girl playing. It got awfully bad. You'd be surprised how many friends my wife and I lost. We considered nobody our friends until after their daughter had graduated."

Lee squirmed. Joe sounded more like a coach than a principal. Finally Joe cooled off and got to the point.

"I wish I had something here for you, Lee, but we're like all the other schools at this time of year. We've hired all our teachers. If somebody here quits unexpectedly, or if I hear of anything any place else, I'll get right on the phone and call you."

Lee thanked him and hung up. For a moment he sat silent, dropping his arm and drumming his fingers against the leg of the chair. He couldn't think of anybody else to call. At the table Jean placed blue napkins to the left of each plate. "It's ready."

Later, while she poured hot water over the washed dishes, she said, "Why don't you call Mr. Henderson?"

Farrell Henderson, who operated an insurance business back at Fairfield, had formerly been superintendent of schools there. It was he who had given Lee his first coaching and teaching job.

"I think it has come down to what you may have to do, not what you want to do," Henderson counseled. "Although I know it's distasteful to you, had you thought about going ahead with the girls team for the present? It beats quitting blindly with no other job in sight. When the superintendent returns to duty, I'd go see him. If he hired you to coach boys basketball, then he'll surely want to do something about this. If not this year, next year. You still have your nice raise in salary. I think you've arrived at the place where you've got to think intelligently, not emotionally, about this. How's Jean? Give her our best."

That night Lee lay awake, staring into the darkness and wrestling with his problem. Jean was asleep beside him, her breathing slow and regular. Why do I coach? he asked himself. Why don't I get into something else?

He turned on his side, smoothed his pillow, and thought about it. He liked boys. He and Jean had even wanted to adopt a boy, but so far they hadn't been successful. Also, he was fond of basketball. Every time he saw a basketball game he wanted to get into it. With him, coaching ranked next to playing. Like an architect or a composer, a coach created an exciting something that the whole community could embrace. It was fun to get wrapped up in a team and all the boys in it, and to watch them develop and mature.

Lee sighed and flipped over on his back. Coaching was like narcotics; once you started, it hooked you. He remembered his friend Jim Fessenden. Jim had a degree in mathematics from Princeton. He had also played tackle on the football team there. On the day they handed him his diploma an insurance firm offered him ten thousand dollars a year to start as a junior actuary. But the position wasn't exciting enough. Jim turned it down to take a job at six thousand coaching a high school football team in Kansas.

But this wasn't Kansas. It wasn't even coaching boys. This was a new town and a new job. He hated to be pushed around, by that surly school board president or anyone else. If he was ever going to get his team back, now was the time. He had to act fast. Enrolment started at nine.

Next morning Lee drove to town early and parked. Most of the stores were closed, but that southwest wind was up and doing business. It rattled the shop-windows, shook the streetlights, and hurled the long rope and chain attached to the town flagpole noisily against the staff. But the air was cool, and water from the sprinkling wagon lay on the freshly washed streets.

Stooky & Son, Attorneys-at-Law. In the amber light of the morning sunshine, Lee read the brown letters on the small, varnished sign. It was early for lawyers to be at work, and Lee had misgivings; but when he tried the glass door, it opened and he walked in. An oldish man with backswept gray hair and a gray moustache looked up from his task of brushing off his steel files with an old-fashioned feather duster. He was wearing black-framed spectacles and had on a coat and a tie. Lee Driskill knew this must be the elder Stooky.

The lawyer transferred the duster to his left hand and came forward. "Good morning, young man. Sam Stooky here. What can I do for you?"

His harsh, jangling voice sounded like bells out of tune, but his extended hand was big and freckled and warm. A mysterious bubbling noise came from somewhere in the rear of the office.

"Does the wind here blow this hard all the time?" Lee asked.

"No, sir," the lawyer answered. "It'll maybe blow this way for a week; then it'll change and blow like the dickens for a while."

They sat down, and Lee Driskill told Sam Stooky all about the broken promise. "I want you to represent me," he concluded. "I want them to stand by their agreement and give me back my team." The bubbling grew louder, and Lee smelled hot coffee.

Sam Stooky stood and retreated behind a partition in the rear. Something moved on the wall to Lee's right. A big yellow cat, its cheeks extravagantly whiskered, rose from its bed amid the lawbooks on a library shelf and stretched luxuriously, thrusting out each foot in turn.

Sam Stooky returned with two bright pewter mugs full of steaming coffee.

"Good morning, Buck," he addressed the cat, "you ought to know something about this. You slept all night on Corbin's treatise on contracts."

"Mmmrrrow," muttered Buck hoarsely. With a soft thud, he dropped to the floor and ambled out the back door.

Sam Stooky handed Lee one of the mugs. "I'd be happy to represent you, Mr. Driskill, but first let's visit a little about it. What does your contract say your position with our school consists of?"

Lee sighed. "It says history instructor and basketball coach. But it doesn't say I'm the boys coach. It just says coach. I should have my head examined for signing something like that."

Sam Stooky held out a white sugar bowl with a spoon in it. "I doubt if that's too damaging. Oral testimony is admissible. Did you ever hear of a thing called 'Reform to Speak the Truth'? That's the legal term for an oral agreement such as you and the superintendent had. Because of it, we can go to Superintendent Bannister, and we can say, 'Look, fellow, you and I both verbally understood and agreed that I would coach the Middleton High School boys basketball team. Either you let me coach them, or I'm going to take you to court.' And I think we'd have a strong case."

Lee blinked, feeling a rush of hope.

The lawyer went on. "But unfortunately Mr. Bannister has just suffered a heart attack, a severe one. I imagine he's in our hospital's intensive-care ward. That means people aren't even allowed to call on him—let alone talk to him or excite him with threats of a lawsuit. And he's obviously too weak, and his condition too dangerous, to submit to a deposition—which is testifying in writing under oath. So until he completely recovers, we'd be powerless to compel him to do anything. That means I can't help you until he gets back on the job, which may take months."

Lee Driskill licked the dryness from his lips. Time was against him. Basketball practice started soon.

He stood. "Thank you, Mr. Stooky. How much do I owe you?"

Sam Stooky also stood. His look was sympathetic.

"Not one cent, young man." He picked up the feather duster again. "Let me ask you something. Purely out of curiosity. You've still got a teaching and coaching job here at a good raise in salary. Why don't you take it? What have you got against girls basketball? Don't you like girls?"

Lee felt wound up like a spring, ready to snap. "I like people who stand by their agreements," he said. He turned and walked out. He was so upset that he forgot to thank the lawyer for the coffee.

As he strode into the school on his way to Hugh Morgan's office, the halls vibrated with the babble of voices, the banging of locker doors, and the rush of hurrying feet. Happy excited voices rang out gaily as boys and girls carrying armfuls of books and supplies paused to greet each other and chat briefly of their summer experiences. Lee saw that this was a much bigger school than the one he had left at Fairfield—bigger building, bigger student body, bigger challenge.

He found Morgan and told him that he would begin coaching the girls basketball team. "But it's only temporary," he warned. "I'm going to have a showdown with Bannister when he comes back to work."

Morgan looked relieved. "That's fine, Lee. I don't blame you a bit. Oh. I forgot to tell you. You'll have one very fine player. Tall girl named Helen Burnsides. Our girls won only three games last season, but Helen averaged twenty-one points a game. She was all we had."

Morgan showed him his office in the gymnasium, a former storeroom reconstructed that summer, so that Bill Hooper's new assistant, Ike Pettit, could have the office of the former girls coach. The principal gave Lee a key and left.

Lee fitted the key into his pocket ring and looked around once at the pitifully small room. Well, he told himself, you walk the ice and hope she's solid all the way across.

Chapter 2

●

Through the Ventilator

Not only did everybody in Middleton defer to the wind, the school named its basketball teams for it. The Tornadoes, as the girls team was nicknamed, practiced at noon. The boys squad—the Cyclones—got the most desirable time, the last period in the afternoon. The school buses that took most of the students back to their homes on the farms and small ranches left promptly at four o'clock, and since most of the students lived in the country, most practices were scheduled during school hours.

Lee Driskill never forgot that first practice. The girls came tripping down the stairs to the gymnasium, twenty of them, hair tossing, heels clicking, trim legs blurring, the scent of their perfume an abomination to his nostrils. To Lee, they seemed like a broken dam with the waters foaming and tumbling about his feet, then spewing into the sunshine to flash in rainbow hues. They were laughing, talking, giggling, whispering, biting their nails and fooling with their hair. Some walked decorously; others slouched. Some skipped; others strolled. As they rushed past him, singly or together arm in arm, to change into their practice gear, it seemed to him that they were thinking about everything in the world but basketball.

When he summoned them with a blast on his whistle and felt all their eyes furtively on him—blue eyes, green eyes, brown eyes, gray eyes—he felt like a man who had blundered into a beauty salon.

It didn't take him long to discover that, except for Helen Burnsides, a tall, imperious girl who habitually stood with her hands on her hips, they knew very little about basketball. They walked with the ball, threw it away, dribbled awkwardly; and when they fell, they lay on the floor laughing. They moved so slowly compared to boys that he lost his patience with them.

"Faster! Faster!" he shouted once. "You run like a frozen creek."

He hadn't realized there were spectators until a scornful whistle floated down from the upstairs balcony. Several boys, some of them wearing red-and-black football jackets, were watching the workout. Each time they whistled, the girls would look up.

Lee stopped the drill. "I want you to keep your minds down here on the court, not up there in the balcony," he lashed them. "The boys aren't whistling at you because they think you're cute. They're making fun of you because you're fouling up down here. I'll bet you couldn't pay them to watch you in a game. They'd be too embarrassed."

The girls listened to him silently, the only sound their shallow, uneven breathing.

Lee Driskill walked over to the west side of the court and faced the handful of boys seated in the balcony above. "All right! The show's over. I want you to get up and leave. We don't want spectators when we practice."

Surprised, they obeyed him, filing out an upstairs door. He saw that one of them was Scott Wells, captain of the boys team.

Lee looked at his watch. Ten minutes to one! Where had all the time gone? He closed the drill by putting the girls around and around the court on the run.

When they trudged to the shower, the spontaneity was gone from them. As Lee undressed, an odd thing happened. Although a solid brick wall separated his new office from the girls' dressing room, he could hear them talking about him above the hiss of their showers in the background.

"He got mad at us before we even walked out on the court," one said incredulously.

"I've never run that much in my life. I don't want any more of that."

"I'm quitting because we've got a man coach. My mother says Mr. Driskill has no daughters, so what does he know about coaching girls? She thinks we need a woman coach, one who understands our physical limitations and abilities."

"Nonsense!" a deeper voice spoke calmly. "Look at Crockett. Girls basketball is cool there. They won the state last year. We talked to them after they clobbered us. The best girls in school go out for their team. They've got a man coach. They like him."

When Lee walked out, dripping from the shower, Oral Cross, the custodian, handed him a towel.

"Thanks," Lee said. "Say, Oral, where are the girls' voices coming from? I can hear them as plainly as if they were right here in the room with us. Sounds like two or three may quit."

Cross listened a moment. Then his eyes fell on the ventilator in the corner. "Might be coming through that." The custodian faced Lee. "Coach Driskill, you'll find out soon enough about these girls. They think basketball is just a big physical education class. The coach last year threw the ball out and let it go at that. He didn't care whether they won or lost. Sometimes I think the only reason we have girls basketball here is to collect the forty-dollar gates their papas and mamas spend coming to see them play."

Seven girls quit that first day instead of two or three. Four more quit after the second workout. Again the reasons came through the ventilator.

"I'm quitting because my daddy says he's against girls playing the first game of a doubleheader. He doesn't want me used as bait to draw a crowd to the boys game."

"Teresa says she's quitting because she's afraid basketball will make the calves of her legs bigger and ruin her figure."

"She's wrong about that." Again the low, calm voice bit through the tumult. "Look at Jane Ann Jayroe of Laverne. She won Miss America after playing three years of high school basketball. There's nothing wrong with her figure."

Lee hurled the damp towel angrily into a corner and moved out of hearing range.

One of the second-day casualties was Helen Burnsides. Lee had stopped a scrimmage to reprimand her. She made little effort to guard or rebound and seemed interested only in shooting.

Finally she slammed the ball down so violently that it bounded into the adjacent seats. She gave Lee a regal, disgusted look. "You can have my suit. I'm not accustomed to being yelled at like this, or to running ten thousand meters after I've had lunch."

Lee Driskill bowed low. "All right, your highness. Since we can't let you practice in the luxury to which you're accustomed, we'll excuse you." Glaring at him, she walked to the locker room and banged the door shut behind her.

He faced the others. "Anybody else feel like folding up and following the star?" One or two looked mutinous, but nobody spoke. When practice ended, Lee stalked off the court stiff-legged as a fighting rooster. He doubted if he could take much more of that kind of attitude.

At the end of the fourth practice, Cindy Butts, a roly-poly blonde, walked up to Lee. She stood only five feet one and had butter-colored freckles on her pug nose. He braced himself for another desertion.

Sweat running down her face, she looked him right

in the eye. "Coach, you can't yell loud enough to run me off. I've been out for basketball here three years now, and I've never played a minute. All I've ever done is ride the bench. But I like the way you coach. Even if you never play me a minute, I'm staying out. All season."

Surprised, he recognized the low, calm voice that had come through the ventilator.

"Thanks, Cindy," he stammered. Afterward he took stock of the situation. Perhaps he had yelled too much and been too gruff in spite of all the provocation.

At the end of the workout he blew his whistle and faced them. "In fairness to the privacy you're entitled to, I think I should warn you that when you talk about me in your locker room, your voices come through the fresh-air ventilator into my office. I can hear you plainly. If you want to talk about me, okay—but if you don't want me to hear you, perhaps you'd better keep away from that ventilator."

The color of their confusion was pink, and it showed along their cheeks and in the tips of their ears. Flustered, they could only stare at him.

"Of course," he went on more gently, "I'd rather you'd come to me and talk about it. We'll elect a captain November first. She'll be a senior, preferably a starter. I want you sophomores and juniors to be thinking about which girl you could talk to best when you have a problem you don't want to bring to me."

Now the squad was reduced to nine, one full team and three reserves. But that became an advantage, Lee discovered. The ones he had left were there for business. More coaching time could be devoted to each. They needed it. None of them could dribble by feel or lay the ball up left-handed. He wished that he was coaching boys and that that surly school board president or Bill Hooper or somebody else was struggling with the girls. But apparently the boys squad didn't need him. Bill Hooper had them working hard, he heard. They had flogged Whitfield, a neighboring town, badly in a practice scrimmage. The *Middleton Mirror* carried a story about it, and the whole town buzzed about the feat.

Lee frowned, sleeving the sweat off his cheek. Girls basketball differed so utterly from the boys game. In boys basketball things happened so fast that each boy seemed a part of the action swirling up and down the floor. When a boy rose gracefully into the air to shoot, he jumped so high that he reminded Lee of a golf ball dropped on a sidewalk. The pace of a girls game went much slower. Girls played on a divided floor and had specialists, three to guard and three to get it in the basket. While half of them worked, the other half stood around like spectators. Lee thought it very dull.

Dull or not, he was saddled with it. The unanimous choice for captain was Cindy Butts. Lee moved Portia Stovall, a tall, bashful sophomore, into Helen's forward position. Portia was the best shooter among the substitutes.

For the next four weeks, his only achievement seemed to be the establishment of discipline. He hadn't realized he had accomplished this until six days before the first game. The girls bungled a simple screening play so badly that Lee decided to stop the workout and make them walk through the pattern. But first he wanted to explain it to them.

"Sit down!" he shouted, and headed for the nearby seats and a blackboard.

To his surprise, they all plopped down suddenly in their tracks on the court. He turned back, facing them."Why are you all doing that?"

Cindy Butts spoke up frankly. "Coach, when you say sit down we think you mean it. We don't even bother to look for a chair." Her remark eased the tension. Everyone laughed.

Lee Driskill grinned. "Okay. I didn't mean to be that tough. I can show you right here."

He dropped to his knees and with a piece of chalk diagramed the maneuver on the floor. The play had one option. If Portia was stopped by her guard, she passed to Cindy who broke for the goal from behind a screen set by Liz Blair. They bungled it as they had all the others.

After he had showered and dressed, he encountered Hugh Morgan on the stairs.

Morgan waited for him. "You might like to know that John Bannister is better. He passed the crisis point and goes home soon. The doctors say that after he rests three weeks, he can probably return to work for short periods."

Elated, Lee walked upstairs with Morgan. Soon he would have his long-postponed showdown with the superintendent.

Next day, Lee went to his office in the gymnasium to make a phone call. As he crossed the end of the court, a girls' gymnasium class was playing basketball. A small blonde pushed a chest pass to another girl, whipped around her guard, took a return pass, dribbled in, and laid the ball in the hoop for a goal.

Neat, Lee told himself. He delayed a moment to watch. When the game ended, he approached the blonde girl. "I'm Lee Driskill, miss. Girls basketball coach. May I ask your name?"

"It's Trudy Blinn, sir."

"You look as if you might learn to play basketball. We need players badly. Why don't you give it a try? We practice every noon."

"I'm in the band, Mr. Driskill. Clarinet."

"Come out anyhow," Lee urged. "Basketball will develop your lungs for clarinet. You might even find it more fun than the clarinet. Why don't you join us this noon? I could have a uniform all laid out for you."

An adventurous gleam lit Trudy Blinn's smoky blue eyes. "Okay, sir," she laughed, "you talked me into it. I'll be there."

"Eleven fifty-five sharp," Lee reminded. The girl was green, but he had liked the way she moved.

For the first twenty minutes Lee Driskill's drills baffled Trudy Blinn. She began to breathe hard. Her face reddened. She didn't dominate the high school squad as she had her gymnasium class, but in time she might become a player.

"We play our first outside game Friday at Brighton," he told her after practice. "We'd like you to go with us. I'll play you some. Why don't you talk to your parents about it? Our bus leaves the school at four thirty. We'd have you back by ten."

"I'll ask my mother, sir."

Trudy went with them to Brighton. On three occasions, she played briefly, and like all the other Middleton girls she didn't play well. Knocked down twice, she bounced to her feet, full of fight.

The defeat galled Lee cruelly. The Tornadoes scrambled hard for a while but eventually grew tired and lost their enthusiasm. He blamed himself. He could do something about their lack of condition—run them until their tongues dangled. He resolved to investigate the possibility of night practice.

After losing two more games, Middleton opened at home against Folsom. Lee winced when he brought his team out to play and saw all the empty seats. He would never get used to playing a girls preliminary. Most fans had just finished their dinners. Through the high west windows he could still see the rose and violet of the sunset. It was too early to go to a basketball game. Besides, no one enjoyed seeing his team clobbered.

To his surprise, Middleton won, 33–28. Folsom was unbelievably bad. Cindy Butts, despite her shortness, scored more points than anyone else—fourteen. Most of the goals came off the simple screen Lee had diagramed on the gym floor with Portia passing to Cindy after Sadie York, the third forward, set the screen. Afterward, the girls yelled and screamed joyfully and jumped up and down. Disgusted with their feminine silliness, Lee found Hugh Morgan, and they sat together at the boys game.

"You had a disappointing crowd, didn't you?" the principal ventured.

"What crowd?" Lee retorted. "Even when we were scoring goals it was so quiet in this place that I could hear the popcorn machine going out in the lobby." He shook his head, staring bleakly across the vacant court.

When the boys game began, the gymnasium was almost full. Lee couldn't keep his mind out of Bill Hooper's problems. He liked the fast break Hooper had brought with him from the university, but he thought the Middleton substitutes could have shown more enthusiasm. During time-outs, they didn't join the Middleton huddle on the floor but stayed on the bench, indifferent to the team effort. With Hugh Morgan sitting beside him, Lee leaned forward, watching Bill Hooper. A tall young fellow whose black sideburns dropped almost to the lobes of his ears, the new coach stood a great deal, frowning when things didn't go right. But he seemed competent enough. Finally, Scott Wells won the game with a lay-up off a fast break in the last four seconds.

The gymnasium trembled with the crowd's joyful shout. Lee Driskill stood and shook his head enviously. That fast break was a crowd-pleaser. He wished he could teach it to the girls, but their game was geared against it. How could you fast break when three guards, alert and rested, always waited for you at the opposite half of the court?

Afterward, when Lee and Morgan joined their wives at the car, they found Jean pale and shaken.

"What's the matter?" Lee asked.

She told him. Jim Stovall, Portia's father, had come up to her after the game. He had said angrily, "You might tell your husband that he has used my daughter as a stooge for the very last time."

Without a word, Lee turned and walked back to the gym. Hugh Morgan hurried alongside. "Stay cool, Lee," he kept saying. "Jim's a good guy, but he's been used to seeing Portia do all the scoring all through junior high school."

In the milling crowd, Lee found Stovall, a gangling farmer attired in blue overalls, black felt hat, and muddy boots. Lee backed him up against a wall. "If you have anything to say about my ball club, why don't you have guts enough to say it to me instead of to my wife?"

Stovall jerked away. "I will say it to you. I feel you're using Portia as a stooge, not taking advantage of her scoring ability."

Lee tried to put a rein on his own anger. "I'm sorry you feel that way, but I can't have one girl just shooting and not doing anything else. That makes it too easy for the other team to stop us. As long as Portia plays on my ball club, she's going to screen and pass and rebound as well as shoot."

The veins on Stovall's forehead stood out like ropes. "Then she won't be playing on your ball club."

Portia walked up just then, carrying her uniform in a plastic bag.

Lee Driskill looked at her. "Here she is. Let's ask her. Portia, how do you feel about the part you've been playing on our basketball team?"

Portia saw her father and her coach glaring at each other. She looked at her father and ducked her head. "Well, I'm not getting to shoot much."

Lee Driskill said, "Well, if that's the way you feel about it, maybe you'd better drop basketball."

Stovall spat angrily on the gymnasium floor. "You bet she's gonna drop basketball!" He faced his daughter. "Give him your suit."

Dutifully she handed Lee Driskill the plastic bag. But she wouldn't look at him. They walked off, leaving Lee standing there. For a moment, he stared at the uniform in his hand, letting the flush of bitterness die. Then he shook his head and looked at Morgan. "That's been the history of my life here at Middleton," he said bitterly. "I'm always left holding the bag."

That night winter blew its cold breath over the land. The north wind cut like a razor. The next morning, Saturday, Lee was up early. He put Alice beside him in the car and drove out into the country, watching the morning sun crimson the buttes and listening to the whistle of the wind in the power lines overhead.

He passed a small farm, and in the cold light of dawn he saw a basketball going up and down against a white backboard nailed to a garage front. Lee sat up. Who in the world could be shooting baskets outdoors in the morning chill? A boy, warmly clad in jeans, sweater, and a corduroy cap with earflaps, peppered shots at the homemade goal.

Lee slowed down, admiring the lad's perseverance in the teeth of the numbing gale. He knew how cold a pair of bare hands could get in that freezing wind, but the boy had solved that, too. A pickup truck stood nearby, the white exhaust from its running motor puffing from its tailpipe. Lee wondered about that until he saw the boy drop the ball, run to the truck, climb in the front seat, and hold his hands over the heater to warm them.

Lee braked his car, admiring the youngster's ingenuity. The boy returned to his goal-shooting, and as he stooped to retrieve the ball, his cap fell off, and his reddish-brown hair, bound by a small crimson ribbon, tumbled down his back in an unmistakable ponytail.

Lee Driskill's jaw dropped with astonishment. The shooter was a girl, a tallish girl; about an eighth grader in school, he guessed. He drove off slowly, watching her stick the ball monotonously through the hoop, but she never looked up.

"We had another girl quit us after the Folsom game," Lee told the squad Monday noon. "Her father wanted her to shoot more. I don't think it's necessary for me to talk to you about that. In any game, basketball included, it all comes down to one thing. Why do you play? Are you in it for what you can do for yourself? Or are you in it for what you can do for your school and your team?"

His hand toyed with the whistle around his neck. "We're going to run more in practice. We've been dying on the vine in the fourth quarter. That's when most games are decided. That's where the gut check comes. Also, we need a better time to practice. I'll see what I can work out."

Hugh Morgan wouldn't rule on that. "I'm sorry, Lee. Mr. Bannister always wants to handle that himself, and I guess you'll have to see Mr. Brawley."

Lee's eyes twinkled roguishly. "You mean Superintendent Brawley?"

Morgan nodded.

Lee knew what that meant. Another brawl with

Brawley. He decided to go and see the tyrannical school board president anyhow. He needed new basketballs, new playing shoes, new uniforms. He would go on Saturday. He didn't like his job, but the girls had a right to decent equipment even if they did butterfinger everything he tried to show them. At least, he had them trying harder.

Trying harder wasn't nearly enough in their next game. Crockett, the defending state champions, and their coach, Chet Chambers, showed Lee Driskill the high quality of girls basketball in the shortgrass country.

From the time they first paraded out onto the court in their woolly blue warmups with each girl's name sewn in gold letters on the back of her collar, until they walked off it an hour and fifteen minutes later, victors by thirty points, the Crockett team exuded class.

Lee sat with his mouth open, envying them. They were organized like a block-by-block Campfire Girls' candy sale. Pride seemed the motivating force behind them—pride in their record, their tradition, their coach, and their school. They talked and yipped to each other like professional baseball players. Their passes lanced in and out, quick and leveled. Their guards stopped everything. Sally Edwards, their best forward, a dark-haired girl whose black eyes flashed with the joy of combat, sank all eleven free throws she tried. The crowd of a hundred that came from Crockett demonstrated noisily.

On the Middleton bench, Lee Driskill squirmed, embarrassed by the contrast between the two teams. Middleton's pre-game drill, with her girls wearing the boys' cast-off warmups and stumbling through their archaic routine, seemed prophetic of the thrashing that awaited them. As Crockett's lead widened, Lee felt grudging admiration for Chet Chambers, his coaching rival. The man had worked hard and built well. Lee couldn't, however, help feeling a twinge of contempt. Why put in all that time and labor on a bunch of girls?

It was in this game that Lee learned something about girl players that he hadn't known before. One of Middleton's guards was Ginger Selman, a thickly built girl with dark curly hair who had grown up in the country. Accustomed to wrestling calves and colts at home, Ginger played her basketball rough.

She did not lack confidence. When Crockett scored its first three field goals by setting a screen and driving down the middle for lay-ups, Lee called time out. As the Middleton players gathered round him, Ginger slapped her hands together. "We'll get 'em, gang! It'll take a little time to wear 'em down but . . . . "

"It sure will," Lee broke in, frowning at her. "Ginger—what have I always told you and our guards about playing defense? Nobody takes the middle of that court away from us. When Crockett comes down that middle as they've been doing, I want you to stand 'em on their heads!" He had in mind what he had shown them so often in practice, that they should shoulder their way through the screens and block the scoring lane.

Play resumed. Again Crockett set up that pick. Sally Edwards glided smoothly around it, took a pass, and drove for the goal. Ginger, guarding another player, left her and met Sally Edwards knee-high with her shoulder, cutting her legs out from under her. The ball flew one way, and Sally sailed another, skidding on her back, feet up, across the sideline.

The referee came running. "That's a disqualifying foul! You're out of the game!"

Stunned, Ginger crawled to her feet. As she walked to the bench, she was crying softly. She didn't like being put out of the game on her own court, even if the bleachers were almost empty. Sally Edwards stood at the free throw line, laughing. Tough as shoe leather, she hadn't minded the hard fall. She sank both free throws.

Lee made room for Ginger beside him. "Ginger, that was pretty intentional, wasn't it?"

Ginger shot an unbelieving look at him, her face taut and tearful. "Coach, I've heard you say a dozen times that when anybody on the other team dribbles down the middle, to stand her on her head."

Lee Driskill swallowed hard and shuffled his feet. Girls were so literal-minded. A boy player would have known that you meant for him to plug the middle but to do it without pulverizing somebody. But girls believed everything you told them. He resolved to be more careful about what he told them in the future.

Between halves, Lee asked Ginger to go to the Crockett bench and apologize to Sally Edwards. And when the game ended, Lee swallowed his humiliation and apologized to Chet Chambers as they shook hands on the court. He also complimented the Crockett coach on his team.

"You start in where we leave off," Lee said.

"You've just begun to build a program in your town," the Crockett coach offered generously. "Next year, I'll bet you'll be hard to handle."

"No, I won't," Lee replied, positively, "because next year I won't be here. I'll be coaching a boys team somewhere."

Afterward he hunted up Ginger and apologized. "When I said for you to stand her on her head, I didn't mean for you to throw that running block on her. But I appreciate the fact that you tried to do exactly what I asked you to." He saw that she limped slightly. "How do you feel?"

Ginger's face was wan. "Mr. Driskill, I'm so sore I can't even put on my watch."

Lee laughed. "Hang in there. We'll get you in shape yet." He walked with her to the refreshment stand and bought her an iced drink.

Later he sat with Jean and the Morgans and watched the Middleton boys thrash the Crockett boys. Lee studied the Middleton boys team closely because he might yet be coaching them. He couldn't help looking for flaws. He noticed that they didn't seem to have the stamina necessary to run Hooper's new fast break offense. In the last half they called lots of time-outs, and their shooting accuracy fell off. But he grudgingly gave Hooper credit for staying with his "Go-go-go" style. And the Middleton crowd loved it.

Lee took it well until his eyes swept the seats behind the Middleton bench, and he saw Gus Brawley and George Brand, the banker, seated with their wives. Every time Middleton scored, Brawley and Brand grinned and looked around boastfully as if to say to the whole town, Look what we brought to Middleton! And look how well he's doing!

The next day was Saturday. Lee drove to town and found Gus Brawley's real estate office. Brawley sat alone at a bare table in a bleak disorderly room. One section of the ceiling had crumbled, exposing the plaster and lath. No wonder Brawley is the richest man in town, Lee thought. He never spends a dime on upkeep. And he'll probably be opposed to spending anything on the upkeep of girls basketball, too.

"My name is Driskill," Lee began. "You're Mr. Brawley, aren't you?" He didn't hold out his hand this time.

Brawley's glittering eyes swung slowly and reluctantly upward from the newspaper he was reading. For a moment they probed Lee nakedly, bright with suspicion and contempt.

"I'm girls basketball coach at the high school." Lee used the title reluctantly. "Can I talk to you here?"

"Here as well as anywhere, sir." Brawley didn't invite him to sit down, so Lee stayed on his feet.

He sucked in a breath and began. "We need new balls, new shoes, new playing uniforms, new warmups. We need a better practice time. We've been trying to work at noon, but it's hard to accomplish much when the girls have to practice on full stomachs right after lunch."

Brawley's broad dimpled chin began to lift, and his bushy eyebrows to come together with hostility. "You used the word accomplish, sir. What have you accomplished here to date in girls basketball? What's your team's record?"

Lee looked at him squarely. "It might be a better record, Mr. Brawley, if we had decent equipment. We need half a dozen new balls so that all our players can shoot at the same time and they'll get more shooting practice. Some of our shoes are so worn they're coming apart. Our playing uniforms are six years old. We're wearing castoff warmups handed down to us by the boys squad." He couldn't help thinking about the new outfits the Middleton boys were wearing. And Bill Hooper had so many balls to practice with that a portable rack with rubber tires had to be purchased in which to keep them.

Brawley snorted disdainfully. "Mr. Driskill, your team's record as of now is one–four. Mr. Hooper's boys team's record is four–one. Obviously he is doing a much better coaching job than you. Your request for new equipment is denied."

Lee's eyes never wavered. He expected to be turned down, but he had to try.

Brawley went on smoothly. "Our school board has even considered hiring a coach who won't run our girls as hard as you've been running them in practice." As he talked, he searched Lee's face as if measuring the effect of his remarks.

Lee fought to keep his composure. "There's more running in basketball than in any other sport, Mr. Brawley. If you run in a game, you have to run in practice. My girls could stand the running lots better if they could practice in the afternoon, when the boys practice. Yet you expect them to do their running right after they eat, while the boys, the stronger sex, wait to do their running until almost four o'clock." He licked his lips, feeling silly. Without meaning to at all he was making a pretty good pitch for a game he abhorred.

Brawley swung angrily at a winter fly that had buzzed him from the cobwebby ceiling. He looked at Lee with open insolence. "Mr. Driskill, I doubt if you'll ever show me you can coach anything. I don't think you've got it as a coach. Your girls team is so poor that our school board has even talked about abandoning the girls game and playing a boys 'B' game as the preliminary."

Lee laughed roughly. "That would suit me fine. I hope you never forget that it wasn't my idea to coach girls in the first place. I don't enjoy coaching girls. But no matter who coaches them, they're entitled to proper equipment. And a fair time to practice. How about letting us take turns with the boys practicing in the afternoon?"

Brawley's black eyes never left Lee's. "Your request to get your practice time changed is also denied, Mr. Driskill."

Lee knew that he was licked, but he was careful not to reveal his disappointment. He nodded crisply. "Good day, sir."

Brawley, not to be outdone, bowed with equal vigor. "Good day to you, sir."

That night Lee told Hugh Morgan about it. Morgan shook his head in puzzlement. "Gosh, Lee, tell you one thing. If you ever shake hands with that fellow, it would be wise to count your fingers."

Lee laughed bitterly. "I don't need to count my fingers because he hasn't shaken hands with me yet."

The incident seemed to draw them closer together. From that time on, the principal talked very frankly to Lee Driskill. They became good friends.

Rankled by Brawley's statement that "I don't think you can coach anything," Lee redoubled his coaching efforts. Nevertheless, they lost the Hollister game at Middleton by one point when Cindy Butts missed three free throws in the final forty-five seconds.

After Cindy's second miss, Lee called time out and walked onto the court to talk to the disappointed girl. "What in the world's wrong, Cindy? Your second shot went way left of the ring."

Cindy looked at him with honest chagrin. "Coach, how can I hit free throws with all those good-looking boys standing under the goal?"

Lee looked beneath the basket, and there they were, the entire Middleton boys squad, clad in their new red and black warmups, each lad's face shining and his hair slicked down. Crouched beneath the goal, they waited for the girls game to end, so they could warm up for their own game.

Later, Lee went to Bill Hooper and told him what had happened. Hooper nodded soberly. "I see. Don't worry about it. It won't happen again." And it didn't. And Lee revised his opinion of Middleton's boys coach.

John Bannister returned as superintendent the following Monday, working an hour and a half each morning and another hour and a half in the afternoon. He had lost color and weight, and seemed quieter and more subdued. Although Lee saw him briefly at the staff meetings, he did not bring up the coaching matter, hoping Bannister would first come to him. Finally, when the superintendent began working six hours a day, Lee could wait no longer.

The day after the girls lost again to Brighton, he walked into Bannister's office. Classes had ended, and the student population was on its way home in the long red buses. The sun slanting into the west window found a miniature in a gold frame on Bannister's desk and projected its shadow on the opposite wall.

Bannister looked up. "Oh, hello, Lee." A slight uneasiness crossed his face, as if he knew why Lee was there. "Shut the door, please. Sit down."

Lee closed the door and sat down. "Mr. Bannister, I don't like to bother you so soon after you've returned to work, but I can't take any more of this. When you phoned me last summer, you asked me to coach your boys. That's what I was doing at Fairfield, and that's what you asked me to do here. We agreed that I should be the boys basketball coach here."

Bannister nodded quietly. "We surely did, Lee."

Elated, Lee kept his voice steady. "Well, then, how about moving me back to coach the boys?"

Pain and helplessness came into the superintendent's face. "Lee, I appeal to you not to try to change what's working so well with our boys. Coach Hooper is doing a fine job. The whole town's excited about his team."

Lee stiffened. "Yes, but he's coaching my team."

Bannister nodded. "I know it. But I'm going to have to tell you that our boys like him very much. They're enthusiastic about him and about his fast break system."

Lee felt his heart pounding and his throat tightening with anger. "I think they would have been enthusiastic about my system. I don't know anything about coaching girls. I detest coaching girls. But I can coach boys. I've been an assistant boys coach five years. That's why you hired me here."

Bannister's eyes pleaded with him. "Lee, please don't press this or start a town fuss over it. It's always unwise to change something that's working smoothly."

Heatedly Lee said, "Girls basketball isn't working smoothly. Everybody in town wipes their feet on the girls program here. I don't see why you even have it. I want the job I was promised, the job I was hired for."

Bannister looked at him helplessly, then dropped his eyes. "I can assure you that if I hadn't suddenly got sick you'd be coaching our boys today as we agreed. But I did get sick. I'm sorry."

Lee stared at him, licking the dryness from his lips. He couldn't speak. But he knew he wasn't going to get his job back.

Bannister went on, lamely, "Lee, some things were done while I was in the hospital that I had no control over. This wasn't the only thing done that I wasn't consulted about. I guess it was impossible to consult with me. Somebody had to take over."

Lee thought savagely, Why didn't the principal take over instead of the school board president? But he stifled the question because of something he saw in Bannister's face.

Fatigue and torment were what he saw. Bannister

said, "You certainly have some redress coming. I don't know how yet, but I'll certainly make it up to you in some way." The superintendent spoke nervously and breathed more quickly.

Swiftly Lee got hold of himself, remembering the frightened looks of the woman and the two children at the hospital the day that Bannister was stricken.

He stood. "I'm sorry if I've pushed this so hard that I've caused you discomfort. I should have been more careful. Why don't you let me drive you home?"

Bannister's smile was pale and wan. "Thank you, but my wife is coming after me. We'll talk about this again sometime."

As Lee walked downstairs, the old forebodings knotted coldly in him again. He hadn't improved his own situation one iota. He knew that he was stuck with coaching the Middleton high school girls through the end of the season.

On the following Monday, the squad lost another player. Lee took the telephone call in the principal's office.

"Coach Driskill speaking."

"Mr. Driskill, this is Harriet Blinn, Trudy's mother. We've decided to take Trudy out of basketball so she can concentrate on the band. She doesn't have time to do both."

Surprised, Lee said, "I'm awfully sorry to hear this, Mrs. Blinn. We need players badly. Trudy was coming along fine."

"Was Trudy playing on your starting team, Mr. Driskill?"

"No, ma'am. But she's a front line substitute. She's played in every game. And I intended to keep playing her. She might develop into a starter by next year."

"Mr. Driskill, I'm going to be perfectly frank with you. Trudy is a starter now in the Middleton high school band. Every one of our one hundred and ten band boys and girls are starters. They're all on the first team. Why should my child play basketball?"

Lee winced. He tried one more tack. "Mrs. Blinn, what does Trudy herself want to do about this? I had the impression that she sincerely liked basketball."

"Mr. Driskill, what Trudy likes has nothing to do with it as long as she's only sixteen and lives with her parents. Mr. Blinn and I will decide what's best for her. Clarinet lessons come pretty high, Mr. Driskill. We've been paying for her clarinet instruction ever since she started in the seventh grade."

Lee knew when he was beaten. "Okay, Mrs. Blinn," he said calmly. "Thank you for calling me about it. Trudy's a nice young lady, and the basketball squad will miss her. Tell her we wish her good luck with the band."

"Good-bye, Mr. Driskill."

Hugh Morgan came in. Lee hung up the receiver and turned stiffly. "Well, I just lost another player."

Morgan's face registered sympathy when Lee told him about it. Lee shook his head glumly. "That cuts my squad to eight."

Morgan tried to ease the pain. "Tell you what, Lee. If you lose any more girls, I'll have to play. Of course, you'd have to get me a wig, a brassiere, and a pair of big black bloomers. I'd solve your crowd problem anyhow. They'd fill the joint just to see old Morgan give and go."

Lee frowned and toed the office rug reflectively. "I wish someone would tell me what's so special about a kid playing in a hundred and ten piece band. She's just a robot. Six steps one way, four steps another. They have no freedom about anything, no chance to freelance, no chance to think for themselves in action." He let his breath out wearily. "Of course, I might be prejudiced about it."

Morgan said, "Have you seen our junior high girls play? They've won eight straight. Their season ends ten days before yours. Then most of them will join your squad. Freshmen are eligible to play, you know. They're little, but at least you'll have more bodies."

The news didn't exhilarate Lee Driskill. Not only would he have more bodies, but also more problems, more interfering parents. One bunch of females was enough without another group joining them and further cluttering things.

He sank into his chair and picked up a book, thumbing through it reflectively. He didn't like anything about his job. Hardest of all to take was the weather. Yesterday the dust had blown so hard that the gymnasium grew dark. They had to switch on the lights. Every fifteen minutes they stopped so that Oral Cross could wrap his wide broom with wet towels and mop the dust off the floor.

Lee shook his head resignedly. He'd be glad when the girls hung up their togs. The long difficult season was nearly over.

Chapter 3

●

The Little Twisters

When Lee Driskill decided to stop bemoaning his dwindling squad and just deal with the days one at a time, doing the very best he could until the miserable season ended, the situation began to improve.

The lunch difficulty resolved itself when the girls decided to bring their lunch pails from home and eat following the noon workout. That saved having to stand in line at the school cafeteria and put them on the court thirty minutes sooner. Lee not only sprinted them harder but gave them two new screening plays, based largely upon what he had planned to use in his boys offense. He also designed new drills stressing rebounding and defense. As he worked and planned,

Gus Brawley's words kept goading him: "I doubt if you'll ever show me you can coach anything. I don't think you've got it as a coach." Lee wished he had the Middleton boys team. He'd show Brawley. He'd show them all.

The Tornadoes won half their games during the three weeks ending in mid-February, and in only one did they absorb a flogging, that one being the return contest at Crockett. When Lee lost Doris Crossett, one of his guards, for a week because she sprained her ankle, his squad numbered only seven, and he diminished the contact and began to emphasize play polish. But he couldn't help worrying. "Only seven players left," he told himself. "One over a full team. If I lost two more girls for any reason, we couldn't put a team on the floor."

The seven became eight later that month. Lee had dismissed a history class and started into the cafeteria to have coffee with Bill White, coach of the junior high boys and girls, when he was accosted in the hall by Helen Burnsides.

"Mr. Driskill, can I talk to you a minute?"

Lee looked at her coolly. "All right." For a moment they were alone near the stairs.

She glanced at him once, then dropped her eyes. "I'm sorry for walking out on you that day I got mad. I'd like to come out again for basketball. I've been shooting at home on a goal on our garage door. I've been doing some running, too."

Lee looked at her suspiciously. "How much running?" he asked dryly. She impressed him as a troublemaker, and he doubted if he should take her back.

"Not as much as I need to, I know. But I think I can help the team."

He frowned, mulling it over in his mind. Her experience and shooting would definitely help his small squad. But he didn't like players who quit. "See me at the three-o'clock study hall. I'll know then."

"Yes, sir. Thank you, sir." He watched her move down the hall with her queenly walk, a tall girl in a blue dress.

"I probably ought to have my head examined," he told Hugh Morgan later, "but I've decided to take her back."

A contrite Helen Burnsides reported for practice the following noon. She worked hard, ran hard, gave no trouble. Lee used her as a substitute at first, but she improved so fast that he had a talk with Cindy Butts just before the Sinton game.

"Cindy, I hate to do this to you but . . . ."

Cindy laughed, her freckled nose wrinkling pleasantly. "Forget it, Coach. I know what you're going to tell me. Been expecting it a whole week now. Helen's playing so well that she deserves to have her old starting position back. She'll team well with Liz and Sadie. That way, we'll have three tall forwards. Don't worry about me. I've sat on that bench so long I know every splinter in it."

Lee looked at her anxiously. Was she really taking it well, or was she just being Cindy? He felt bad about benching his captain to promote someone who had quit.

But the team braced, winning two games in a row. Helen scored sixteen points in one, seventeen in the other. That raised Middleton's seasonal record to eight victories, ten defeats. It didn't rank with the thirteen–seven record of Bill Hooper's Middleton boys or with the ten–zero rating of Bill White's Little Twisters, as the junior high girls were called, but it was progress. Lee Driskill sighed. Soon the season would end.

Lee drove the school bus to the Austin Creek game. Before his squad boarded, he saw Helen Burnsides laughing and holding hands with Art Fletcher, the football captain. Then Helen approached him.

"Mr. Driskill, can Art ride to Austin Creek with our squad? There's plenty of room in the bus."

Lee scowled. "No," he told her quickly and flatly. He didn't want any boy friends along. He wanted them to keep their minds on Austin Creek.

Helen's hands went to her hips, and she looked at him oddly. Then she turned to say good-bye to Art. Their leave-taking became so protracted that Lee and the others were kept waiting a full minute, sitting in the bus with the motor running.

The game wasn't decided until the final moment. Helen Burnsides scored twenty points but seemed to play with a slight irritation that took the edge off her accuracy. Lee wondered if she was upset because he hadn't let Art Fletcher ride with her on the bus.

With thirty seconds to play, Helen came to the foul line with the score tied. It was a one-on-one situation. If she made the first free throw, she would be given a bonus toss.

She seemed to discharge the ball carelessly and too quickly. It rolled off the hoop. Austin Creek rebounded and called time out.

Lee was on his feet in a flash. He looked around him on the bench. "Cindy!"

"Yes, sir!" Cindy Butts stood at his elbow, her eyes eager.

"Go in for Helen. Cover them on defense, but try not to foul."

Austin Creek played it coolly. Watching the clock, their forwards milked the time down to the last four seconds, then took a final shot. Lee set his teeth together, breathing in deeply. Maybe the shot would miss.

It didn't. The ten-foot jumper went through. Middleton had lost again. This time the girls didn't weep openly, although their eyes looked red. Their main emotion seemed to be disgust. They had failed by a point to do something they hadn't done all season, to win away from their home court.

Lee frowned at them as he picked up equipment and stuffed it into a bag. "Don't get mad, get even," he told them. "We play 'em again next Tuesday at home."

After the squad showered and dressed, everybody milled for a moment in the Austin Creek lobby. Lee saw Art Fletcher standing with Helen Burnsides' parents. Helen's father managed the Middleton cotton gin. As the team got on the bus, Helen came up to Lee. "Mr. Driskill, I don't feel well. Can I ride home with my daddy and my mama? So I can get to bed early?"

Lee stared at her. How dumb did she think he was? Art Fletcher was probably riding with her parents, too. He had probably ridden with them to the game. "Helen, when we take a bus our whole squad rides together in it, going and coming." Shifting his feet, he eyed her keenly. "And something else. See me Monday morning in my office ten minutes before classes begin. I want to talk to you about how you played tonight."

Anger clouded her face. Again her hands went to her hips. She was probably born with her hands on her hips, Lee decided. But she climbed obediently into the bus and rode all the way home without saying another word.

On Monday Helen Burnsides quit the squad for the second time. Lee hunted up Cindy Butts and apologized. "Worst mistake I ever made in coaching was demoting you. Or letting her come back after she quit once. I'm sorry, Cindy. Awfully sorry."

Cindy's grin blazed. "Coach, it's just like I told you. You can't run me off. I like the way you operate."

That made him feel worse. Gus Brawley was right, he told himself bitterly. I can't coach anything. At home two hours later, sleep came slowly. His guilt and helplessness nagged at him until a late hour.

Next afternoon he watched Coach Bill White's Middleton junior high school girls play their final game of the season. The all-victorious Little Twisters were matched with Grundy, a team they had defeated twice. Lee knew that could be fraught with danger. It was hard to defeat a team three times consecutively. It was hard to develop enthusiasm for it or to persuade your players to regard such an opponent seriously. Sitting with Hugh Morgan, Lee watched curiously as they shared a box of popcorn.

Surprise ruled him the minute the Little Twisters

poured out of their dressing room onto the court. Lee's right hand was full of hot popcorn, but instead of putting it into his mouth, he sat there holding it, enthralled. They averaged only fourteen years of age, but Lee soon saw why they were champions.

"Go get 'em, Twisters!" Hugh Morgan yelled in his deep bass voice as they sprinted past, but none of them paid him any attention. In their uniforms of plain white cotton, they only had eyes for the goal they warmed up on. They attacked it with shrill yelps. They had apples to pick, and the quicker they got at it, the better. Lee Driskill sat up, impressed.

"They know they're going to join your squad Monday," Morgan told him. "They know that you're here watching them tonight."

Lee Driskill doubted that. They hadn't even looked at him as they tore past, nor at their mamas, papas, boy friends, or anyone else. They had only one thing on their minds—beat Grundy and close the season all-victorious.

They did it 57 to 35. As Lee slowly munched the popcorn, he couldn't keep his eyes off one of their forwards. A trim, rangy freshman, she was the team's leader, and her clear, far-carrying voice rang out all over the court. She didn't look particularly fast, but when she drove around an opponent, she took such a long first stride that she got half a step advantage before the ball hit the floor for the first dribble. She wore a tiny crimson ribbon in the back of her rust-colored hair, and as she darted about the court, that ribbon and the portion of her hair it enclosed joggled saucily up and down.

Lee Driskill frowned. Something about her looked familiar. "Who's that forward?" he asked Hugh Morgan.

"That's Pat Thompson. She transferred last year from Eagle City. Her father used to play professional baseball. They live on a farm out there near you."

Then Lee recognized that here was the girl with the ponytail who had shot goals in the morning chill.

Another girl caught Lee Driskill's attention, too, a little doll-like brunette thing with enormous shining eyes and nostrils that seemed to quiver like those of a wild horse.

Lee felt Hugh Morgan's elbow punching his ribs. "That's Candy Brown. Isn't she a pretty little dish? She's the one the boys all want to go with. She's the junior high beauty queen."

Lee watched her flash in, eyes stormy, lips curled in a snarl, and jerk the ball away from a Grundy forward. Then she whipped a pass to Pat Thompson, who long-strided around her guard for another goal.

Lee stroked his chin. "Not very big, is she?"

Morgan chuckled. "Even the smallest hair throws its shadow." He looked at Lee apologetically. "A fellow named Publius wrote that two thousand years ago."

A third player also attracted Lee's interest. She had a long neck, and when she took the ball to the division line, stretching that neck and looking for somebody to pass it to, she reminded Lee of a lookout goose acting as sentinel for a wild flock feeding on a green wheat field. Although her passes lacked finesse, she always threw them to the right girl.

Lee's hand dipped into the popcorn box. "Who's

that one?" he asked. Her hair was straight and dark, and when the ball went to the other half of the court, she'd reach behind her with a movement of her hands and smooth the belt at the back of her shorts.

The principal's smile went out. "That's Frances Bonner." When Lee Driskill got a closer look, he saw green eyes and an oval face, strangely immature.

"She's had a rough home life," Morgan went on. "Her father's a country minister and awfully strict. Her mother is a quiet little woman with a sweet mouth and a meek disposition. But when anybody mentions going to the movies, her mouth hardens into a straight line and her body becomes rigid. They don't believe in dancing or wearing jewelry. They think a pack of playing cards is a lure of the devil. Our daughter Mary used to be Frances' best friend, but they broke that up, too."

"Why?" asked Lee Driskill, curious.

"Her father is so peculiar. He figures that Frances came into the world to be a shining example to all the young people in town. You know—as the minister's daughter who can do no wrong. They didn't let Frances join the pep club because all the girls in it wear short dresses. They let her work Saturday at the Variety Store but they take all the money she earns. Afraid she'll spend it for something worldly, I guess. They don't let her date. When she looks at a boy, her father whips her with his razor strap."

The principal looked disturbed. He crossed his long legs, shifting uncomfortably on the narrow seat. "I could talk all day about Frances Bonner. Frances and our Mary decided to be chums. Our families lived across the street from each other. The girls talked about the secrets they would have. They began walking home together with their arms around each other. One day they agreed to start to school half an hour before the first bell. Frances' father put a stop to it.

"He asked Frances why she wanted to sneak off to school half an hour early. She told him the girls wanted to go early and play tag. He told her he would whip her if she went early to play. He told her it was her natural inclination to do wrong, and he intended to prevent it. He wanted her to fear him. That's his idea of how to enforce discipline."

Listening to the strange story, Lee wiped the salt off his lips with his handkerchief and watched the girl in action on the court. She seemed to think with her feet as well as with her mind. He liked the way she pressed the Grundy guards when they tried to bring the ball to the center line. With flashing feet, she anticipated the direction they would take and covered them closely and cleanly every step. Leaning forward, Lee decided that she would have been a natural at one of the pleasures her parents seemed determined to deny her—ballroom dancing.

Middleton was to play its final home game on the following Tuesday—the return contest with Austin Creek. Lee had only one practice day to blend the junior high team with his own squad. But the Little Twisters couldn't practice at five o'clock in the afternoon, the substitute time Lee had arranged. They were having an end-of-the-season victory party at six o'clock in the upstairs lobby of the high school. It was a big event for them, Hugh Morgan explained, because they planned to surprise Bill White, their coach, with a gift. Reluctantly Lee had to practice without them.

It was a strange setting for a practice. While the gay laughter from the Little Twisters' party floated down from the lobby above, Lee Driskill drilled the Tornadoes on the court below. But all through the festivities, he was aware that the Little Twisters, most of them wearing the first high heels and party dresses of their lives, kept leaving the party and strolling in twos and threes to the balcony railing, a piece of fried chicken in one hand, a napkin in the other, staring with big eyes at the practice beneath them.

Amused, Lee knew what was passing through their minds. They idolized Bill White and probably wondered if they could ever play for any other coach, especially a hard-boiled one named Lee Driskill.

Lee turned away, provoked. Don't fret your pretty heads, he wanted to tell them. I don't want to coach you any more than you want to play for me.

Next night occurred the union of the Tornadoes and Little Twisters in the game against Austin Creek. The two Middleton squads hadn't practiced together. Although Lee had asked the Little Twisters to report at six o'clock, they were all there at five thirty, shoes polished, uniforms freshly pressed, scrubbed faces gleaming. The older girls, the Tornadoes, wore faded crimson twill; the Little Twisters, their plain white cotton jerseys and shorts. Lee watched them stumble through the warm-up drill together, then sent them to the dressing room.

When he entered five minutes before the tip-off, the tension lay thick as low country fog. Instantly he could sense the rivalry between the two groups. The Tornadoes sat on one side of the room, the Little Twisters on the other. Even the yellow-haired Crossett sisters, Doris and Dorothy, were caught up in the civil war and sat apart, Doris with her Tornadoes, Dorothy with her Twisters. Polite but in deadly earnest, each group eyed the other. The senior high girls knew the reputation of the junior phalanx, knew that some of them might appropriate their places on the team.

Planting one foot on the bench, Lee looked around him at the two divided units and decided that a little honesty might help. "Okay. Stop glaring at each other like the Cheyennes and the United States cavalry at the Medicine Lodge peace conference. You're not battling each other tonight; you're battling Austin Creek. You all go to the same school and play on the same team—Middleton. Okay. Let's covey up. On your feet." He looked around him. "Captain Cindy?"

Everybody got up and locked hands, forming a ring. On his left Lee Driskill had a Tornado by the hand, on his right a Little Twister. As the connecting force between both factions, he could feel the rivalry and hostility go out of them, and togetherness flow in like a current of warm, clean air. They weren't two groups anymore.

The ball went up at center, and Lee Driskill saw that his team had come to play. The Tornadoes, their pride aroused, were determined to do well in front of the crowd that filled a third of the gymnasium. Sharper than they had been all year, they began to pull away from Austin Creek. At the quarter, Middleton led by four. With three minutes left in the first half, their margin ballooned to nine, and Lee Driskill stood and looked around him at his bench. Tonight there were eight girls on his bench instead of the usual two, and he felt a sense of security.

"Pat!" Pat Thompson, the Little Twisters captain, stepped quickly to his side. "Go in for Sadie." She had her warmups half peeled off before he finished the sentence. "Just play it by ear," he told her. "You haven't had a chance to learn our plays."

With a flash of steady gray eyes, she looked at him coolly. "Yes, sir," she nodded, her ponytail jerking up and down.

Lee watched her, a lithe unruffled girl who didn't stumble or bump into anyone as she ran to the scoring table. Then he sat down, making room beside him for Sadie York whom Pat replaced. Sadie frowned as she slipped into her warmup shirt. She didn't like being taken out, but he wanted to test his reserves.

He looked up just in time to see Pat Thompson get her hands on the ball for the first time. The freshman forward took one dribble and faked a set shot, drawing her guard to her. She faked it so well that Lee, like Austin Creek, raised his head, looking for the loft of the ball. Instead she passed, buzzing the ball past her guard's left ear.

Cindy Butts swung out to meet the pass, beat her opponent to the goal and banked the shot right-handed. For a moment Cindy looked astonished. Despite her lack of size, somebody had finally got the ball to her. A glad grin overspread her face, and she and Pat Thompson ran together, embracing. That play made Pat solid with the Tornadoes.

A moment later Pat screened perfectly for Doris Crossett, who drove in for a lay-up. The ball came again to the Middleton forwards, and Pat faked a set shot. Then, jumping around her guard with that long stride, she glided in to score left-handed.

In the last half, Lee played his starters until the lead over Austin Creek swelled to seventeen. Then he substituted the six Little Twisters. Using their junior high plays, they fought the bigger Austin Creek girls to a tie in the fourth quarter alone. Pat Thompson scored twelve points in her first high school game, playing only ten minutes.

Lee Driskill stroked his chin meditatively and resolved on the spot that thereafter Pat Thompson would be his starting forward, even if she was just a freshman. The team needed her every minute, not just occasionally.

At home that night, Jean waited until she'd served Lee's favorite dessert, hot apple pie, before she told him the news.

"I've been offered a job."

Lee almost dropped his fork. Jean sat quietly, one hand twisting a lock of black hair over her ear. "At the Ford Company."

Lee wedged off another piece of pie and forked it into his mouth. "Gosh, honey," he kidded. "The Ford Company? Are you going to sell cars or work on the grease rack?" He knew it sounded corny, but he needed time to get used to the idea of his wife even considering a job.

Jean ignored his banter. "It's the bookkeeping job

Mrs. Phillips had. Joe Daniels phoned this morning. He said they'd heard I had worked as a stenographer before we got married. He said Mrs. Phillips is moving to Texas."

Lee swallowed the pie and suddenly found it tasteless. "Did you tell him we're not going to be here next fall? That any job you took would only be temporary?"

"I told him we weren't sure. That we might move."

"Might move? You know darned well we're going some place where I can coach boys."

She met his look squarely. "That's another reason I thought it wouldn't hurt for me to try the job for a while. You may not be able to get another school right away. Meanwhile, I'd save what I make. We might need it before you catch on somewhere else."

Lee fell silent. It made sense. But he didn't like the idea of his wife supporting him. He was wedded to the old-fashioned principle that the husband should earn the living.

"I told him I'd talk it over with you and let him know tomorrow."

Lee ran his fingers through his hair. Tomorrow seemed awfully soon.

Tomorrow dawned, and practice began for the district tournament. In the first round they would meet Ragan's Switch on the neutral court at Mesa. Eager and alert, the Little Twisters worked hard trying to learn Lee's offense although it was the first pattern play of their lives.

The final workout came at night. The girls trickled through the gymnasium door in informal attire—

mostly blue jeans, sandals, and jerseys of every hue in the spectrum. All except Frances Bonner. Her plain brown dress hung conspicuously four inches below her knees, and her low-heeled shoes seemed in keeping with the sartorial decorum demanded by her parents. She didn't say much, but Lee saw that basketball meant a lot to her.

Lee stationed her at forward on the second team, and after the first workout, kept her five additional minutes while he drilled her on set shots from all around the circle. She shot clumsily, beelining the ball at the hoop. Lee worked patiently with her, teaching her to arch her shots. She tried hard.

"Thank you for working with me, Mr. Driskill," she said shyly as they walked off the floor together.

Next morning Lee was awakened by the hiss of frying bacon. Jean was getting breakfast early so she would have plenty of time to dress for work. She liked her new job. "I meet a lot of people."

Lee dressed and reached for his razor.

Jean went on. "I even saw Gus Brawley yesterday morning. He never noticed me. He was looking for a pickup. Mr. Daniels took him around himself and showed him the different models. I think the other salesmen are afraid of him."

Reaching down by his knee where he knew her head would be, Lee stroked Alice's long silken ears, and the big gray setter shut her eyes in ecstasy. Lee said, "He hasn't been coming to the school so much since John Bannister came back to work. Say, honey, you got my coaching gear washed?"

"In your drawer." Jean kept her eyes on the bacon. Lee shot a look at her as he walked to the chest of drawers. Her new job affected her housework very little. She knew how to budget her time. She's organized, he told himself as he lifted the freshly pressed trousers and jersey out of the drawer, and switched his mind onto the coming game with Ragan's Switch. Big and experienced, Ragan's Switch had won sixteen of nineteen games. They'll beat us, maybe drub us, Lee told himself. Irritation gnawed him. Although this would be his last game ever coaching girls, defeat of any kind rubbed him raw.

Next afternoon, when the school bus hauling the team to Mesa arrived at the gymnasium, Hugh Morgan grinned from behind the wheel. "Climb aboard, Tornadoes!" he boomed, his big hand thwacking the horn button. "Get a good grip on the furniture. We're making no stops. This hack's traveling like a two-forty trotter on a shell road."

Everybody laughed. Morgan, a careful driver, rarely drove more than fifty miles per hour.

Standing outside near the door, Lee watched the girls mount the steps, one by one. Frances Bonner stood in line, confusion and shame in her face. She wouldn't look at him. Puzzled, Lee saw standing close behind her an older woman, a quiet little body with brown eyes and a sweet mouth. Like Frances, she wore no jewelry nor lipstick, and her dress fell almost to her ankles. Obviously she meant to accompany the team on the bus.

Lee moved closer. "I beg your pardon, ma'am. Aren't you planning to take the wrong bus? This is the girls high school basketball team. We're on our way to Mesa to play in the district tournament."

Her smile was trusting, almost benign. "I'm Mrs.

Bonner, Frances' mother. I always go with her on the basketball trips."

Lee Driskill felt as surprised as if the north wind had gusted and suddenly blown off his hat. "You do? Why?"

Her eyes glowed with righteous dignity. "To chaperone her." At her mother's words, the girl flinched as if she'd been struck.

Lee frowned. "To chaperone her? In the name of heaven, why does she need a chaperone on a trip with thirteen other girls, the principal, and the coach?"

"Mr. Driskill, the devil tempts young girls on a trip, same as he does anywhere else. The devil's ways are devious as the windings of a snake. Mr. Bonner and I don't intend for Frances to wander from the right course."

Astonished, Lee stared at her. "That's all very admirable, Mrs. Bonner. But it's not necessary. Frances is a fine girl. So are all the rest of our girls. And I'd rather not have parents or relatives or boy friends on my team bus. I just want the players. Then there will be no distraction, and they can keep their minds on the game."

Mrs. Bonner's sweet mouth tightened primly. "If I don't go, Frances doesn't go, either."

Lee looked her right in the eye. "Mrs. Bonner, we want very much for Frances to go. But I also want her to do as the other girls do, and none of them bring their mothers."

Her chin lifted piously. "Mr. Driskill, their mothers don't care what happens to them, or they'd be here going with them, too."

He tried a new tack. He knew the girl wanted desperately to play and needed the companionship of the other girls. "Why don't you and Mr. Bonner drive over behind us and see the game?" He had noticed the small sedan parked nearby. "I'll get you some tickets and leave them at the door in your name. Mesa isn't very far. About fifty miles. It would take only about an hour. Be my guests."

She shook her head. They were now alone in the line. Everybody else had boarded. From the interior of the bus, the hum of conversation and of laughter floated invitingly through the open door.

Lee said, "I'm sorry, Mrs. Bonner."

At his words, a stricken look fleeted across Frances' face. Turning, she began walking back to the family sedan, head down, shoulders trailing dejectedly. The mother followed.

On the bus, Hugh Morgan looked contrite as he wound the steering wheel vigorously. "I'm sorry. She always rides with Frances on trips. Bill White lets her. I forgot to tell you."

Upset, Lee took off his coat and settled himself behind Morgan. "I wish you had told me."

All the way to Mesa, Lee Driskill was depressed. Although he knew his decision was right, he had deprived a lonely girl of the chance to travel with her team and play a basketball game in another town, always an exciting experience. Apparently basketball was about all Frances Bonner was given much freedom to do.

Overpowering the Middleton guards, Ragan's Switch scored field goals on their first four possessions and whirled into an 8–0 lead. They had brought along a pep band and four hundred followers. Each time they scored, those four hundred would leap to their feet, waving black and gold pennants and roaring with joy while the pep band's slide trombonist would sink to one knee, flutter-tongueing his instrument to get the husky vibrato he wanted as he reached for the rhythm of "Hot Time in the Old Town Tonight."

Lee substituted Candy Brown, the freshman doll, for Sadie York, and Middleton began to do better. Pat Thompson hit a twenty-foot set shot from the front. Candy Brown flashed in front of a Ragan's Switch pass for an interception and bounced to Pat. Going clear by her guard with that long first stride, Pat drove but put the ball too heavily against the backboard and it twisted out of the ring. But Candy Brown, following hard, pounced upon the ball and forked it back in.

On the bench, Lee shook his head in awe, wiping his face with the towel. He had never seen a player that small go up so high for a rebound. As he watched Candy race back to her position, clapping her hands joyfully, he thought that, even if she did attract boys the way a sugar bowl attracts flies, if the next coach could teach her to go to her left, she could make quite a player.

Then Middleton's guards settled down. Seeing their forwards getting tough, they got tough, too. At the quarter, the Ragan's Switch lead had melted to 14–10. Midway in the second quarter, Candy beat her big guard to a rebound and did what she always did first—looked for Pat. With her back to the goal, Pat faked right, then cut left. Candy's bounce pass led her. With a screech of suction soles, Pat braked herself, jumped into the air, started her shot, then slipped a side pass to Cindy Butts all alone beneath the goal. Cindy carefully laid up the ball.

On the Middleton bench Lee Driskill bit down joyously on his lip. The game was tied.

In the third quarter, Ragan's Switch became unglued, and as sometimes happens in basketball, the game departed unbelievably from its script. When Middleton twice forged ahead by five points, Lee felt a chilled sweat prickling the back of his neck. The four hundred Ragan's Switch followers looked at each other incredulously, and their pep band's pipes of pandemonium were stilled, the musicians letting their instruments dangle dejectedly. Lee Driskill positioned Cindy and Candy in opposite corners and stationed Pat out in front, where she could drive. Grinning to himself, he sat back and enjoyed the mischief he had created.

But Ragan's Switch was a good team, and a good team keeps trying until something works. Their coach, a big, frowning man in a tan slip-on jacket, who looked as if he had come straight from the plow handles, used up three time-outs calming his troops and figuring out the situation. After that, his superior personnel and experience began to exact its toll. Two of Middleton's little guards fouled out. When the Ragan's Switch forwards assailed the Middleton substitutes for goal after goal, the faithful four hundred found their voices, and the pep band's trombonist again bent his knee and recovered his husky vibrato. On the Middleton bench, Lee Driskill writhed in torment and wished that he had Frances Bonner. Ragan's Switch won, 38–31, and headed for the district tournament.

After the game, the Middleton players shook hands with their conquerors, then hurried toward the dressing room where they burst into tears. As he picked up the loose towels, Lee thought he knew why. For the first time all year they had almost felled a giant.

To his surprise, Pat Thompson and Candy Brown sobbed just like all the others. Lee snorted. What foolishness! Why couldn't girls lose like boys? Boys hated to lose, but you rarely saw one cry.

Jean stood before him, reproof in her calm face. She had ridden to the game with Morgan's wife, Dell. Lee had a fleeting impression of how attractively she was dressed and how pretty she looked, even when she was agitated.

"Aren't you going to go into the dressing room and say something to them? Girls are more emotional than boys, you know."

Lee's mouth fell open. "I'll say they are!" He wanted no part of trying to comfort thirteen weeping females.

Her reproof changed to displeasure, and with a sense of guilt he remembered that on the few occasions his wife disagreed with him, she usually was right.

She said tautly, "You could at least tell them they played well. After all, they almost won the game. And they weren't supposed to come within twenty points of Ragan's Switch."

The Ragan's Switch coach had walked up and heard part of their conversation. To Lee, he thrust out one big hand, but he spoke to Jean. "They all cry when they lose, ma'am."

Lee said, "They're not going to cry on me any more."

The stormy lights in Jean's violet eyes held him. "They're not crying on you now," she reminded him. She nodded pleasantly to the opposition coach, and they both watched her leave, threading her way neatly through the crowd back to the Morgans.

"I'm George Hoggett." The Ragan's Switch coach pronounced it as if it were spelled *Gawge Hawgut.* "You dawgone neah upset me. That new fo'ward of yours is slick as calf slobbers. She got twenty-two on me tonight."

Lee shook hands. "She's liable to get twenty-two on anybody." He felt deflated. He always felt deflated when Jean disapproved of him.

"You gonna have yo'sef a good team next yeah with that crew."

Lee set his jaws and shook his head. "Not me." He enjoyed the surprise that came into Hoggett's face. "This is my last year at Middleton. This is my last year anywhere coaching girls. Let's go look at the boys game a little while. Want to?"

Side by side in the bleachers, they watched Bill Hooper's Middleton high school boys play Mesa. Lee leaned forward, watching keenly. Although the Middleton boys had a season's record of 16–8, he couldn't help being critical.

He didn't like the way Hooper defensed Pete Price, Mesa's fine forward. Middleton wasn't doing a good job of stopping him and Lee thought he knew why. Price had to have the ball. The Mesa star thought no play started until he got his hands on it and no play ended until he discharged it at the goal. Lee would have given a month's salary check if he could have sat down with Bill Hooper and showed him what to do. You covered a player like that closest when he didn't have the ball. You played him at the point of the ball. The idea was never to let him get the ball in the first place.

In the small knot of Middleton spectators, he recognized Gus Brawley and his satellite, the banker George Brand. One of the Middleton cheerleaders, in her crimson sweater and pleated white skirt, looked familiar, and Lee saw Pat Thompson and recognized her shrill, far-carrying voice.

Middleton's fast break won. Afterward, Gus Brawley crawled through two rows of seats to clamber down onto the court and personally congratulate Bill Hooper. Outside, Hugh Morgan had the bus's motor running. Dry-eyed and composed now, the girls began to climb aboard. Lee counted them. Thirteen. They were all there. Depressed by the defeat, they talked very little.

As the bus bored through the darkness, its lights illuminating the pavement and its motor droning loudly, Lee folded his hands and felt relieved. The long season had finally ended, and he was free. His mind kept thrusting back to the Ragan's Switch game, sifting the details in and out. There were some good scrappers among those Little Twisters. They played to win.

In the front seat across from Hugh Morgan, Lee closed his eyes, settling back comfortably. Two miles passed before Morgan leaned across the aisle and spoke: "You sure had our team ready tonight. The game reminded me of something my father once told me. Dad said that the glory consists not so much in winning as in playing a poor hand well."

Lee opened his eyes, listening to the roll of the tires on the asphalt. He said modestly, "It's not such a poor hand any more. The next Middleton coach might build himself a pretty good team if he plays his coaching cards right."

Morgan steered around the carcass of a rabbit in the road. "I sure hate to see you leave. If you ever change your mind, let me know."

Chapter 4

●

Marathon on Capshaw Road

After debating all summer, Lee did change his mind, bracing himself for one more year of punishment.

He had no choice if he wanted to stay in coaching. He had hoped to catch on as boys coach at Varney where his friend Joe Brody was now superintendent. And then Joe had telephoned him the night after he met with his school board.

"They won't let me hire you, Long Knock," Joe reported glumly. "They're kinda proud of their boys basketball here. They don't want a boys coach whose only previous head-coaching experience has been a ten-twelve season coaching girls. No matter what I tell 'em, they keep coming back to that. I can't talk 'em out of it. If you had a better won-and-lost record, even with those girls, I think I could persuade 'em."

For the same reason, no other school wanted to hire him either.

Having decided to get out of coaching, Lee accepted a summer job selling real estate. It involved a cut in salary while he was learning, but Jean still held her position and liked it. They'd get along. But when goldenrod blazed along the roadside, nights grew cooler, boys began running to get in shape for football, and the whole town became electric with the impending start of school, Lee felt a powerful excitement and discovered that coaching was still the thing he most wanted to do in all the world. And even if he couldn't coach boys, he could at least be around them and feel stimulated by the association.

The challenge of it motivated him, also. His mind kept harking back to what Gus Brawley said that day he went to the school board president about new balls, shoes, and uniforms for the girls. Every time Lee thought about that encounter, his spine chilled and his head rocked with anger. He wanted to make Brawley eat his scathing words. He wanted to show them all what he could do. If he made a decent record, Joe Brody's boys job at Varney might be his.

So Lee telephoned Hugh Morgan. Luckily Middleton still hadn't hired a girls coach. They had offered it to Bill White. "Not me!" White had told John Bannister. "It's harder to win in high school. You have more problems. I'm staying right here in junior high where I won't get fired."

On a night in early September, Lee Driskill drove to

the gymnasium to hold his first meeting with his new squad. They had asked for it, he couldn't imagine why. It was dark, and having forgotten his flashlight, he had trouble fitting his key into the lock. That accomplished, he stumbled across the gymnasium floor to the dressing room and entered.

Groping blindly about for the light switch, he thrust his bare hand into something soft and sticky. Startled, he sniffed twice, trying to identify the odor. It smelled like fresh paint.

Fresh paint it was, he discovered when he found the light switch. The color was green, and he had got the paint all over one hand and the sleeve of his jacket as well. Angrily he looked around the small room. Not only had they daubed their lockers with green, but they had strung new green curtains across each window and wired a dark green ruffle around the mirror on all four sides.

"Murder!" Lee Driskill exclaimed with displeasure. "Next thing they'll do is try to sew green ruffles around the cuffs of my pants!" He stalked into the janitor's room to find some turpentine.

When he returned to open the front door, they were all there, giggling, talking, laughing. "Hello, Mr. Driskill," each one greeted him cordially. He could smell their perfume, light and sweet and girlish. The combined whiff of it unnerved him. It always unnerved him to stand close to so many young females. "They're too clean," he muttered to himself. "I swear, they must use all those soaps I see advertised in *Girls' Life.*" His nose longed for the sour whiff of a boy's unwashed sweatshirt.

He locked the front door and walked downstairs to the gym. They were seated on the lower seats. Although a few still looked coltish, others had blossomed into legginess and had started filling out.

"Well!" he asked gruffly, "what's this all about?" He was still provoked about the paint.

They looked hesitantly at each other, waiting for somebody in their group to speak.

Pat Thompson, now a sophomore, found her voice. "Mr. Driskill, we wondered about training rules."

Puzzled, Lee asked, "Training rules?" No boys team he'd been around had ever mentioned the subject. Boys regarded training rules as a spider's web in which to become entangled and caught.

Candy Brown sat up straight, her enormous eyes shining, her arms folded in front of her. "You know, Mr. Driskill. Things we need to do without. Like, what do you want us to eat? What time do you want us to be in bed each night?"

Looking at their earnest faces, Lee realized that they were not jesting. He thought, they've probably read about college teams having training tables, study halls, and curfews, and figure they need them, too. They'll probably obey the restrictions for a week or two, then forget all about them. He decided to humor them for the present.

"Okay," he said, "but when do you want to start all this?"

They agreed to start November first, after the football team had played six games. Most of them were in the pep club, and Pat Thompson was one of the cheerleaders. They felt that they should heavily participate in all phases of school activities until the end of October. Then basketball would come ahead of everything else, although they would still stay as active as possible in other things, too.

To his surprise, Lee found he needed to protect them against themselves. When he let them fix the restriction, they penalized themselves too severely.

For example, the curfew. When they voted to be home and in bed by nine thirty every night except Saturday, Lee was doubtful if they could do this for four consecutive months. "That would be pretty hard on the boys you go with, wouldn't it?" he asked.

"I had in mind eleven o'clock," he temporized. "So why don't we make it ten thirty?" He figured most of them would be home that early anyhow.

Since most of them were sophomores and had just started dating, that seemed no problem. Pat Thompson pointed out that if any of them were dating boys who were also under football or basketball training regulations the early curfew would help both teams.

They still didn't look satisfied. It was plain to Lee Driskill that they couldn't consider themselves an athletic team unless the range of their sacrifices covered something they liked very much.

"How about fountain drinks?" Sadie York asked. "You know—the kind we buy at the drive-in? Shouldn't we give them up, too?"

Lee's eyes swept them shrewdly, right to left. He knew how fond high school girls are of any fountain drink mixed with soda water—especially of something called Nectar, a new beverage that was taking the school by storm.

"Girls, from the first of November until the end of the basketball season, I don't want you to drink anything with carbonated water in it."

That silenced them. Their eyes grew big and round. But they accepted it. Lee could see the resolution come into their faces. Before the meeting ended, they punished themselves still further by voting to eat no more than one candy bar a week. He told them that practice would start the following Monday.

"One more thing." He looked sternly at them. "Next time you decide to paint your locker room, tell me about it. Then I won't get my hand in it when I stumble around in the dark trying to find the light."

As the comedy of the situation struck them, he saw dismay and self-reproach come into their young faces. Candy Brown was laughing at him noiselessly, the heel of one hand pressed against her nose. And yet she seemed sorry for him, too.

Lee turned away roughly. He didn't want anybody feeling sorry for him. As he led them up the stairs to the front door, he thought it had been a pretty good meeting at that. At least they seemed serious about the coming season. He wondered how long their enthusiasm would last.

On the Sunday afternoon before practice started, Lee was at home with Jean. Somebody's knuckles rapped loudly, commandingly, on the front door. When Lee opened it, he saw a car parked outside with a woman seated in the front. And the man on the porch before him was Jim Stovall, the farmer who had withdrawn his daughter Portia from the squad the preceding season. Stovall and Lee had not spoken to each other since.

Stovall stood proud and stiff and glaring. Lee thought, it looks as if we're going to have it out all over again. And I've just eaten a big dinner.

Stovall said, "Driskill, if I let Portia come out for basketball this year, will you give her a square deal?"

Lee's tongue felt an inch thick when he tried to talk. He struggled to control himself. "She got a square deal last year. So has everyone else I have ever coached, and I don't appreciate your implying that your daughter didn't." He stood in the doorway, glaring right back at Stovall.

Some of the hostility went out of Stovall's face, and his voice became more conciliatory. "Well, now, let's don't get all foamed up about it, like we did the other time." He lowered his eyes and toed the porch bashfully. "That's one of the things I came up to do anyhow—to apologize."

Lee said unyieldingly, "If Portia comes out this year, she's going to have to start at the bottom and work her way up, even if she was a starter last year when she quit."

Stovall's jaw came up with a swooping motion, and again they glared at each other. Again Stovall dropped his eyes. He said, "Portia wants to come out for basketball. My wife thinks we ought to let her. Sometimes my wife isn't very smart. She thinks you're a pretty good coach."

Lee stepped out on the porch and closed the door softly behind him. "Well, I think she's smarter than you give her credit for," he replied, "except I wonder how she got stuck with you." His hands twitched as if he'd enjoy wrapping them around Stovall's skinny neck.

Again Stovall backed down. His voice became more friendly. "Well, now, Driskill, let's not get all excited, like we did last year. I just wanted to be sure that it wouldn't be held against Portia this year." Although it was Sunday, he still wore overalls and his black felt hat, but he had on a clean shirt and his boots were polished.

Lee pulled a long breath and felt the tension in him subsiding. "We'll be glad to have her. This is a new year. But I feel it only fair to warn you that we have some good shooters, and I'll probably have her screening for them again. She'll also have to learn to guard and rebound, or she may not even make our traveling squad."

Stovall turned and spat off the porch. Then he faced Lee again and nodded. "I understand. I'm sure you'll treat her fair and square. I'll stay out of your hair."

Lee walked out to the car with him. He smiled at Mrs. Stovall. "We're glad to have Portia back with us, Mrs. Stovall. Our practice begins Monday, and we'll look for her. Won't you get out and come in? Jean's back in the kitchen making green-tomato relish."

They were on their way to a friend's and declined. As Lee stood watching them drive off, he wondered if he'd been stupid again. He thought of Helen Burnsides and of how she had quit, begged to come back, quit again. He hoped he had done the right thing.

He decided to call on the Bonners and try to reach some sort of understanding in regard to Frances. He would ask Jean to go with him the following night. Her calming influence might help.

The next morning he was tidying his desk at the gymnasium office when Miss Rogers, the superintendent's secretary, appeared. "A lady to see you, Mr. Driskill."

Lee looked up, surprised. "Thank you." He got to his feet. There in the doorway, looking shy and out of place, stood Mrs. Bonner, Frances' mother, a smile on the sweet mouth that was entirely unadorned by lipstick.

"Good morning, Mrs. Bonner," Lee greeted her. Uneasily he stepped back. She had beaten him to the punch, called on him before he could call on them. "Won't you come in and sit down?"

She glided past him and sank timidly into the only chair in the room, pulling her ankles out of sight beneath the folds of her long dress. "Mr. Driskill, I want to talk to you about the uniform you want Frances to wear when she plays basketball."

"All right, Mrs. Bonner. What about her uniform?"

She reached down, smoothing her skirt virtuously. "Those red twill pants you expect her to play in—they're far too short."

Licking his lips, Lee saw that he was facing trouble. "Too short, Mrs. Bonner? They have to be short, or the girls can't move on the court—run, dribble, guard, shoot. Besides, didn't Frances wear shorts last year all through junior high basketball? Why should she change now?"

Her chin lifted piously. "Mr. Driskill, Frances is an older girl now. The devil dearly loves to work his wiles with older girls. I want your permission to sew an extension on the bottom of each leg of the uniform Frances will wear. I've checked, and I can match the red twill at Wagner's store."

Horrified, Lee sagged back against the wall, looking at her unbelievingly. "Mrs. Bonner, that would make Frances ten times more conspicuous than all the other players on the court. It would be terribly embarrassing to her."

He shook his head. "I don't agree with you that shorts are improper for girl basketball players, and hundreds of thousands of mothers around the nation support that view. If Frances plays basketball here, she should wear the same uniform as our other girls, just as she should travel with the other girls on our team bus, eat with them, and be governed by the same eligibility rules. Frances needs basketball, and our basketball team needs Frances, but if she plays, she must conform. I cannot make exceptions. I want all our girls to look alike when they play."

She folded her hands primly in her lap. "What did you mean, Mr. Driskill, when you said that Frances needs basketball? She's certainly crazy about it, but Mr. Bonner and I aren't sure that it's good for her—all that concentration on winning."

Lee hesitated, collecting his thoughts and searching for words. "Mrs. Bonner, I think it's great for girls. And for boys, too. Young people should be taught that winning is a proper goal whether it be in choral singing, debating, needlework, science, English, stock raising—you name it. They should be taught to compete hard."

Lee saw her wince, and a small shadow of doubt cross her eyes. He pressed the small advantage he seemed to have. "Here's how I look at basketball, Mrs. Bonner. It's great fun, and young people are entitled to lots of fun. It teaches them discipline, too. My players have to take abuse from me that they probably wouldn't take from their own parents. They don't talk back to me. Basketball teaches them how to rely on themselves. They find out that no matter how much money their parents have, it won't buy them a place on my team. They have to make that team themselves. Basketball teaches them values they can use all their lives—how to work hard for something they want, how to win and how to lose gracefully, how to get along with people, how to take care of their bodies, how to buckle down when things get tough. It teaches them that they must forget themselves and subordinate everything to a harmonious team effort."

She got up. Her mouth hardened, and she set her lips precisely. "Mr. Driskill, I still don't want Frances to look indecent. Mr. Bonner and I don't aim to give the devil that much head start. We want her to stand squarely in the light. Do I have your permission to sew extensions on her uniform?"

Lee shook his head. "I'm sorry, Mrs. Bonner, but if Frances plays for us, we'll expect her to wear the same uniform all our girls wear." He thought, there goes one of my best prospects. He felt sorry for the girl.

Mrs. Bonner walked out slowly and hesitantly, as if she didn't know where to find the exit. Lee escorted her to her car in the parking lot and opened the car door for her, marveling at how one frail little body could contain so much obstinate blindness.

To his surprise, Frances reported for the first practice. Lee didn't understand it. She was the first one on the floor and the last to leave. He decided to ask her about it.

"Your mother told me she didn't want you to play because she thinks the uniforms are too short."

Frances ducked her head in mortification. "I know," she breathed, her voice barely audible.

"I'm sure sorry your folks aren't going to let you play this year," Lee continued. "We need you."

She looked up, surprised. "Why, Mr. Driskill, I think they're going to let me play in the home games." Then the look of shame returned to her face. "It's the games we play in other towns that they don't want me to play in. Because they won't be there to check up on me."

"Do you think it would do any good for me to talk to your father?"

Fear flashed across her eyes. She shook her head. "No, sir." Then she added, "I can't practice much at night, either."

"You can't? Why?"

"Because I have to help Father and Mother at the revival."

Lee restrained his curiosity about the nature of her help, but later he asked Hugh Morgan about it.

"Her father runs a mission near the railroad tracks," the principal explained. "It's really just a big tent with a stove in it. Her parents make her go among the castaways who come to the tent for food, the drunks and derelicts of all description. These are men no other high school girl would be allowed to look at, yet it's Frances' job to pass among them, distribute printed tracts, and inquire about the condition of their souls."

Lee didn't like using a player who appeared only in home games, but his sympathy for the girl ran so deep that he decided to do it anyhow, so that her life wouldn't become wholly intolerable.

They practiced three days a week during October. On the two odd days they did roadwork outdoors. Lee had his theories about that. He believed that good physical condition preceded mental toughness, and that discipline preceded team morale. On Tuesdays and Thursdays he loaded all sixteen of them, dressed in shorts and sneakers, into the school bus and drove them five miles into the country. In the bus or under a tree they would eat the lunches they had brought from home, then walk back to school while Lee drove a mile ahead of them, waiting for them to pass him at each mile crossing.

On the first Tuesday, Lee parked the bus off the highway at the end of the first mile and waited for them to pass him. In Oklahoma it was still hot in early October, and a wind that had crossed thousands of rows of green cotton curving symmetrically in the red sand fields made the roadside sunflowers bob and curtsy.

Down the road he heard them approaching, the sound of their voices becoming louder and louder. Frances Bonner, Pat Thompson, and Ginger Selman were setting a stiff pace.

As they came by, walking steadily, he leaned out the window near the driver's seat. "Gee, whiz! I never saw so many fat, lazy people in my life. At the rate you're getting in shape we couldn't win a game from Mrs. Colbert's fifth-hour physical education class."

Grinning, they swept past him, the hot wind whipping their legs. Then he saw them slow down and huddle, whispering. Then they deployed in a long loose line, and giggling, began to leapfrog over each other's backs, moving at a trot.

In the bus, Lee laughed to himself. They think they're going to show me that they aren't fat and lazy. But playing leapfrog is a strenuous business, even for boys. After a hundred yards of that in this temperature, they'll be played out and be glad to start walking again. He pressed the starter, put the big yellow bus in gear, and followed them slowly.

To his astonishment, they went the whole mile hand-vaulting each other's bent-over bodies, trotting between each vault. A whole mile of skipping and hopping and jumping and laughing in the blazing shortgrass heat. They tired toward the end, but they did not quit.

On the following Tuesday, he drove them five miles northeast on the old road toward Capshaw school. "Walk west on the section line," he told them after they'd eaten their light lunch. "Stay off the main highway, so nobody will hit you or try to pick you up."

He drove past them and waited at the crossroads, marking the end of the first, second, and third miles. Each time they passed him, walking briskly. He drove to the end of the fourth mile and waited. They did not appear. He looked into the rear-view mirror but failed to see them. Turning the bus around, he retraced the entire fourth mile slowly, but they seemed to have vanished. A vague uneasiness filled him, and then he remembered that it shouldn't be difficult to track fifteen girls walking along a country road.

In the dust, he saw where they had crossed a bar

ditch and entered a wheat field. Standing on the bus steps, he scanned the field but saw nothing. They're probably staying behind the terraces, so I won't see them, cutting straight across the fields to the school, he told himself. He got in the bus and started to drive back to school.

One block from the gymnasium he met them coming in the opposite direction. He stopped the bus. Sweaty but cheerful, they were dogtrotting. Laughing, they all tried to talk at once: "We played a trick on you." "Did you think we were lost?" "Mr. Driskill, we ran to the school without stopping." Murder, he thought, they're insane with energy.

He faced them. "Get in." They did, plopping down gratefully in the leather seats. Lee Driskill turned the bus around and headed for Capshaw Road.

"Where are we going?" they asked. Lee never spoke until he reached the spot where they had left the road to enter the wheat field. He stopped and flipped the ignition key, killing the motor. Then he stood and faced them.

"You did a very foolish thing today," he said sternly. "You're under my supervision during the noon hour, yet you paid no attention to my instructions. A teacher just doesn't turn sixteen girls loose in the country without keeping an eye on them all the time. I want you always to remember that. Okay. I want you to get out of the bus and walk back to school—on the road—the way I told you to do the first time. Don't cut across the fields. Stay on the road."

He threw the lever to open the door and stepped out of their way. Without a word, they filed past him, one by one. Surprised and hurt, they refused to look at him or to speak. To Lee their silence was deafening. Ordinarily they were as chattery as a bush full of sparrows going full blast on a July morning.

Again they started walking. This time the only sound was the slap of the soles of their shoes striking the hot roadway. Lee followed them in the bus. If they slowed down a little, he tooted the horn.

At the school, Hugh Morgan waited anxiously. It was after two o'clock, and they had missed one class. When Lee explained what had happened, Morgan wrote each of them an admit slip, and after they showered and dressed, he sent them on. They were all good students, and Lee knew it wouldn't hurt them to miss one class.

None of them spoke to him the rest of that afternoon when he passed them in the halls, but he knew that he had been right. They had to learn to obey him. It was they, however, who had the last word. When he locked his office door that night, he discovered that they had greased the knob with what looked like face cream.

He didn't like that. At home, later, he found Jean outdoors, a basket half full of wet wash at her feet, trying to hang clothes in the violent Oklahoma wind. He told her about it. "If they're going to retaliate every time I discipline them . . . ."

Jean laughed. "They were probably hidden someplace nearby watching to see how you took it. After all, you made them walk an extra mile and a half. If they can take that, surely you can take a little face cream on one hand."

Next morning he decided that he didn't know anything about girls. His first homeroom class was full of them. Lee stood by the window, listening to the rustling of their dresses and the clicking of their heels as they hurried to their seats.

Candy Brown sailed past looking fresh and cool in a white shirtwaist and pleated skirt. She slowed down, smiling. "Mr. Driskill, are you still mad at us?"

Confused and off-balance, Lee stared at her. "Of course not," he replied huffily. "I just don't want you wandering all over the country like a pony with its bridle off every time we go out to do our roadwork."

Still smiling, she moved off. Frowning, he glared after her. Why had she even brought it up?

He walked testily to his desk and sat down. Girls were such baffling people. In their basketball uniforms he could cope reasonably well with them, but in their freshly starched school dresses, with color on their lips and polish on their nails, and their perfume giving off scent like a bed full of honeysuckle, they were creatures from another world.

Later, during a break, he encountered Portia Stovall and Sadie York. Portia's blue eyes sparkled. "Mr. Driskill, that's the prettiest sports shirt I ever saw," she gushed enthusiastically.

Embarrassed, Lee heard himself mumbling something meaningless in reply, and they moved off smiling. On his way to the lobby canteen to brace himself with a Coke, he ran into Hugh Morgan.

The principal eyed him with concern. "What's the matter? You look upset about something."

On his third savage thrust, Lee got his dime into the

machine's slot. "Hugh, do me a favor, will you? Give me all-boy homerooms next semester. I'm not cut out to deal with these girls. They see right through me."

Taking a long pull on his iced drink, he told Morgan about it. The principal laughed extravagantly.

"Oh," he remembered, "Saul Myerson, editor of the *Mirror*, wants to see you. He wants some quotes about girls basketball. Yesterday he talked to Bill Hooper. He's writing a story about our basketball prospects, both boys and girls."

Next afternoon, Myerson came to the gym. He was a fat little fellow with a permanent crook of the four fingers on his right hand, the result of constantly carrying a portable typewriter. The case was so scuffed and aged that it looked like something left over from the last century.

"Gotta minute?" he asked, peering at Lee with shrewd brown eyes.

"Sure." Lee cleared space for him on the desk.

Without taking off his topcoat, Myerson unlatched the battered case and pulled from it a small black typewriter. Tossing the case carelessly into Lee's wastebasket, he put the typewriter on the desk, ran a sheet of paper into it, sat down, and thrust both arms upward and outward like a concert pianist about to go into action. Again he surveyed Lee with those sharply appraising eyes that seemed to say "I dare you to lie to me."

"Shoot," he said, putting his gnarled fingers on the keys.

Amused, Lee asked, "You mean you want me to talk about girls basketball?"

"Yup. Give out with how things seem to you—prospects, schedule, returning stars, departing stars, anything about the upcoming season you want to gab about."

Lee Driskill belonged to that school of coaches who, when talking for publication, paint their prospects about 15 percent gloomier than they really are. It was a defensive stratagem designed for consumption by the public so that the public wouldn't expect too much. "I feel that since we have no seniors and our starting ball club will run largely to sophomores, we'll probably lose five of our eight games before the Christmas break," he said.

Like striking hawks, Myerson's fingers attacked the keys, some of which were so worn that the identifying letter was gone. He typed so fast that he had no difficulty keeping up.

When Lee finished, Myerson ripped out the paper and looked keenly at Lee, his brown eyes dancing with fun. "You sound like the fellow who had inscribed on his tombstone, 'I told you I was sick.' But I'll print it as you said it."

With the first game only a month away, Lee dropped the outdoor roadwork and began to drill his squad five days a week. One noon, during practice, he was called to the telephone in the superintendent's office.

"Go ahead and work on that inside screen," he told the girls. "Set it deep. Drive around it hard. Just as if we were playing a game."

When he finished the call, he decided to scout them, a maneuver he often used with boys. He went to the balcony and, staying out of sight, watched them from aloft. He wanted to see how faithfully they would work, or if any of them were working at all.

To his surprise, they were still practicing that inside screen enthusiastically. They were working as hard as if he were there with them. He stared thoughtfully. A boys squad would have stopped work the minute I left the court, he reflected. They'd be playing dodge ball. He shook his head in bewilderment. It was hard to believe.

Gradually his team began taking form. It ran heavily to sophomores from last year's Little Twisters. Pat Thompson and Candy Brown looked like fixtures at forward, just as Ginger Selman, Doris Crossett, and Liz Blair did at guard. The third forward position seemed a tossup between Portia Stovall and Frances Bonner. Portia was the better shooter, but Frances excelled at guarding and rebounding. Lee watched Frances with interest. She looked an inch taller and five pounds heavier, but in the halls and classrooms she still walked around with that lonely, frustrated look.

A few days before the first game, Lee and Jean attended the annual football banquet at the high school. The sophomore girls served the food. Pat Thompson was there with a date. Wearing a coral apron over her white gown, she served Lee and Jean.

Pat seemed disturbed about something. Nodding to Jean, she set Lee's plate of roast beef and baked potato in front of him, and he heard her sniff a couple of times.

Lee looked up to see a pair of disapproving, level gray eyes. Big tears were welling in them.

Pat said, "I saw the paper tonight. Evidently you

don't have much faith in us. You said we were going to lose five of our eight games before the holidays."

She began crying softly. "We're going to show you! I'll tell you what I think. I think we're going to win all eight."

Surprised, Lee spoke with open directness to her: "Pat, that was just newspaper talk. You wouldn't want me to predict that we were going to win them all, would you? No coach talks that way. The fans would think him crazy and when his own squad read it, they'd get too cocky. We'd be ripe for a fall."

From her sleeve, Pat extracted a handkerchief and dabbed at her eyes. "You could at least have told them the truth." Lee could think of nothing else to say. She seemed totally uninterested in his coaching propaganda.

The team's inaugural game against Big Sandy came four days later. Wearing a tight-fitting brown dress with a white lace collar, Cindy Butts, last year's captain, came bouncing into the pre-game meeting. "I hitchhiked a ride home from the junior college," she bubbled happily. "Coach, I just had to be near the team."

Lee felt flattered. It was nice knowing that someone missed the ill-starred previous season. You missed basketball most the first year after you graduated, he knew. He welcomed his first captain cordially, taking her into the dressing room with them before the tip-off and including her in their pre-game circle. During the game, Cindy sat on the bench, keeping the ball control chart.

Pat Thompson, still smoldering from the newspaper

story, scored thirty points. Although just a sophomore, she had quickly become the team's natural leader. When she drove past her guard and another guard would leave her assigned opponent to check her, Pat would pass unselfishly to the open Tornado forward. "Anytime your guard checks off, I'll score you! I'll get the ball to you!" she would call shrilly.

Remembering Helen Burnsides, Lee wondered how Pat, his new standout, would take discipline. Not until the Hondo contest did he find out. Although Pat scored twenty-eight points, she loafed on a rebound. Instantly Lee called time out. It always helped team morale to dress down the star just like anybody else if she deserved it.

"Pat, if you're just going to stand out there and not rebound, I'm going to get you some pompons so you can cheer 'em on," he said.

"Yes, sir." Pat stared humbly at the floor, nodding her head so vigorously that her red ponytail bobbed up and down like a railroad brakeman's oscillating lantern at night.

In the Glendora game she walked with the ball while trying to shoot right-handed, driving to her left. At half time Lee scolded her for it before the whole squad.

Apologetically, Pat hung her head and shook it contritely as if to say, "I'll never do anything *that* dumb again."

In a later game, she threw a pass behind Candy Brown and into the crowd. When Lee rebuked her during a time-out, she looked at him so gratefully that he suspected she had erred on purpose so she could take her turn at being disciplined like all the others.

She's putting me on, he decided, and resolved to stop wasting his time trying to correct this dedicated player.

Although Ginger Selman, the ranch girl, was only a junior, the squad had elected her captain. There weren't any seniors. Black-haired and sturdily built, Ginger knew what her trouble was—food. She never left any on the table. After each practice Lee made her run three laps around the court. "I may give out, Coach, but I'll never give up," she told him.

Ginger's father owned a small red-soil farm and ranch. Because of the drought it wasn't very productive. "We can't afford to live in town," Lee had once heard Ginger say. "There are seven kids in our family. Dad has to live in the country so he can raise enough food to feed us all."

Frances Bonner's father personally brought her to the gymnasium for the Bolton game, fifth on the schedule. To Lee, he was courteous and smiling, but before finding a seat in the stands, he turned and beckoned to Frances.

"I should like to see her alone for a moment, Mr. Driskill."

Out of hearing of everyone, the minister faced his daughter. Lee saw Frances cringe at her father's words. Pale and disturbed, she rejoined the rest of the team and played listlessly in the game.

On Monday, Hugh Morgan told Lee what Mr. Bonner had said. Frances had told Mary Morgan at school that morning. "Now remember," the minister warned Frances, "it is your natural inclination to do wrong. But that's no sign that I'm going to permit you to do wrong. I'm going to keep my eye on you. Don't make any attempt to deceive me."

That night, Lee listened to the hooting of the owls until a late hour, worrying about Frances. With her parents peering suspiciously over her shoulder, she couldn't play well at home. And they wouldn't permit her to play in the road games. Restless, Lee propped himself up on one elbow and turned his pillow. What could he do?

Chapter 5

The Beulah Tournament

The first road game, Lee knew, would truly test the mettle of his green squad. Mesa, the city that had entertained the district tournament the year before, was the host for a December game. At the half Mesa led by four. With the unfriendly Mesa crowd roaring, Lee wondered how his sophomores would respond.

They responded as if somebody were trying to push them off a raft into a river full of crocodiles. They scored the first five field goals of the last half and kept going.

Candy Brown, the freshman beauty queen with the face and figure of a delicate doll, with one gesture epitomized the dauntlessness of this new Middleton team. In the midst of the rally that moved Middleton ahead to stay, Candy snagged and painfully tore a fingernail on her left hand. Without taking her eyes off the game, she popped the finger into her mouth and sucked it.

Suddenly a loose ball rolled near her. Ignoring the broken nail, Candy raced a big Mesa guard for the ball, wrestled it away from her, and whipped it to Pat Thompson, who was fouled.

Lee called time and bandaged Candy's finger on the court.

Candy, smallest gladiator in the game, was still panting lightly. "Mr. Driskill, that's the strongest girl I ever saw. I thought I'd never get that ball away from her."

As he fastened Band-Aids both laterally and vertically across the nail, Lee needled her gently. "Why don't you pick on somebody your own size? If that big girl had met you solid, she'd have knocked you so high that the crows would have built nests in your hair."

Candy looked at him fearlessly, her nostrils quivering like those of a wild filly. "Mr. Driskill, when I put on my uniform I feel as big as anybody."

"Murder!" Lee grunted to himself as he secured both Band-Aids with a strip of tape. "I've been wanting to coach boys. Shoot! I've got me a boy right here." He sent her back, and she played the rest of the game with her bandaged nail half off.

With Frances Bonner staying home, Lee used Portia Stovall as a playmaker in the Montgomery game. The Tornadoes won handily, but Portia only scored seven points. Afterward, Jim Stovall came up to Lee on the court. He and Mrs. Stovall had driven over to see the game.

"Portia sure passed up some good shots tonight. Didn't she?" Stovall said.

Lee gave him a direct look. "Yes, but she made some fine passes."

Stovall started to spit, then restrained himself. "She sure did," he nodded. "She sure did."

Next morning, at the Crescent Café on Main Street, Lee was stopped by another father, a big man who walked with a slight limp and wore black horn-rims, boots, and a Western hat. His stomach spilled over his belt in a well-fed roll. He reminded Lee of a bale of cotton with the middle wire broken.

"I'm Frank Thompson, Pat's dad," the man boomed in a resonant voice that carried all over the room. "Say, I like the way you coach. Can I buy you a cup of coffee?"

Lee shook hands. "It's good to meet you. We're sure proud of Pat. She's going to be a good one."

"Hoo haw!" bellowed Frank Thompson proudly. "What do you mean, going to be? She's a good one already!"

Lee laughed. Joe Daniels, Jean's boss, had told Lee that it had been Frank Thompson's dearest ambition to have a son whom he could steer into professional baseball. Instead, he had had a daughter. Thompson had been a minor league catcher whose knee was torn so badly in a home-plate collision that his own career terminated before he had the opportunity to try for the big salaries paid by the majors. So he became a farmer and an auctioneer. Lee decided that Pat must have inherited her competitiveness and far-carrying voice from her father.

They settled themselves at a table. Thompson produced a cigarette paper, filled it with tobacco from a small pouch, wet one edge of it with his tongue, and rolled it on his hip, away from the wind that intruded every time the front door opened.

His face wrinkled good-humoredly. "Pat tries to get me not to smoke." He scratched a kitchen match on the seat of his brown twill pants, looked at Lee, and chuckled. "When Pat first went to junior high school, she thought any girl who smoked had a bad reputation."

Lee spooned sugar into his coffee. "She works well with the little kids, I've noticed. Likes to be around them. I saw her coaching both boys and girls at the church gymnasium last Saturday."

"Hoo haw!" scoffed Frank Thompson. "That's where she is right now." He touched the tiny flame to the tip of his freshly rolled cigarette. "Waste of time fooling around all those little runts. That'll never make her any money."

Squinting his eyes almost shut, he drew smoke into his lungs. "Pat's a farm girl," he went on proudly. "Drives the tractor, hoes cotton, milks the cows." Disgust showed in the curl of his lip. "Her mother's teaching her to cook and sew. If she'd been a boy, I'd had me a pitcher who'd be drawin' a hundred grand. There's big money in baseball today."

In spite of Frank Thompson's preoccupation with baseball, Lee knew he was secretly proud of Pat and her basketball feats. He would sit in the stands wearing a blue plaid shirt and black Western hat. When Pat shot a goal, he would pull the hat forward over his eyes. When she missed, he would claw it back on the crown of his head, revealing sorrel hair, just like hers.

In the final December contest, Middleton shouldered the Beeville girls aside, 55 to 39. The team had swept its first eight games, just as Pat Thompson predicted. Dee Daniels, a carpenter who was an elder in the Bonners' church, escorted Frances to and from the game. Mr. Bonner was preaching in the next town, and Mrs. Bonner was ill with influenza. Lee liked the way Frances pressed the Beeville guards when they tried to bring the ball to the center line. Quick-footed and fast-reacting, she attacked them so cleanly and furiously that several times they failed to get the ball across the middle in the required ten seconds. She was cool and relaxed, and played twice as well with her parents absent.

The gymnasium was only one half full even for the start of the boys game, though there were grade-school youngsters all over the place. Saul Myerson, pausing a moment at the bench to chat with Lee, had the explanation: "Been too hot and dry. People are stuck for cash. They're living on wind pudding. Unless we get some rain, not even the papas and mamas of the players can afford to come."

Lee had taught his players to face the scoring table when a foul was called on them, hold one hand high, and turn so that the scorer could get a full view of the number on their backs. Three minutes before the game ended, Frances Bonner made her first foul and, facing the scoring table, raised her hand and turned her back.

"Mr. Driskill, look at that." Sadie York spoke from the bench.

On the front row of seats across the court, a small boy stood at the sideline, watching Frances. In plain view of the crowd, he also faced the scorekeeper, raised one hand, then turned his back, grinning with enjoyment as he went through the same ritual as Frances. His imitation was so perfect that thereafter every time a Middleton girl fouled, other small boys and girls in the lower seats would step out onto the floor, slowly face the press table, raise one hand, then solemnly turn their backs.

Lee grinned. "At least, the small fry support us."

They had other support, too, much of it from the parents of the players. Patsy Prickett's family never missed a game. Patsy's six-year-old sister brought her dolls and played with them in the stands. Her three-year-old sister spent most of the time beneath the bleachers, picking up discarded paper cups. Patsy's father, Jed, an introverted druggist, usually held the baby.

On the night Middleton defeated Beeville and Patsy scored her first field goal of the season, Lee looked behind him and was astonished to see Jed Prickett stand up and shout joyfully, swinging the baby from side to side as if he were about to toss her onto the playing floor.

His wife squealed in fright and, reaching across him, snatched the infant from his arms. "Well, Lord, Ivy," Jed protested, "I wasn't going to drop her." While they argued, the baby leaned forward in her mother's arms and grabbed the spectacles off the nose of the man who sat next to them. Mrs. Prickett, still flustered, restored them to the owner and apologized.

Then she turned to Jean, seated nearby with Dell Morgan. "Heavenly days, Mrs. Driskill, isn't this exciting? I intended to visit my mother in Kansas this winter, but I guess I'll just wait until the basketball season is over. I didn't know we'd be winning."

After the Beeville game, Lee took Jean with him into the dressing room and talked to his squad. "We're still making too many mistakes. I like the way you battle, but Candy still can't go to her left, Ginger makes too many wild passes, Portia got outfoxed twice on rebounds, and Pat missed three free throws. We've a lot of hard work ahead of us to do during the holidays. So don't get cocky. All you've done to date is beat some weak teams. After the holidays we start taking on the strong clubs. What can you do against them?"

Later, Jean walked out with Lee. "You shouldn't have been so harsh with them," she said seriously. "Sometimes those girls look at you as if they almost liked you."

Lee checked his wristwatch. "I don't want them to like me too well. Because I'm not going to be coaching them forever." He looked at her and held up a single finger. "Just this one year."

In the lobby they encountered Bud Foglesong, an old friend with whom Lee had played basketball at Southwestern College. They sat with him watching the boys game. On the court before them the Middleton boys were having trouble with the Beeville boys. Bill Hooper had lost Scott Wells and another starter who had graduated. His new team had won only two of five games. Middleton went ahead with five minutes to play but kept trying to fast break, beat Beeville down to the goal with the ball.

Lee sat stroking his chin, studying the action. He thought Bill Hooper came close to being a good coach. Hooper's main flaw was that he went all out in one direction. He'd shoot down to the wire with you. Even if he had a two-point lead with a minute to go, he'd keep jacking the ball up at the goal instead of retreating into a delay game to protect his lead.

A long Beeville shot in the last fifteen seconds beat the Middleton boys. Afterward, Lee and Jean took Foglesong home with them for coffee and conversation.

"What are you going to do during the holidays?" Foglesong asked. "Hunt birds?"

While Jean spooned ice cream on three helpings of chocolate cake in the kitchen, Lee filled his friend's coffee cup from the pot. "I'll hunt some. But mainly we're going to practice."

Foglesong looked up. "Practice during the holidays? Your kiddos won't like that, will they? Holiday time is courting time and staying-up-late time."

Lee handed him the sugar bowl. "When they're winning, you can work them as hard as you want to."

He didn't know that it would be their idea to work even harder. When they began their Christmas-season practice, the girls asked to work five days a week, instead of the three Lee suggested. That cut into Lee's quail-hunting time, and Alice looked at him reproachfully each time he walked out of the house without wearing his hunting gear or picking up his pump gun. But Lee decided that if his players could give up more of their holiday, he could sacrifice more of his. On the second afternoon of the holiday season they began their special practice.

Brown-legged and flat-stomached, they were variously dressed, ranging from Sadie York in tan trunks and a short-sleeved white shirt with a big green "M" inscribed on the front to Pat Thompson in a black sleeveless jersey and cut-off blue jeans with the bottoms raveled, the frizzed threads trailing. There were no distractions. They had the gym all to themselves. Eager to please him, they worked like harnessed young mules.

"Hut!" Lee yelled. The long line of girls broke from the east wall, sprinting their fastest. Lee let them get only a third of the way down the court. "Hut!" They stopped suddenly, spun round facing the direction they had started from and, leaning forward with arms extended in front of them, did stationary running, sixteen pairs of feet stamping the floor.

"I like to hear those shoes cry," Lee called challengingly. "That means everybody's working."

"Hut!" Still facing the east wall, they ran backward until they traversed the middle third of the floor. "Hut!" With a shriek of rubber, they put on the brakes, whirled facing the west wall, and again did their stationary running, arms extended, feet blurring.

Another "Hut!" sent them winging on their final dash to the west wall. Using this routine, they raced up and down the floor, arms swinging, hair tossing, dividing the court into thirds. When he granted them a short rest they bent over, hands on knees, and all he could hear was their shallow, uneven breathing.

"You've got to learn to push yourselves when you're tired," he lashed them. "Anybody can get tired. Anybody can quit."

Patsy Prickett, wearing brown corduroy shorts and a green short-sleeved jersey, reclined against the wall, her chest heaving.

"Patsy! Is that why we built that wall? So you could lean against it?"

Patsy pushed herself away from the wall as if it were hot.

"Candy, where are your knee pads?"

Candy Brown, in a red blouse and cut-off jeans, looked down at her knees. They were bare. She grinned. "Oh, sir, I forgot 'em."

Lee walked up, facing her. "Candy, look around you."

Candy shot a hasty look around her. "I know, sir. Everybody else is wearing theirs."

Lee frowned at her and switched to a rebound drill. Three girls, each with a ball, lined up five yards from the wall, facing it. Three more girls faced the passer, backs to the wall.

"Hut!" Each passer shot the ball high off the wall. Each guard whirled, leaped with both hands high and came down with a ball clutched to her stomach.

"Drop your tails! Spread your legs! Backs straight! Heads up! Spread those fingers! Keep those hands out in front of your forehead, not behind it!"

They did a dribbling drill, then a cut-off drill to break up the give-and-go, then a bear walk forward and backward on their hands and toes to build up their shoulders and stomachs. Finally, he put them through a passing drill in which they lined up in four-girl squares and shot crisp, leveled passes at each other, the *whoot* of the caught ball the only sound violating the gymnasium quiet.

As he stuck his whistle into his pocket, Lee grudgingly gave them credit. They were all there. They did everything he demanded at full speed and then looked at him as if to ask, "What else you got that you think we can't take?"

It was warm for December, about seventy-five, with the south wind kicking up the dust. He knew where they'd head after they showered—to the drive-in. He knew their throats must be parched and how greatly they must thirst for a cold drink made with carbonated water.

I don't think I could punish them if they did cheat a little, he thought. In fact, I'd think they were more human if they did. But when he drove to the drive-in and checked up on them with Charley Smack, the proprietor, he got a surprising answer.

"No, sir, Coach Driskill. None of those girls have touched a Coke, or a Nectar, or a Seven-Up, or anything with phosphate or fizz juice in it. They come here quite often, but they always order plain water cherry limes. And they're never here after ten o'clock at night, either."

With the bottom of his white apron, Charley wiped his sweaty face. "I can't say as much for some of our boy players. They hang out here till midnight and tank up on all the belch water they can drink. But not those girls. Hot, ain't it?"

Lee started his motor. "Sure is. Thank you, Charley." Frowning, he backed out, heading for home. Nobody could be this perfect.

The girls liked to have fun along with all the excruciating work. Lee had called an early morning practice so he could go quail hunting afterward. To tease him, they came wearing robes over their pajamas with their hair twisted in rollers, as if they had just climbed out of bed.

Smiling to himself, Lee said, "The reason I asked you to report so early was because the *Seymour City Sun* photographer is coming to take your pictures." That panicked them. They were thrown into mass consternation and protested in a medley of soprano voices. Not for a full moment did they realize that he was only teasing them in turn.

They revenged themselves upon him in a novel manner. When the practice ended, he went to his locker for the bar of soap he always used to wash his hands. To his surprise, it would not lather although it always had. Baffled, he took it home and showed it to Jean.

"Don't ever buy any more of this brand for me," he told her, "it won't make suds."

Jean picked up the soap, scratched it with her nail, and smelled it. She began to laugh. "No wonder it won't lather," she said. "They coated it with fingernail polish."

In the final scrimmage of the holidays, Lee made a memorable discovery. With Sadie York home with a cold, he needed a second-team guard. Frances Bonner, a forward, stood nearby.

"How'd you like to play guard for us today?" Lee

asked. "We need somebody tall to cover Pat." Without a word, Frances stepped across the line alongside Pat Thompson.

In the action that followed, they waged a hammer-and-tongs duel. As a guard, Frances was green. Pat, smart and experienced, took her over all the jumps. But Frances had the fastest feet Lee had ever seen. With Lee coaching her, she improved so steadily that soon she gave Pat fierce opposition. And when Lee put her on Portia, Portia seldom got off a shot.

Although she strengthened the team defense immeasurably, her uncertain availability presented a problem. Her parents still refused to let her accompany the squad on games away from home. Without her, Middleton's margin of victory in the road games became slimmer.

At Cottonwood, Lee first noticed that his team warmed up with their jackets open. The floppy effect seemed to bind their arms. When he divided the squad, the forwards shooting free throws while the guards practiced dribbling, he summoned Ginger Selman, the captain.

"Why are the girls wearing their warm-up jackets open?"

Ginger's honest eyes looked down at her own jacket, also open. "The zippers are broken on three of them, Mr. Driskill. The rest of us leave ours open so we'll all look the same, like a team."

Lee felt a slow vexation rising in him. He had gone to Gus Brawley last year about new equipment and had been turned down. Meanwhile Brawley had bought Bill Hooper's boys fifteen new red and black uniforms last year and new matching warm-up pants and jackets this season. The jackets the girls wore were castoffs from the boys. He resolved to see Bannister about it in the morning.

John Bannister rose, smiling. "Nice going last night, Lee. Let's see, your record now must be about nine and nothing, isn't it?"

"Something like that." Lee sat down, hooking one leg over the other. "John, our uniforms are about shot. This year, we're wearing those old warmups handed down to us by the boys. Boys are bigger than girls, and these jackets are about two sizes too big. Also, last night at Cottonwood the zippers broke on three of them, and we had to practice with them open. When we do that, they not only bind the girls' arms, but we look as floppy as a bunch of scarecrows."

"I see." Bannister had lost some of his heartiness but seemed sympathetic. "We barely broke even financially last fall on football. Crowds are down. The cost of equipment has gone sky high. I doubt if we can afford an expenditure that large. But I'll see what I can do."

Two days later the superintendent sent for Lee. "Lee, I tried hard to sell our school board on those new uniforms for the girls. They turned me down."

Lee stared at him coldly. Damn it, he wanted to say, the school board just bought the boys team a full set of uniforms and warmups, and we're playing better than they are. But he restrained himself.

"What reason did they give?"

Bannister looked apologetic and spread his hands. "Just that times are hard, and there's a drought on. We have to cut expenditures."

Lee felt his temper rising. "Patsy Prickett ripped her

shorts the other day in practice. She put her hand over the torn place and took off running to the dressing room. What am I supposed to do when this happens in a game?"

Bannister drew himself up stiffly and pushed back his shoulders. "Take your gear to the cleaners this week and tell them I said to have every single article gone over carefully and mended. Also, tell them to put new zippers in every warm-up jacket. We'll pay for them out of the school activity fund."

Lee stood. "Thanks," he said not very warmly, and walked out. Why am I fighting this so hard, he asked himself later. Even if they get new uniforms next year, I won't be here to coach them.

Next morning Hugh Morgan had news for him when they met at the coffee-vending machine. "Lee, from now on, your girls are going to get hot beef sandwiches, cold milk, and a salad delivered to them in the dressing room after all home games. John's having it done for the boys team, too."

Lee brushed a raveling off his sleeve. "That's fine. Whose idea was this?"

Morgan grinned modestly. "Well, I made the suggestion. But John went for it. The Home Ec department will do the cooking."

Lee said sincerely, "I appreciate it, Hugh. The girls will, too. It'll pep them up. How's the school going to pay for all this food?"

"Out of the student activity fund."

While he sipped his coffee, Lee computed the cost in his mind. "We could take that money and make a substantial start at buying new uniforms."

"That's what I told John," Hugh replied.

Lee snorted. "At least, he seems conscious that we have girls basketball here. That's progress." He looked at the coffee cup in his hand. "I hope the student fund can stand the strain. We have some pretty good eaters on our squad."

The telephone call came next morning during Lee's homeroom period. He took it in the superintendent's office. "Lee Driskill speaking."

"Mr. Driskill." There was no mistaking the hostility and contempt in the silky, deliberate tones. "I understand that you have given your basketball team the idiotic instruction that drinking carbonated beverages is unhealthy for them and therefore you forbid it."

Lee felt the muscles around his mouth tightening and for the first time he remembered that among his various other enterprises Gus Brawley owned the city's Nectar agency.

"I did tell them not to drink them during the season but I didn't say that it was unhealthy."

"Don't quibble, Mr. Driskill. It's the same thing."

Lee felt his scalp prickling with irritation. "Mr. Brawley, it isn't the same thing. Carbonated drinks aren't unhealthy. I understand they contain fast sugar and sometimes a little bit of stimulant—caffeine I believe—which shouldn't be harmful to young athletes, provided they don't drink it too close to practice or competition. Actually, the main reason we banned them was because the girls wanted to do it as a disciplinary measure. They didn't feel they were really in training unless they sacrificed something they liked very much, and . . . . "

"Mr. Driskill," Brawley interrupted, "I want you to listen to me very carefully. I'm sending four cases of iced Nectar to your office in the gymnasium at eleven o'clock this morning, just before your practice starts. I want you to revoke—take back in the presence of your whole squad—this stupid rule. I want you to tell them they are invited to refresh themselves after each workout with a bottle of ice cold Nectar, compliments of the Gus Brawley agency. Do you understand?"

Lee flushed and thought, he talks to me as if he owns me. As if I work for him personally instead of for the school. Lee felt a rash, uncontrollable urge to nettle the bullying school board president, to shock him out of his attitude of arrogant authority.

"Mr. Brawley, I believe that you also own the controlling interest in a sporting goods store here, don't you? While you're sending over all that free pop, why don't you send over—also gratis—a dozen new girls basketball uniforms with zippers that will work? Be sure to make the jackets small enough so they'll fit my girls instead of just enclosing them, like tents."

For a moment there was deadly silence on the line. Then Brawley's voice, soft and menacing. "Your attempts at humor, Mr. Driskill, are very crude. They are also unwise. Most unwise and imprudent as you will learn. I know how to reach difficult people like you, Mr. Driskill. I've always known how to reach them. May I suggest that in the future you—in your stumbling fashion—take care of the basketball coaching and let me take care of the soft drink business?" He hung up so softly and with such apparent calm that the click of the instrument seemed not at all like a threat.

Lee stood looking at the transmitter in his hand. Now that he had stung Brawley he felt better. The man had to learn that he couldn't wipe his feet on him.

Ten minutes later Bannister, his face tense, hurried into Lee's gymnasium office.

"Lee, I just had a call from Mr. Brawley. He seemed upset that you had told your girls they couldn't have carbonated drinks. He says you admitted they weren't harmful. He says this hurts his business, gives his product a bad name. Don't you think we could rescind a small training regulation like this? Do you think it absolutely necessary? After all, Mr. Brawley is president of the school board and he helps us in lots of ways. He's done a lot for the school and for the town."

Lee described, word for word, how the girls had asked for the pre-season meeting to discuss training regulations and what had transpired there.

"It all comes down to this, John," Lee concluded. "He's attempting to serve as dietitian to my squad. If I let him take that over, he'll probably move into the coaching next, telling me what players to use and how to run my offense. No coach in his right mind would permit this."

Bannister frowned and squared his jaw. "I think it best for all concerned if you yield on this one small point. I'm sorry. You're doing a good job. But I've got to have peace between my faculty and my school board."

Lee wet his lips and drew a deep breath. "That's not peace. That's surrender to outside interference. You'd better get somebody else to coach your girls basketball team. Maybe Mr. Brawley would like to coach them. It wasn't my idea to coach them in the first place, remember? I was hired to coach the boys."

Bannister stared at him haggardly and walked out. When the four cases of Nectar arrived, Lee carried them into the basement and stacked them behind the door where nobody would see them. He wished everyone would leave him alone. He needed time to plan. The next competition was an all-girls invitation tournament sponsored by Beulah, a small town located one hundred miles distant in the northwest wheat belt. A power in girls basketball, Beulah had won all its games, too. The tournament fell on their home court, which meant that Middleton would have to play without Frances Bonner.

Although times were hard at Beulah, that small metropolis, settled mostly by German people, knew how to have a tournament. They had invited seven girls teams besides their own. No boys teams were invited. During their three-day stay, the visiting girls would be fed free of charge at the school lunchroom and would live in the homes of Beulah citizens.

Beulah sponsored something Lee had never heard of, a sports club composed principally of businessmen and of the fathers and mothers of the high school girl and boy athletes. When Middleton's bus entered the small town, Lee saw that there was a basketball goal erected on nearly every house or garage and that the kids, many of them girls, were also using them.

At the red brick high school, Lee and his players got out. Lee looked around. This was very different country from that around Middleton. The Beulah school sat in a quiet spot between two hills, each dotted with green cedars.

"How do you feel, Mr. Driskill?" somebody asked. "Tired?"

Lee stretched. "I keep falling down. No wind here to hold me up."

A big, friendly-looking man in a black jacket and fur cap stepped forward. "I Chris Schiffner," he announced. "Wife and I belong to the Beulah Sports Club. We want Portia Stovall and Candice Brown and Patricia Thompson and Frances Bonner stay at our house."

He had a rosy complexion and gray hair. Behind him, his wife and two teen-age daughters stared shyly at the red and black Middleton bus. They were neatly dressed, their faces shining and expectant. Other Beulah families were walking up and tendering similar invitations to the remaining Middleton players and to other teams arriving in other buses.

Surprised that they knew the names of his players, Lee extended his hand. "I'm Lee Driskill. It's awfully generous of you to put us up. We'll be glad for you to have the girls you named. However, Frances Bonner couldn't come. Would you like to take another of our players in her place?"

Chris Schiffner turned and faced his wife and daughters. They smiled and nodded.

"Yah," he said, speaking for them all.

Lee turned, surveying his squad. "If you're sure you have plenty of groceries, we might give you Ginger Selman." Laughter swelled among the Middleton contingent.

"We take her," Chris Schiffner replied jovially. "But she can't eat more than my Hilda. Hilda will eat anything that don't bite her first."

Behind him, the older daughter ducked her pretty head and stammered shyly, "Father. Please."

The four Middleton girls named stepped forward, surprised to be known by name one hundred miles from home. With his big gnarled hands, the father picked up their luggage and looked at Lee. "What time you want them back at the gym, Coach?"

The famous Beulah hospitality lasted until Saturday night when the final game, Beulah versus Middleton, started. The small gymnasium was packed with people. Beulah had won both its tournament contests. So had Middleton. Each took a 11–0 record into the championship final.

Early in the first quarter, Lee discovered that Beulah had the best girls basketball team he had ever seen. In their uniforms of orange and black, they played tough defense and rebounded with smash and authority. Twisting the white towel in his hand, Lee watched them with a fatalism he could not fight down. Big, fast, and experienced, they rarely made a mistake and did their rough job with a minimum of errors and fouls.

Lee soon realized that Middleton was going to be beaten. He felt sympathy for his team. A proud group, they weren't accustomed to losing and wouldn't understand defeat. In the third quarter, he felt a choking lump of pride in his throat when the Tornadoes poured out all their resources to rally and draw within four points. But Beulah redoubled its efforts and despite

Pat Thompson's twenty-one points, which kept the fiery numerals dancing on the small electric scoreboard, Beulah won, 34–27. Afterward, the Tornadoes looked sober and dazed as they congratulated their conquerors.

In Middleton's dressing room, Candy Brown raised an ashen face, her wet eyes aglow with the light of a new discovery. "Mr. Driskill, we played our dead level best tonight. But sometimes your best isn't good enough, is it?"

"That's right." His eyes swept over the Tornadoes compassionately. Before he knew it, he was talking. "I think Beulah won because they have a heck of a team, and they were playing on their home floor. Everybody gets whipped once in a while. You made me real proud of you when you pulled up your socks and launched that rally, coming from twelve points down to only four. You played better then than you really are. I'll remember that for a long time."

To his amazement, they all burst out crying. For the first time it occurred to him that his opinion and praise were important to them. Confused, he walked from the room. He hadn't intended to say anything.

After they'd had their cry, Ginger, the captain, led them back onto the court, and mingling with the crowd, they found the three Beulah families who had housed them, and thanked them for their hospitality.

Glum and silent, they showered and climbed onto the bus. Lee stood outside, watching them. It was their first defeat, and instead of looking licked or humiliated, they only seemed confused. A sweeping humility surged through him. When two all-victorious teams clash, one has to lose no matter how strong and proud it may be. And tonight the losing club was his own. He hadn't enjoyed congratulating Joe Buckingham, that sharp Beulah coach, but he certainly respected him and his team. They were a fine group.

Sighing, he grasped the handrail and swung aboard. "Oh, well," he consoled himself philosophically, "if you don't stumble once in a while, you don't know you're moving." But he knew the pangs of defeat would linger all the way home, and it was a long drive.

Inside the bus, Lee counted his squad. Dropping into the driver's seat, he reached into his pocket for the ignition key. To his astonishment, he couldn't find it.

"That's funny," he muttered and searched his trousers again. The whole squad helped him to look for the key on the floor of the bus, under the seats, and back in the Beulah gymnasium, but it was gone.

"Sir," Susan Grove, a substitute, stood shyly at his elbow. "I'll start the bus if you won't tell on me."

Lee stared at her, nonplussed. "You'll what?"

Susan stood her ground, a flicker of confidence in her brown eyes. "I know how to hot wire it. My brother showed me. You can do it two ways, under the hood or under the dash. It depends upon whether the car has a button starter or a key. All I need is a piece of insulated wire."

Lee found it for her, and the gifted young lady ducked under the dashboard and went to work, wiring two posts together to activate the ignition, then touching the wire to the third post. The starter hummed, and suddenly the motor burst into a triumphant roar. A faint cheer rose from the squad. The whole operation had taken about a minute.

Susan emerged, her blonde hair fallen over her eyes. With the back of her hand, she pushed it back and accepted the piece of Kleenex somebody handed her.

Lee looked at her with admiration. "Looks like you saved us about a hundred-mile walk. Thanks."

All the way home he explored in his mind the necessity for developing a ball control offense. That shrewd Beulah coach had scouted every minute of Middleton's first two victories and knew how to set his defense for their regular attack. But if Middleton had had in reserve a second offense that Beulah hadn't seen . . . .

Ahead a car approached. Lee pushed his toe against the foot button, dimming the bus lights. Installing a ball freeze would take lots of planning and teaching. Why take time for that when soon he'd be all through coaching girls anyhow? Behind him, the girls dozed. He thought about the Beulah Sports Club in which the whole community participated. Middleton needed a program like that, but Middleton had a long way to go.

Most of all, Lee thought about Middleton's next game, a contest against an opponent more highly rated even than Beulah. Crockett's defending state champions, coached by Chet Chambers, were coming to Middleton Friday. Sally Edwards, their all-state forward, would be with them.

Lee planned a surprise for them, a secret he kept from everybody. Frances Bonner could play in that game. Lee decided that Frances would guard Sally Edwards.

Chapter 6

Lorrie Sue

At noon on the day they were to meet Crockett, Lee brought them into an empty classroom. He knew that he didn't have to arouse them to play Crockett or any other team. They always played as if they were mad at losing. But he wanted to talk to them anyhow.

He stood before them, one foot on a chair, a piece of chalk in one hand. "Most of you have never played against Crockett. They're the blue bloods of girls basketball in our state. They have a real tradition. Hundreds of their fans will follow them over here tonight. They have great personnel. Only one or two of our girls could probably make their starting lineup. They have us beat in equipment, too."

He shifted his shoulders. "They'll be wearing those woolly blue warmups with each girl's name sewn in gold letters on the backs of the collars." Out of the corner of his eye he could see them edging up to the front of their chairs. They knew why they were there.

"You have a wonderful opportunity tonight. If you put everything together, you might win. I don't have to tell you that girls basketball at Middleton is an orphan, a stepchild, a poor relation. It's just barely tolerated here. Tonight you have it in your power to write a Declaration of Independence for your sport. If you beat Crockett, you'd shake this sleepy town to its roots. You'd rock the whole state."

To himself Lee admitted, I still don't like this game, or like to coach it. But I do like the way these girls hustle. They know all about hard work and sacrifice. They want to win.

As he talked, he began tossing the chalk into the air and catching it with the same hand. "I know forwards score all the points, but I've always said that our guards win or lose our ball games. The newspapers don't know it, the fans don't know it, but our forwards know it, and all of you know that I know it. Crockett's forwards were the best in the state last year, especially Sally Edwards, their all-stater."

He shot a long, deliberate look at Frances Bonner. "Sally Edwards scored forty points on Daingerfield last week. She made thirty-two on us here last year. There's not a whole lot of finesse to guard play. It's mainly a matter of determination. How badly do you guards want to win this game? How tough are you going to play tonight?"

He stole another glance at the guards. Ginger and Liz Blair looked steamed up enough to move the gymnasium, brick by brick, to Main Street and back bare-handed, but he still wasn't sure about Frances Bonner.

A loner, she sat on the end of the back row, an empty seat between her and the next girl. As she listened, she kept reaching up with a graceful movement of her hands to smooth her hair behind her ears and press out the wrinkles in the black ribbon that bound it. It was then that Lee noticed that Frances' lips were colored a pale pink. A flicker of admiration for her courage ran through him. She was probably putting the lipstick on and taking it off at school, but he liked her independence anyhow.

Lee put the chalk in his pocket and leaned forward. "One thing more. You'll be playing for somebody else tonight, somebody who considers each one of you his or her idol—the little kids at the game. When each of you was a grade schooler, you idolized somebody on the high school team and tried to pattern yourselves after every thing they did.

"Tonight it's turned around. Some little peewee is watching you. Watching how hard you play, admiring you, wanting to be like you. You don't know it, but they watch you at school in the daytime, too. They watch how you dress, how carefully you drive, how loudly you talk, how closely you sit next to your boy friend when you ride in a car. They imitate you, try to pattern their lives after you. You'll be playing for them tonight, too."

He brushed the chalk dust off his hands and swung

his foot off the chair. "I'll see you at the gym at six o'clock."

Although the Middleton gymnasium that night looked only one-half full, even with Crockett's contingent, it seemed that all the children in town were there. Lee had taught the girls when they first ran out on the court to form a ring and start clapping their hands in unison, slowly at first then gradually increasing the tempo until the noise reached a crescendo. It gave them a feeling of togetherness. Tonight the grade schoolers in the crowd, watching for it, began to clap right along with them. Soon the sound of their hands became so loud that the Tornadoes on the court began to look around at the youngsters and grin. When the Middleton spectators, catching the infection, joined too, the noise swelled into a roar. At the other end of the floor the blue-clad Crockett team, smartly executing a three-girl roll, occasionally stole a look at the proceedings, too.

Lee met Chet Chambers at the scoring table. The Crockett coach wore a new suit of gray hopsack, and his black tie was knotted neatly. As they shook hands, Chambers stared intently at Lee. "I thought you told me last year that you were all through coaching girls."

Lee frowned. These rival coaches had memories like computers. "I am—after this season. I got drafted one more year."

When the buzzer sounded the summons to play and the rival teams shucked their sweat clothing, Crockett's sartorial advantage was even more apparent. Her players wore new uniforms of powder blue on the backs of which their large white playing numbers were thinly outlined in gold. Middleton wore its old-style, oft-mended red satin tops with tattered black numbers that each year became harder and harder to read.

The ball went up and the tip went to Sally Edwards. Then Lee Driskill's breath snagged in his throat, and he felt the blood pounding in his ears, for Frances Bonner pounced on Crockett's all-state forward like a chicken on a bug, slapped the ball out of her hands, beat her to the recovery, and raised the ball triumphantly above her head with both hands to protect it. She took her time, her head pivoting on her long neck so she could see the court's entire width, and again Lee was reminded of the lookout goose acting as sentry while the rest of the flock dined on the new green wheat.

"Frances!" Pat Thompson's strident voice rang out. Frances looked for Pat, saw her, passed her the ball. Middleton maneuvered coolly, passing and faking and overloading one side of the court so that Pat was left alone on the other side with Crockett's best guard. That guard had never seen Pat play.

Pat faked a long shot, rocking back just enough to get the Crockett guard coming her way, then long-strided around her with the dribble to bank the shot. Lee's heart leaped, and his hand tightened into a fist. Middleton 2, Crockett 0.

An official gave the ball to Crockett's forwards and they began weaving off their screening attack. But when Sally Edwards drove dribbling around the screen, Frances Bonner clung to her so closely that Sally saw she couldn't turn the corner going into the goal. Instead she swung back out, stopped, and slapped the ball twice, a look of annoyance on her face. Lee knew that she was signaling the other Crockett forwards back into alignment and that they would send the play around the opposite side.

But Frances was there, too. The screen worked this time, pinching off Ginger, but when a platinum-haired Crockett forward tried a shot, Frances leaped and swung a long arm.

Blam! Liz Blair dove on her stomach to recover the blocked shot.

Kneading his knuckles into his palm, Lee watched enthralled. When Sally moved, Frances moved with her. They reminded Lee of a dance team with Sally leading and Frances the girl partner. And as Frances continued to anticipate nearly every lead the Crockett star made, dissolving neatly into her footsteps and denying her the drive, Lee felt the blood pounding in his temples and thought of the old song "Me and My Shadow." Sally Edwards was certainly being shadowed tonight.

And then he saw something else that made him grin proudly and let his breath out fast between his teeth. As they stood together at the middle line and the ball was down at the other end of the court, Sally, the enterprising senior, tried to bait Frances, the sophomore, by smiling and relaxing and giving her six inches of position to get her off guard, and then when the ball approached, exploding suddenly in front of her to take the pass. But Frances, an intelligent girl who made all A's and B's in the classroom, saw what was going on.

Soon she, too, began relinquishing space at the

division line as she smiled and chatted and helped the Crockett star regain her composure. But the minute a Crockett pass zipped Sally Edwards' way, Frances shot to the point of the ball, fiercely disputing its possession and often intercepting.

Lee grunted in admiration at the schoolgirl theatrics. Frances learns fast, he thought, twisting his fist into his palm with satisfaction. She's sweet and gentle when the ball's someplace else, but once it comes her way, she goes after it.

Three times during the contest, Chambers, the Crockett coach, stood and, with the fingers of one hand forming a right angle to the palm of the other, sued for time. On each occasion, he talked calmly to his star, instructing her how to shake off this frowning sophomore leech, and Sally Edwards would wet her lips and frown and nod. But when play started, Frances Bonner resumed her grim stalking of the Crockett star, and that was the story of the game.

Crockett drew even at 27–27 late in the third period, but Lee, experiencing one of those strange moods of confidence that any coach who has stood at the brink of adversity will recognize, didn't substitute a single player. His young fighters were matching Crockett in everything—spirit, speed, avoidance of errors, desire. He knew they had a good chance to win.

Portia Stovall put away the last two field goals on passes from Pat Thompson that lanced through the Crockett defense like rifle shots through tassels of corn, and Middleton upset the defending state champions, 36–32. Afterward, the Tornadoes swirled around Frances, hugging her happily. Lee's elation spilled out as he yelled like everybody else in the wild, thin crowd. He knew where the credit belonged. The first play of the game, when Frances Bonner collared Sally Edwards and cleanly slapped the ball out of her hands, was the battle's chapter heading.

Chet Chambers, his shirt and tie still immaculate, found Lee and offered his hand. "Say," he drawled laconically, "I'm glad you're gettin' out of this game. You're tough!" Limp with joy, Lee could only smile and shake his head unbelievingly.

As he walked to his office, pausing every few feet to shake the many congratulatory hands thrust toward him, Lee thought, I've got to watch myself. I don't want to get too fond of these girls and their plodding game. But his joy was overwhelming.

Hugh Morgan waited for him at the office door, his face grave and concerned. First he shook hands. "Great, Lee. You've earned it all. I'm glad for you." Then he added, "But I have bad news. There will be no beef sandwiches tonight or any other time. Gus Brawley and his board met before the game and ruled it out."

Lee stared at him incredulously, all the conversation knocked out of him.

Morgan went on, "Brawley told John Bannister between halves, and John told me. Brawley explained to John that times are hard, and our crowds stay thin. The boys team still gets its meal. Brawley says the boys play the main event—that they're what the crowds come to see."

Lee looked shrewdly at Morgan. "He's hitting back at me because I crossed him on the carbonated-drink deal."

Morgan nodded. "Probably."

Lee straightened his shoulders and made up his mind. "I'm going to take them out to eat myself. Steaks. At Hannover's. They've earned it. Go find Dell and Jean. We want you with us. I'll tell the girls."

It cost him twenty-seven dollars. Brawley had probably foreseen that, too. He's making my last year of coaching girls a memorable one, Lee thought bitterly.

With and without Frances Bonner, the Tornadoes kept blowing down opponent after opponent. The hostility of the school board gave the team an extraordinary unity. By the time their record reached 15–1, Lee noticed that parents of several players were following the team to see the out-of-town games.

He was pleased. Parent enthusiasm was a fine endorsement. For the first time it occurred to him that with Frances the team might make an impact in the approaching state tournaments. What could he do about Frances? Why do I try to do anything about her? he asked himself. After one more month I'll be all through coaching girls. We'll have a fine record without Frances. Then he shook his head wearily. These girls were dedicated. They deserved to have their best combination for the tournaments.

He decided to seek the advice of the mothers of his players. The mothers were his staunchest allies, he had learned. When he told the mothers that the pre-game meal should consist of honey, dry toast, and a poached egg, and that he wanted the girls at the gymnasium by six o'clock, the mothers looked at him as if he were the Apostle Paul; and they always followed through. It was the mothers who washed and pressed their daughter's uniform, put white polish on her playing shoes, repaired jammed zippers, cooked the pre-game meal, sat with the daughter while she ate it, and drove her to the gymnasium. Then they hurried home again to serve the family dinner before rushing back to the gymnasium to see the game.

"I think these shortgrass girls get it mostly from their mothers," Lee told Jean the next night as they dressed to attend a church social. "These mothers are so competitive. The dads are proud of their daughters, but all they do is stand out in the corridor at the games and smoke and brag."

He stripped a necktie off the rack behind the bedroom door. "It's the mothers who really sweat out the games, too. When the girls peel off their warmups to start the game, they glance at their mothers sitting in the bleachers, and mama will nod, square her jaw and double one fist. When I helped coach boys at Fairfield, we'd get a new class and a new bunch of parents each year. We'd scout the parents as much as the kids, because whenever we had a good team, we always had a good bunch of parents. Bloodlines tell in basketball same as they do in horse racing."

Jean stood before the mirror fitting a small blue hat on her black hair. "You sound like a genetics professor," she laughed.

Lee looped the necktie over his head. "Basketball is great for teaching kids how to be competitive. That's what life is all about—working, scheming, sacrificing, helping, trying to win. Everybody needs a worthwhile goal. Every town and community needs something they can work together on and be proud of, like that sports club at Beulah. Something they can do for the young people, something that the fathers and mothers and everybody can get their teeth into . . . ."

And now they were trying to get their teeth into this problem involving Frances Bonner.

Dorothy Thompson, Millie Brown, and Mary Grove—the mothers of Pat, Candy, and Susan—drove in from their farm homes to talk.

"What can we do to help?" they asked as Lee escorted them to the school cafeteria and they discussed the matter over cups of hot coffee.

They decided to try Millie Brown's idea first. "Ray and I could ask the Bonners to go with us in our car to the road games as our guests. We'd even follow the team bus to and from the games if they wanted to."

But when she called on Mrs. Bonner, Mrs. Brown got a sweet smile and a refusal. "She didn't give me a reason. But I think it's because she wouldn't feel comfortable associating with women who dress fairly stylishly, wear lipstick and a little jewelry, and occasionally go to a movie or belong to a square-dance club," Millie analyzed it.

Dorothy Thompson suggested that they might justify Mrs. Bonner's presence on trips by electing her the squad's team mother, so she could travel with the players, act as chaperone, and handle any of the small emergencies that were constantly arising. Lee liked the practicality of that but when he broached it to Mrs. Bonner, she declined.

"The church has started a new mission downtown, and Mr. Bonner and I will be needed there." Then she added something that made new fear knot his stomach.

"Mr. Bonner wants Frances to help us in the mission at night."

A little before nine o'clock the following morning, Lee went to his office to get his grade book. As he walked across the basketball court, he heard something crashing violently against the steel lockers in the girls' dressing room and the sound of a girl's voice choked with emotion.

Surprised, Lee knocked on the door. Nobody answered. He pushed it open and saw Frances Bonner snatch up a small glass vase of flowers and hurl it against the brick wall. The shattered glass sprayed on the floor.

"I hate him!" the girl cried, her voice rough with anger. "I hate him! And I hate her, too!"

"Wait a minute, Frances," Lee called out. "You're wrecking the room."

She glared at him, her mouth a tight line, then resumed her bitter cries. "I hate them both!"

It was obvious she was talking about her parents. When she continued to throw things, he walked toward her, feeling the broken glass crumbling beneath the soles of his shoes.

He grasped her by the shoulders, shaking her roughly. "Cut it out!" he commanded. "Get hold of yourself. You don't talk that way about your own folks, no matter what they've done."

For a moment she looked at him, as if seeing him for the first time. Then to Lee's astonishment, she threw both arms around his neck, laid her head on his shoulder, and broke into agitated weeping.

As he looked down at her plain brown dress, old-fashioned, darned along the sleeves, the white lace jabot hanging dejectedly crooked, he thought he knew what had upset her. Her father and mother were probably taking basketball away from her. The game meant a great deal to this proud, lonely girl. It was the only thing she was given any freedom to do. He patted her shoulder, pitying her profoundly. Although high school was a girl's brief time for blooming, this girl's blooming would never develop past the bud.

When her sobbing subsided, she pushed herself away from him, sniffing. "Thank you, Mr. Driskill," she said, tremulously. "I'm sorry."

While he swept up the glass with a broom, she composed herself and told him that she was afraid her parents would forbid her to play even in the home games thereafter. Then she went to class.

As he hunted for the dustpan, Lee felt helpless and discouraged. There seemed nothing further that he could do.

So the team went to Floyd City without Frances. It was the first time Middleton had played at Floyd City, an oil town that prided itself on its semiprofessional baseball teams. It proved an unforgettable experience.

As the Middleton bus halted at a red stoplight on Floyd City's main street, handfuls of loose gravel rattled noisily off the windowpanes, tossed by small boys who were lying in wait in the street, and the girls squealed in fright and shrank away from the windows. Slowed by traffic, the Middleton bus was pelted at every stoplight as the urchins raced alongside, discharging their gravel with shouts of glee. Finally they tired of their sport and fell back.

At the game, a boisterous crowd, many of them baseball spectators, filled the auditorium. The Tornadoes, in their warm-up, were victims of more harassment than in all their other games put together. The Floyd City students had heard of Pat Thompson. Every time she launched a shot in practice, they would grunt in unison, "Oomph!" If she made the shot, the students, pretending delight, murmured in prolonged unison, "Ah!" If the shot missed, they moaned in mock disappointment, "Oh!"

"Wait 'til Lorrie Sue gets ahold of you, Thompson," a deep voice kept chiding from the balcony.

"Who's Lorrie Sue?" the Tornadoes asked each other.

When Ginger Selman, whose pudgy build set her apart, trotted past the scoring table, somebody called, "Hey, blimp! When do you get your landing instructions?" and Ginger's face flamed.

Lee Driskill was also a victim of their banter. Every time he walked out onto the court, they chanted in unison, "Hut! Hut! Hut! Hut!" in time to his footsteps.

"Pretty lively crowd here," Lee observed mildly when he huddled the Tornadoes before the tip-off. "Just what we need to keep us on our toes. Don't get to listening to them and forget to play basketball. This team hasn't lost all year on its home court."

In the introduction ceremony, when players of both teams stripped to their uniforms, Middleton got its first good look at Lorrie Sue. Six feet two inches tall, 180 pounds, with legs as big as logs, she drew the biggest cheer of any player on the floor.

And when the game began, gum-chewing Lorrie Sue

showed what she could do. Floyd City used a zone defense with Lorrie Sue planted in the middle, like a goalie in ice hockey, and Middleton had trouble shooting the puck past her. They seldom got a rebound. She smothered Middleton's drives, blocked shot after shot. When she snagged a rebound, she would spin and, firing from behind her ear, rifle the ball to her forwards with a long cross-court pass that sailed like a javelin.

She was rough, too, and one of the officials, a swarthy little man with low sideburns that needed clipping, overlooked most of it. Once Lorrie Sue and Candy Brown, plunging side by side for a rebound, collided and Lorrie Sue's shoulder propelled Candy across the distant sideline. Like a defiant terrier, Candy jumped up, the ball in her hands, but the official ran up and pointed to her.

"Personal foul on you!" Raising her hand, Candy obediently turned her back to the scoring table.

In the third period, one of the Floyd City forwards, reflecting the mood of the crowd and the pace of the game, backhanded Ginger Selman across the mouth. Quick as a flash, Ginger slapped her, staggering her. Neither official saw the fight, but Lee did. Standing, he called time and withdrew Ginger, sending in Susan Grove.

The Floyd City forward who had been guilty of the original blow came to the Middleton bench and faced Ginger. "I'm sorry. I started it."

Still seething, Ginger wouldn't look at her.

Lee, sitting next to her, nudged Ginger in the ribs. She looked at him, then at the Floyd City girl. "Well, I didn't help it along any. I'm sorry, too."

With Lorrie Sue and the Floyd City guards staying back in the zone, the Middleton forwards began to hit from outside. Portia potted three straight from fifteen feet. Pat hit twice on short jumpers. Candy scored from the corner. But not even Pat could drive around Lorrie Sue. The thick-legged Floyd City amazon kept jumping in front of Pat, throttling the drive, and often fouling roughly although the fouls weren't called. Finally, Pat quit trying to drive around her, whereupon the Floyd City crowd began to chide Pat and boo her.

The swarthy little official with the low sideburns assessed foul after foul on Middleton. Soon Sadie York fouled out. With four minutes left to play Middleton led, 50–45. Ginger's fifth and final foul followed on a play in which she scarcely touched her opponent.

Lee stood, facing the official, a cold knot of anger tightening in his stomach. He asked mildly, "Does the visiting team draw all the fouls over here?"

The official walked up and thrust his face saucily into Lee's. "You want a technical foul, or do you want to sit down?"

Then Lee, who had never drawn a technical foul in his life, felt himself coming completely unbuckled. "I might as well have one while you're so drunk with power. You've been putting fouls on us all night."

The official turned to the scoring table. "Technical foul on the coach," he intoned. The Floyd City forward made the shot.

Again the official walked up and stuck his face into Lee's. "You want another?"

With an effort, Lee kept his voice even. "Heck," he

said coolly, "I didn't want the first one. But go ahead. Two's an even number. That would be the closest to an even break you've given us all night."

Again the Floyd City forward looped the free throw. Lee sat down. The official retrieved the ball and, facing Lee from the court, held up his hand and looked at Lee, mockingly asking with his gesture if Lee wanted another foul. Lee ignored him.

With two starting guards fouled out and Frances Bonner back in Middleton, the Tornadoes had little defense. Floyd City won by six.

"What did you think of the officiating?" the Floyd City coach asked after Lee took the long walk down the sideline to congratulate him.

Lee still felt the knot in his insides. "Now that you mention it, I thought it was rank. Of course, in my present state of mind you couldn't expect me to like it. I'm sorry I blew my stack and took those technicals. Apologize for me to your superintendent, will you?"

Out on the court Lee saw the flash of Lorrie Sue's white teeth as Pat Thompson slid an arm around her and congratulated her. Other Middleton players were observing the most difficult social grace of all, felicitating an opponent who probably wouldn't have won without the assistance of an official.

Tight-lipped and silent, the Middleton squad filed onto the bus. There was no crying this time. Lee liked what he saw in their faces—the force of an unbeaten will.

After he counted them, Lee stood in the aisle, facing his team. "I'm sorry I got my quills up out there tonight and drew those two technical fouls. All season I've been lecturing you about how important it is to control your tempers and accept the decisions of the officials. Looks like I need to take my own advice."

Then he sat down and drove them home. It was only their second defeat, and the season was nearly over. As he steered, he thought about it. It was fun working with these girls. Too bad their game wasn't pulse-pounding or heart-shattering. He wondered how the boys team at Varney was doing.

The next day was Saturday. In his office just off the court, Lee was reviewing his notes on Oklahoma history for his Monday class.

Susan Grove stuck her head through the doorway. She had on a blue sweater, plaid skirt, and knee-length blue woolen stockings. A black purse with long straps dangled from one shoulder. "Mr. Driskill?"

Lee glanced up. "Why, hello, Susan."

She seemed worried. "Candy had a car wreck just now and rammed her knee against the dash. She's all right, but she's afraid her folks will think it's her fault." With one hand, Susan hitched the purse higher on her shoulder. "She's sitting out in front in the car. She wants to talk to you."

Lee got up and locked his office. Most high schoolers drove too fast, he knew. "Has she talked to her parents yet?" Susan shook her head, and her hair, cut so that a fold of it curved provocatively upward along each cheek, brushed her nose on both sides. "She wants you, Mr. Driskill."

They walked outside. Candy sat slumped in the front seat of the Brown family automobile, her shoulders stooped dejectedly, her doll-like face smudged with tears. The car's right rear fender was crumpled.

Lee softened when he saw her. "What's the matter

here?" he asked sympathetically. Placing both hands on the door, he leaned inside.

Even in her distressed state, Candy Brown was a very pretty girl. Her voice was high and tremulous with a catch in it, like that of a small child. Somebody in a cement truck had run through a stoplight and hit her.

"Let's go look at the spot," Lee suggested.

He sat on the outside of the front seat. Susan drove. Candy sat between them, sniffing and dabbing at her eyes with a handkerchief so moist from tears that it seemed to be in mourning with her. Lee stared straight ahead down the street. It was a new experience, seeing a fighter like Candy so pale and agitated.

At the site of the collision, Candy described it all over again and cried once more. Lee saw that she was blameless. "Did you get his license number?" She nodded. "Did you call the police?" Another nod.

Lee looked at her. "Do you want me to go with you and talk to your father?"

She nodded, sniffing, her hands in her lap. Susan put the car in gear.

Lee handed her his clean dry handkerchief. "Why did you come to me?"

Candy's eyes dropped to the tips of her fingers. "Because—because—you and the team—we're all like a big family together. You always solve our basketball problems so well that I knew you'd have the answer to this one, too."

Lee laughed. "You're loading me like a shotgun. I don't think I solved anything the other night at Floyd City."

Candy raised her enormous eyes to his. They were loyal, shining eyes. "You took up for us against that awful official—in front of all those people."

Lee grunted. "Darned if I didn't! And helped get us beat by drawing those two technical fouls." He didn't feel like a hero.

Susan spoke from behind the wheel, "It bucked us up when you talked to him, Mr. Driskill. We were already busy enough battling that team and that awful crowd. It's hard to play against an official, too."

At the Brown home, Lee went in with them and explained to Candy's parents what had happened. The fact that he sometimes taught the driver's training class at school seemed to help. They thanked him. The police report cleared Candy. The truck firm's insurance paid the damages. Candy limped a little in practice, but with the district tournament approaching, she healed fast.

As Lee walked to school on Monday, a cloud bank boiled out of the northwest. Forks of lightning illuminated the darkening sky. The faraway rush of the wind came to his ears. On the school ground ahead, he saw it strike the young elms and honey locusts, bending them almost flat. A raindrop spattered against his cheek. He began to run and, beating the deluge, trotted downstairs to his office in the gym, exhilarated by the exercise.

He had visitors. Gus Brawley, in a black slicker that glimmered eerily in the gymnasium lights, and John Bannister were waiting for him. Brawley's face was as dark as the cloud outside. What have I done now? Lee wondered.

"Good morning," he greeted them, unlocking the door. "Won't you come in?"

Brawley came in and to the point, almost simultaneously. "Mr. Driskill," he began in his suave, insolent tones. As usual, he put the emphasis on the *mister.* "I understand at the basketball game last Friday night at Floyd City you made a nuisance of yourself. You bawled out an official before your own team and before the Floyd City team and before the crowd. I have been reliably informed that the only way the official could subdue you was to call a foul on you for unsportsmanlike conduct."

Lee held up two fingers. "Two fouls," he corrected. Would he ever be free of Brawley's meddling?

Brawley's shaggy eyebrows came together ominously, and the look he gave Lee was that of a farmer getting ready to cut a pig's throat.

"Mr. Driskill, here's what I want you to do. You will write a letter of apology, a *full* letter of apology to"—he spread the fingers of his left hand and pointed to them one at a time with the forefinger of his right—"the Floyd City superintendent, the principal, the athletic director, the basketball coach, the official, and the president of the school board"—Lee saw that he had run out of fingers and was obliged to count on one of them twice—"You will do this today, and you will mail copies of all the letters to me."

Lee turned to Bannister. "John, I did lose my head over there. When one official fouled out our two best guards, I told him off. He gave me two technical fouls before I got everything off my chest and sat down. I'm sorry. After the game, I apologized to their coach and told him to express my regrets to his superintendent. I also apologized to my own team coming home."

Relieved, Bannister looked at Brawley, hopeful that the explanation would satisfy. His hope was doomed. Brawley's broad, dimpled chin began to lift and his eyebrows to come together again. He gave Bannister a long, imperious stare, and the superintendent cowered and dropped his eyes.

"Mr. Bannister." Again he stressed the *mister*, and the superintendent seemed to suck for air through his open mouth. "You have heard this genius whom you employed as our coach admit his disgraceful behavior at the Floyd City game. I understand it to be the duty of the superintendent to administer our school in accordance with the policy defined by the board. You heard me tell him what the board expects of him. I want the carbons of those letters in my post office box in the morning."

"Yes, Mr. Brawley," Bannister stammered and cringed.

Lee was astonished at the degree of Bannister's submissiveness. Brawley glared at Lee and walked out, his slicker rustling menacingly.

Bannister looked at Lee with naked helplessness. Lee pitied him.

"I'll write the letters, John."

A slow anger filled him as he thought of Brawley's continual interference. But he still blamed himself for losing control.

As he and Jean drove past the drive-in on their way home that night, they saw Frances Bonner and a boy for the first time. They were riding in an old gray coupe that had the words "Rolls Rough" painted in yellow letters on one side. Its broken fenders seemed to wave at all passers-by.

Lee didn't know the boy, a small, timid-looking blond with a cigarette in his mouth. But there was nothing timid about the way he drove that old chariot. He had even tampered ingeniously with the exhaust so that it seemed to cheer as well as roar.

As they drove off, tires squealing, Frances waved at them gaily. She still wore the pink lipstick.

Chapter 7

The Black Blazer

Frances didn't play in the final home game against Ragan's Switch. She didn't even come to the game. Mary Morgan telephoned Lee Driskill an hour before the tip-off.

"Frances asked me to call you, Mr. Driskill. She says that her father and mother want her to help tonight at the mission. Dad said for you to come by our house, and he'll try to do something about it."

Lee stiffened, feeling the futile anger beginning to stir. Thanking Mary, he hung up, staring at the wall. For a moment the wild, cruel idea assailed him that never in this world would there be basketball and parties and fun for Frances Bonner. He could see her moving timidly among the derelicts at the mission.

Unable to abide the fury he felt, he walked outside. Big, cottony clouds pumped out of the north by the wind scurried across the sunset and were dyed yellow and crimson by it. Lee felt the dust particles sting his cheek. He knew it was what the natives call a "dry blow" and that no rain would come of it. He got in his car and drove to Hugh Morgan's home.

They talked a moment, then the principal picked up the telephone. With a big forefinger he dialed the Bonner residence and asked for the girl's father. The minister wasn't home, but Mrs. Bonner was. For ten minutes Morgan talked quietly, patiently, persuasively. Finally he said good-bye and hung up.

He looked at Lee incredulously. "Do you know what she told me? She says that the underlying cause for all of Frances' unhappiness is the devil. And that the devil is motivated by sin. 'You can hear the hiss of the serpent when you say the word,' she told me."

Lee sat for a moment, silent and brooding. "Well," he said finally, "the team will wonder where I am. Thanks, Hugh."

As he drove to the school, the woman's words hung in the violent wind, in the angry sky, in the town's flickering lights. There remained some solemn echo of them even in the clarinetting of a departing freight train, the sound curiously flawed by the gale.

Lee parked his car behind the school, walked into the building and onto the court. The crowd had just started to come. He saw Gus Brawley, standing in front of the Middleton bench, talking to some of the girl players. The school board president moved off before Lee arrived. The girls looked surprised and disconcerted.

"What happened?" Lee asked, looking from one to another.

Big-eyed and a little awed, Ginger raised her head. "Mr. Driskill, he just walked up and scowled at us. Then he said, 'A lot of you ought to be at home sewing.'"

Lee put his hands in his pockets, frowning. "He did, did he? What did you tell him?"

Ginger looked at Sadie York. "At first we didn't tell him anything, we were so surprised. Then Sadie said, 'Why, Mr. Brawley, we all sew. I made the dress I wore to the game tonight. I made it all myself. Pat made the dress she wore, and she also made another just like it for her mother. Candy makes a lot of her own clothing, too, some of it in her home economics class. Our whole team does a lot of its own sewing.'"

Proud of Sadie, Lee said, "Nice going, Sadie. What did he say then?"

Sadie spread her hands. "Nothing. He just looked angry and left."

Lee turned away. He thought, Brawley probably expects us to sew our own new uniforms, too. That's the only way we'll ever get them—make them ourselves.

A big fellow in a tan slip-on jacket, who looked as if he had come straight from the plow handles, walked up, sticking out a big, hairy hand. "I'm George Hoggett, Ragan's Switch coach." He still pronounced it as if it were spelled *Gawge Hawgut.* "Say, you been goin' good this yeah. I thought you told me last yeah you wasn't gonna coach girls any more."

Lee flushed. "I got drafted. But this is my last season."

Although Ragan's Switch brought along their pep band and their slide trombonist, they had very little opportunity to play "A Hot Time in the Old Town Tonight" because Pat Thompson was sharp as a locust thorn. She hit thirteen of fifteen field goal attempts, half of them jumpers from out on the court. The Tornadoes won by eleven with Lee using all his substitutes.

Hoggett came over and shook hands, but he still looked defiant. "You beat me at basketball, but ah'll Indian-wrestle mah girls against yours any old time."

Laughing, Lee declined.

Afterward, he and Hoggett watched Bill Hooper's Middleton boys race away from Ragan's Switch.

Chin cupped in one hand, Lee frowned when Hooper began to send in his substitutes. Excited, the boys tore off their handsome sweatsuits, stood on them, and trampled them in their eagerness to join the action on the floor.

Murder, Lee thought. If my girls had new equipment like that, I'll bet they'd take better care of it. They'd probably bring coat hangers from home and hang 'em up on the goals.

The game ended, and Gus Brawley and George Brand, grinning proudly, shook hands with Hooper on the court. Lee knew that probably they would later mingle with the coach and the boy players while they ate those hot beef sandwiches in the dressing room. Bitterly he turned away.

The final practice on the afternoon before they left for the district tournament at Hondo was the most frustrating of the year for Lee.

He didn't understand the girls' attitude. They forgot to pack their duffle bags. They didn't practice like a team heading for the decisive tournaments of their season. Instead they seemed gay and secretive.

"You act as if you're going over there just for the trip instead of what the trip's for—to play two hard games," he scolded them. "You act as if you've never made a trip out of town before."

When he halted the drill to go to the office for his whistle, he saw them through the window whispering conspiratorially as they peeped at him over their shoulders. He lifted the whistle out of a small drawer and slammed the drawer shut. Hummm, he told himself, they're probably talking about me—about how hard I'm working 'em. Well, they haven't seen any hard work yet!

He put them into a shooting drill that called for banking the ball in the hoop while moving at top speed. The penalty for missing the goal was one lap around the court. They bungled it so badly that soon the entire squad was trotting around the floor while Lee, his patience gone, stood in mid-court trying to figure it out. Finally, he blew a blast on his whistle and huddled them.

"If you're going to practice like this we might just as well stay home," he stormed. "We'll call the whole thing off."

They stood silent, the only sound their rapid breathing. He looked at them with exasperation, perplexed by their strange remoteness and evasiveness. Their minds seemed a thousand miles away.

He closed the drill with the toughest thing he could throw at them, the sprinting forward and backward up and down the court. He ran them until their tongues hung out, but there was no word of protest from any of them. After six lengths of the floor, he stopped it. They still looked dreamy and intoxicated.

Tight-lipped and weary, he checked his watch. "When you shower, don't forget to turn on the cold water at the end. Keep your heads covered. Don't walk around barefooted. We don't want any colds."

Later, when Jean picked him up in the car, the wind pressed her short coat and belted tan skirt against her. A scarf protected her black hair from the breeze, and he saw she'd been to the beauty shop.

"Climb in," she invited, "we're not eating at home tonight." Busy with his problems, Lee supposed they were dining at some restaurant downtown until she stopped in front of the two-story brick residence of Dr. Paul York, Sadie's father.

Jean got out from behind the wheel. "Come on," she urged.

Puzzled, Lee looked up. "Where are we going?"

She smiled mysteriously. "I can't tell you that. I promised not to." Baffled, he walked with her to the front door. She pressed the white pearl button, and they waited.

The door opened, and they entered. The doctor and his wife introduced themselves and led them into a large family room filled with smiling girls attired in party dresses. At first Lee didn't recognize them. Their prettiness and their fragrance made him feel as if he had stepped into a florist's shop.

"Surprise, Mr. Driskill!" "Surprise!" "Surprise!"

they called gaily in a medley of fresh young voices. To his astonishment, he saw before him his basketball squad.

"Shall we give it to him now?" somebody asked. A girl in a green gown stepped forward, a long box in her hands. Tonight she wore red lipstick, and her eyelashes were brushed with blue mascara.

"Why," Lee Driskill stammered, "it's Ginger!"

Grinning, the captain handed him the box. "It's from—all of us," she said. "We hope you like it."

He finally got it out of the box and unfolded it. It was a new black blazer of Dacron and wool with three silver buttons. On a patch on the breast pocket was inscribed in red the figure of a tiny whirlwind. Lee's mouth fell open. The coat was beautiful. Times were hard, and he couldn't imagine how they had raised the money it must have cost. He took off his suit coat and tried on the blazer. It fit perfectly.

"We got your size from Jean," they bubbled happily.

As he picked up the varnished wrapping paper, Lee remembered the unpacked duffle bags, the poor shooting drill, the whispering that stopped when he walked up—all the little things they hadn't done well in practice because they were excited about doing this bigger thing for him tonight. He felt humble and ashamed.

He looked into their radiant faces. "Now I know why you couldn't practice well." Blushing, he looked at his shoes and shook his head. "I feel like a dime's worth of dirty ice."

They laughed uproariously. Then they all had dinner together, buffet style. All evening Lee wore the new blazer.

It was on the Tuesday following their sweep of the district tournament at Hondo that the long-distance call came. Summoned from an afternoon homeroom, Lee took it in Bannister's office. The superintendent was out, but Miss Rogers and two student secretaries were there, stuffing letters into envelopes.

"Long Knock?" Joe Brody's teasing voice came on the line. "You still wanta come out here and be my boys basketball coach?"

Lee's heart leaped exultantly. "You dawgoned right."

"You still unhappy there?"

"Well—not entirely. But I'm not satisfied with several phases of the program. And I've always wanted to coach boys."

On the other end of the connection the Varney superintendent chuckled softly and dragged the conversation out a little, postponing the purpose of his call as was his way. "You still got that old gray bird dog that can't smell anything?"

Lee pretended indignation. "Let me tell you what she did last fall in a plum thicket east of here. I got a double on a rise, killed one bird, crippled another. Alice picked up the dead bird first, then caught the cripple, and carried them both. The cripple fluttered loose and got away. Alice spit out the dead bird, caught the cripple again, put it deep in her mouth, picked up the dead bird with her front teeth, and brought 'em both to me." It had happened just as he told it.

Joe laughed. "Tell you something, boy. You haven't seen quail hunting like they've got out here."

He became quiet. Lee waited, heart thumping.

"Long Knock. This boys job is yours. I've already talked to two board members. They're for you. Two others have favorites of their own, but I can swing 'em. The fifth one will do anything I ask. We read about you upsetting Crockett. We hear you've won twenty of twenty-two ball games. That right?"

Lee modestly flipped a thread off his trousers. "Oh, something like that. We're only a sophomore team."

"Why don't you drive over here and see what we've got? Bring Jean. Bring your fishing gear. Stay at our house. I want you to meet our board."

Lee propped one leg over the knee of the other. "How about salary?"

Joe laughed. "Goin' commercial on me, huh? We'll beat what you're gettin' there, beat it pretty good. We'll talk about that when you get here."

Lee thanked him. "I'll talk to Jean. I think we can come after our season ends here."

He turned triumphantly and dialed the Ford Company. "Jean? I just had a call from Joe Brody at Varney. They've offered me the job coaching their boys . . . ."

When he hung up, Miss Rogers spun round from her desk. "Sounds like congratulations are in order. I couldn't help overhearing."

At practice next day, Lee was late. As he hurried onto the court, stuffing his white cotton coaching jersey under his belt, all the girls were waiting for him at the sideline. They looked quiet and subdued, a hurt expression on their faces.

Although Ginger was the captain, Pat, the natural leader, did the talking. Honest and direct, she wasted no time.

"Mr. Driskill, you don't like us, do you?"

Her words astonished him. "I don't think I understand. What do you mean?"

Her steady eyes, gray as stone, fixed on him accusingly. "You don't want to coach us, do you?" She stood there, trim and stiff-backed, waiting for his answer.

How could he tell them the truth without offending them? How could they know how exciting it was to coach a game in which all the players moved freely all over the court, instead of half of them standing idle while the other half played three on three?

Pat's eyes were suddenly wet and her voice tremulous. "It's all over school that you're going to Varney."

Troubled, Lee looked at them. They deserved an honest answer. "Do you want me to level with you?"

They all nodded.

"No, I don't want to coach girls."

He saw the shock whiten their faces. For a moment they looked as if they hadn't heard him correctly. "Why not?" Pat asked, an odd, girlish squeak in her voice.

Lee wet his lips and plunged ahead. "I just want to coach boys. I've always wanted to coach boys. I was hired to coach the boys team here. It was to have been my first head coaching job after I'd been an assistant boys coach for five years at Fairfield. But when I got here, they welshed on their agreement. They gave my job to another man."

Surprise in their faces, they all listened carefully. He saw Pat Thompson's lips part and understanding come into her eyes. "And that's why you're stuck with us," she concluded for him.

For a moment there was silence. Then Pat spoke, the hurt coming back into her face. "Have we done anything wrong? Are you upset with us for losing those two games? Have we ever broken training or displeased you in any way or made you ashamed of us? Haven't we always tried to do everything you told us? Have we ever given up in a game?"

Lee shook his head. "No." It was hard to face those steady eyes.

Pat's face softened and her voice became almost pleading. "Mr. Driskill, we don't ever want any other coach but you. We tried to tell you that when we gave you that blazer the other night at Dr. York's house. Please reconsider your decision. We'd rather have you than any coach in the world."

Lee looked at her but couldn't speak.

Pat managed a grin, a brave, tearful grin. "It's kind of a standoff, isn't it?"

Lee drew a long breath. "I honestly don't think I'm that important. I think you would have had a good team this year no matter who coached you. I think you'll have a better team next year."

Points of fire showed suddenly in Pat's eyes. "I'll tell you one thing, Mr. Driskill. We're not giving up on this." She looked around her resolutely as if enlisting the support of the others. "You've taught us how to fight hard to win in basketball. We're going to fight hard to win this, too. Varney hasn't got you yet."

While Lee stood there with his mouth open, they turned away and began jogging around the court.

A queer bitterness twitched his lips. They were making too much of this. Every basketball team changed coaches now and then, usually for the better. He wondered how many of Varney's starters returned next season.

Hugh Morgan stopped by the practice and handed Lee forty-five dollars, which had to take them to Pemberton and back for the regional tournament. "This is all the money we have left in the student athletic fund. I hope you can make it do. There's a little left in the activities fund, but Brawley wouldn't let Bannister give that to you. He said it might be needed later for boys track."

"Thanks, Hugh." Lee folded the bills in his wallet and pocketed it. He'd be done with Brawley when he went to Varney, but he felt sorry for the next coach of the Middleton girls.

"If you get in a jam and need more, phone me and I'll figure out something," Morgan added. "Dell and I will drive over Saturday night if you hit the finals. We'll bring Jean. Good luck."

Lee drove his own car, taking Jean along to drive it back so that she would have transportation to and from her work. Parents of the players furnished two other cars, and the drive to the regional tournament was accomplished without mishap.

It was a sunny day, warm for late February, and

there was no indication that anything could mar its peace. Pemberton, a college town, was filled with motels, but there was little tourist trade in winter. Mindful of his tight budget, Lee bargained successfully with a motel manager to house his team for two dollars per girl.

They won the first game, an afternoon contest, by eight points. Half an hour after Jean started home, the wind growled out of the north, and a slate-colored cloud bank appeared, obliterating the sunset. It grew colder. The first snowflakes, big and wet, came floating down softly and lazily, like butterflies meandering in spring.

Next morning, Lee was awakened by a knock on his door. "Lee, Lee." It was a man's voice, soft and urgent—Sam Bradshaw. "Take a look out your window." Sam Bradshaw was the father of Bonnie Bradshaw, one of the freshman players. Lee blinked the sleep out of his eyes and pulled back the curtain. He stared, unable to believe what he saw.

Off to the south the hills were gone, erased in a drab grayness that hid the sun. Lee dressed and had breakfast with Sam.

"It's six inches deep on the flat and getting worse," Sam reported. "All of us who brought cars are going back home right now, before we get snowed in. Then we'll all come back tonight to see you play Yoakum, if the weather lets up so they can start the snowplows."

But it didn't let up. Instead it grew worse. All vision died at fifty yards. The wind rose, and now the flakes were small and hard and stinging. Excited, the girls would have liked to go out in it, snowballing and sledding, but they had a game to play, and they stayed inside to rest. Yoakum, a big team, had lost only four times and had won its last eleven games in succession. The winner would go the following week to the state tournament to play in the last round of eight.

Caught with only his new black blazer, a thin purse, and no transportation to the Pemberton gymnasium, Lee began to feel uneasy. Game time was six o'clock, and the gymnasium a mile and a half uphill from the motel.

When he looked outside at four o'clock, all minor depressions had been evened off by the drifts that now lay level over everything. By five o'clock, it had snowed twelve inches. All the highways were closed, and he had to figure some way to get twelve girls and the student manager to the game. While the team dressed in the motel, Lee hitchhiked a ride to the gymnasium, found some Middleton students who attended college at Pemberton, and asked them to go back to the motel with him and bring the team to the game.

The game became a nightmare. Pat Thompson didn't have her shooting touch, and when Pat was off, the whole team sagged. Yoakum's big forwards shot so well over Middleton's little guards that with two and one half minutes left to play Yoakum led by seven and was stalling, refusing to shoot.

With a Yoakum free throw coming up, Lee called time out and faced them. "If you'll start doing half the things you can do—and do them right—we can still beat this team." He saw Ginger, the captain, look at him as if asking herself, I wonder if he really believes that?

Lee looked around at them. "We have to gamble a little. When that big red-faced forward gets the ball and starts stalling, we've got to foul her, but it mustn't be flagrant or they'll get two free throws. I want Ginger to foul her. Ginger, do it cleanly but put her on the free throw line where she can't rebound. If she misses the free throw, we ought to get the rebound. We can win this game yet."

Ginger stared at him. "You mean that?"

"I sure do."

Ginger jumped straight up into the air. "Whoopee!" she yelled as if Middleton had already won.

Like a railroad turntable reversing a locomotive in a roundhouse, the game changed direction. From the foul line, the big Yoakum forward put the ball squarely in the hoop, but it ran capriciously around the ring and curled out, Sadie rebounding. With two minutes to play, Pat long-stepped around her guard and scored left-handed. With a minute left, Portia fed Pat who drove right-handed and was roughly spilled on the court. Twice she trod the foul line, twice her ponytail wiggled, and twice she dropped the free throw dead center. Then the defense dropped off Candy, and she sank a twenty-footer.

Nineteen seconds remained, Yoakum led by one and Yoakum had the ball. The Yoakum coach called time out to reorganize his shaken forces. In the Middleton huddle, Lee, fearing that his small guards would never get the ball, resorted to strategy. "Pat, change positions with Susan. You go to guard and get us that ball. Then I'll call time and put you back at forward."

He looked around at them, trying to keep the tension out of his face. "Stay relaxed. The pressure's on them.

If you don't intercept in the first five seconds, foul her again while going for the ball, and we'll risk their missing the one-and-one."

The climax play followed Lee's script as precisely as if he had written it out in longhand. A Yoakum forward tried to pass, but Pat Thompson, now playing guard, leaped catlike to slap the ball away. Ginger pounced on it and called time out. Twelve seconds were left, but now Middleton had the ball. Then Lee made the exchange everybody expected, Pat trotting back across the middle line to her forward position.

All eyes were on the referee standing on the sideline with the ball. Ginger, at his elbow, held out her hands. On the court, the players crowded and jostled each other gently. Each Middleton girl was hounded by a gold-clad Yoakum lass, a look of mighty resolution on all their faces.

With an exaggerated gesture, the referee handed Ginger the ball. Ginger bounce-passed to Pat. A roar of approval was wrenched from the crowd. Middleton's crack forward had the ball, and every person there knew what she could do.

Expecting Pat's long-striding drive, Yoakum clogged the middle, all three guards watching her with clenched faces. With the clock in its countdown, Middleton's forwards faked, dribbled, and moved, trying to probe the defense for an opening. None showed. The crowd was screaming. On the bench, Lee stared in horrified paralysis. Do something, Pat! Do something!

With four seconds to play, Pat drove toward the goal with every ounce of speed in her slender body. All three Yoakum guards converged on her. But Pat was looking as well as dribbling. Suddenly, she doubled into the air and hook-passed to Portia Stovall standing all alone beneath the goal.

And Portia dropped the ball!

Afterward, the Yoakum victory celebration threatened to overrun everything. Portia walked woodenly around it to the bench. When Lee and the team tried to console her, the girl buried her face in her hands.

Dry-eyed, she finally looked up. "It was a good pass, Mr. Driskill. I should have looked the ball all the way into my hands."

Hot food helps to assuage the pangs of defeat. Lee sent his saddened squad to the college cafeteria, then got rides for them back to the motel. As he lingered to pay the dinner bill, the cafeteria manager walked to the front door and with a key locked it from the inside.

"We're closed," he announced. Lee hadn't eaten. And when he paid and it took the last of his funds, he realized he couldn't have eaten anyhow.

He had no money left. They couldn't drive home to Middleton because the highways were buried under fifteen inches of snow. The motel manager would have to give them credit for the night's lodging, and Lee didn't know what he would do in the morning about breakfast for fourteen. He'd cross that bridge when he came to it.

As he stepped outside in his black blazer to walk the mile and a half to the motel, he felt his ears numbing. The snow had been trampled down enough to provide a rough path, but the cold shut down on him so hard that he ran the last mile down the long hill. Every breath he drew was a cold stab in the chest. The wind had died, and the stars were blazing.

Ahead he saw the motel lights. Stamping and scraping his feet to get rid of the crusted ice, he ducked into the lobby and was grateful for its cozy warmth. His run had made him ravenously hungry, but he had no money and every café in town was closed anyhow.

In his room, he draped the blazer over a hanger. Ginger Selman came by to report on the bed check. "All the girls are in their rooms, Mr. Driskill."

He hung the blazer over a hook in the closet. "Did everybody have dinner?"

"Yes, sir." She paused, squinting at him shrewdly. "Mr. Driskill, that cafeteria closed while we were eating. Where did you eat?"

Lee blew on his hands and laughed. "I didn't. Got too busy. I'll eat in the morning. Good-night."

Her quick footsteps echoed down the hall. Lee felt too restless to sleep. It was cold in the room and he put his blazer back on. Relaxing, he took off his shoes, dropped into a chair, put his cold feet on the gas heater, and played the exciting game over in his mind. Yoakum didn't beat us, he told himself. We beat ourselves. Actually we made the moves that should have won the game. We made them because these girls believed me when I told them they could win even when they were seven points down. A boys team wouldn't have believed me no matter if I'd talked until I was blue in the face.

Staring at the cheap carpeting on the floor, he marveled at the credulity of girl athletes. They believed everything you told them without doubt or skepticism. If you told them to push a Santa Fe diesel from the depot to the section house, they would try to do it. Girls were so dedicated and coachable. They were more fun to coach than boys.

He rubbed his hands together for warmth and thought about it. Why was he leaving all this? When you came right down to it, it was the people in the game that counted, and whether a coach enjoyed working with them. What kind of people did he prefer coaching, boys or girls?

A soft knock on the door interrupted his musing. He got up and opened it. Kitty Thurston, a freshman, stood there smiling, a shiny red apple in her hands. It was a big, meaty apple and as Lee stood there eyeing it, he felt his mouth watering.

"Mr. Driskill, we know you haven't eaten," Kitty said. "We checked and this is all the freshmen girls could find. Pamela found it in her suitcase." She handed him the apple.

Grinning, he thanked her and told her good-night. How about that! he asked himself as he bit hungrily into it.

He plopped down again into his chair, chewing and meditating. What would he be heading into when he went to Varney? Boys participated in so many different sports that it was hard for them to give their loyalty completely to one. But basketball was the only sport available to girls; consequently it became the dominant interest of their lives. A coach could calculate this interest by the attention he got when he talked to his team. When he talked to a boys team, the five starters listened but the substitutes gazed out the window. But every girl on the squad drank in a coach's remarks with rapt absorption. Even the greenest girl in the group thought she was involved.

Lee finished the apple and sat studying the core. The two games differed in spectator appeal. A boys game was mostly run and shoot. The goals came so fast that the audiences got little emotional relaxation, and it was often difficult to stay abreast of the scoring.

Frowning, Lee tossed the core into a wastebasket. Spectators could follow a girls game more easily because play occurred in a smaller area, the pace was slower, and fewer girls competed. The crowd had time to see the screens form, the defense check off, and the players jockey for position on rebounds. Spectators had time to breather and think, and to drink in the drama of the moment.

Another knock rattled off the door, startling him. He swing both feet down and opened it.

"Surprise, Mr. Driskill!" With glowing cheeks and an easy laugh, Candy Brown stood in the doorway. Behind her Pat Thompson and three other sophomores stood smiling.

Candy's laugh rang out merrily. She said, "We bought thse at the cafeteria to eat before bedtime. We want you to have them." She held out two chocolate bars.

Knowing how all healthy young people liked a snack before going to sleep, Lee Driskill protested, trying to refuse. But they insisted.

As he sat alone stripping off the paper wrapper, it occurred to him for the first time that running off to

Varney would be the act of a very selfish person. He'd be rid of Brawley and the problems, but the girls wouldn't. They'd still be struggling with a low budget, ragged uniforms, thin crowds, an inconvenient practice hour. Could he look at himself in the mirror after leaving them like that?

While he considered it and finished off the second candy bar, there was a third knock. Lee padded to the door in his stocking feet. What now?

Portia Stovall and the juniors filled the doorway, smiling. Lee blinked in amazement. The team had no seniors, so he figured this constituted his final nourishment of the evening. But he hadn't reckoned on its originality. In Portia's hands was an ice bucket filled with a snowy substance that gave out the pleasant aroma of vanilla.

Portia saw his mystification and grinned. "We ransacked all our luggage but we didn't have anything to give you. So we talked to the old man who runs the motel. He gave us all he had—a cup of milk, some sugar, and a little vanilla extract. He loaned us the bucket and this spoon. We got some snow and stirred it all together. It's snow ice cream."

"Murder!" Lee Driskill laughed, "you're spoiling me rotten. But I appreciate it. I'll sure eat it. And I know it's delicious."

It was, too. And before he finished wolfing it down, Pat and Candy brought the second-place trophy, a handsome little silver figurine of a girl player mounted on a walnut pedestal. They set it on his table and left. They didn't want him to be lonesome.

Amused and touched, Lee chuckled to himself as he

finished off the ice cream. Murder! he thought, what a bunch of natural mothers! They're all trying to mama me. And that's when he knew that he wasn't going to join Joe Brody at Varney.

Right then, he phoned Hugh Morgan long distance and told him of his decision to stay on as coach of the Middleton girls.

"We'll come and get you tomorrow," Morgan promised. "We just got the bus fixed. The snowplows will start clearing the highways in the morning. I'll bring enough money to pay all your bills."

While Lee warmed his hands over the gas heater, the last and most timid knock of the night came.

"Come in."

"I can't, Mr. Driskill. I'm in my pajamas and robe. We have a problem down in our room." Lee recognized Sadie York's voice.

"Go on back where it's warm and I'll be down in a minute," he told her. "Let's see, you're in Room 119, aren't you?" He pulled on his shoes and waited until her running footsteps died away, then walked down the hall to their door and rapped.

It took somebody the better part of a minute to unfasten both the door and its safety latch.

"Give me time to get back in bed, then come in," Sadie directed.

Lee waited until he heard a bed creak. He knew there were four girls in the two beds—Sadie York, Ginger Selman, Candy Brown, and Pat Thompson.

When he stepped into the room the lights were on. All he could see on the pillows were what looked like four sets of nylon bristles on wire frames, but he knew there was a girl under each set. He chuckled to himself. Probably hair rollers.

"What in the world's wrong?" he asked, amused by their girlish propriety.

The quilts were lowered an inch, and he saw four pairs of eyes.

"Our pilot light went out." Sadie's voice was muffled. "We're about to freeze to death. We were afraid to light it. Afraid it might blow up."

With his back to the beds, Lee got down on his knees by the stove. He had only two matches. Neither would ignite. "Somebody hand me some matches," he said, holding his hand out behind him.

The bed creaked, and he felt a match being pressed into his hand. "Now somebody please push this button on the stove." The other bed creaked. A hand slid past his ear, engaging the button. He scratched the first match, held it over the vent. "Now." A soft detonation, and the pilot light burst into flame.

"That ought to do it," Lee said. "Better open the window an inch, so you won't get gassed." He stood and turned around, heading for the door.

They were all out of bed, and they all wore red flannel pajamas. Pat still held the packet of matches. Ginger had pushed the button of the burner.

Lee began to chuckle. "Why were you so bashful? You're covered from head to toe. Wearing all that insulation, you're almost decent enough to go down into the lobby."

Like quail exploding from a grass clump, they scattered. Bare feet drummed, bodies collided, quilts flew, both beds squeaked, and when Lee walked out, he saw again only the tops of the four sets of hair rollers.

"If you're still cold, wear your warm-up suits over your pajamas," he advised as he shut the door. He laughed to himself all the way back to his room.

As he turned down the quilts of his own bed, he decided that next year they would have chaperones to travel with the team and handle all such emergencies. He liked Dorothy Thompson's suggestion about enlisting a mother of the players for the duty.

His mind became a ferment of planning. With his whole team returning, they might just as well shoot for the summit, the state championship. If somehow they could secure the full-time services of Frances Bonner, they might mount a solid challenge. Most of all, they needed new uniforms. If ever a team had earned them, this one had.

The rules recommended two sets of playing uniforms, one of light color, the other dark, so contesting teams wouldn't duplicate colors, but Middleton owned only one set, and it was shabby from several years' wear. He decided to talk to Hugh Morgan about all these things tomorrow.

When Morgan came after them in the bus, he seemed quieter than usual. After all the girls had boarded, he beckoned to Lee. "Sit behind me. I have something to tell you."

Face grave, he turned the vehicle around slowly and pointed it home through snowdrifts bladed back three feet high on each side of the road.

"It's about Frances Bonner." Morgan leaned toward Lee but kept his eyes on the highway. "She ran off and got married. To some little blond kid from Folsom. She phoned her folks from Amarillo. They told her not to come back."

Shocked, Lee stared down the narrow ribbon of road. He knew what that meant. Many schools automatically expelled students who ran off and got married because one marriage in a school sometimes encourages several. Lee remembered the boy he and Jean had seen with Frances at the drive-in. Pink-cheeked and immature, he hadn't looked a day over sixteen.

Lee shifted his feet uncomfortably. "When did it happen?"

"Thursday afternoon. Same day you and the team left for Pemberton."

Angrily Lee figured it out. The girl got very little affection at home. She felt insecure and unwanted. The boy looked a little the same way. They had probably married for the most pathetic reason of all—for mutual sympathy and understanding, two lonely young people trying to get something they had failed to get at home.

The sun emerged, but Lee felt no warmth nor elation. All the way to Middleton he sat brooding as he listened to the drone of the motor and the swishing of the tires through the slush. The divorce rate for youngsters who married in their teens was appalling. What kind of life lay ahead for Frances Bonner?

Chapter 8

Ball Freeze and Fiscal Squeeze

Spring settled into summer; summer melted into fall; and on a foggy Saturday morning in October, Lee summoned the squad for the first practice of his third year at Middleton.

As he stood by an open window in the school foyer, the girls began arriving, the twin pools of their auto lights shining faintly through the fog's pearly thickness like tiny electric bulbs through gauze. Sound carried with remarkable fidelity through the damp haze, and long before he saw them, Lee heard car doors slamming. He could follow their approach by the scuffling of their shoes on the walk and the murmur of their voices, soft and plaintive in the morning damp.

Out of the fog bank, as through a curtain, the girls

began appearing in twos and threes. Lee was amused by the variety of their attire. They wore jeans, old slacks, hip huggers, and a collection of sweat shirts that in lettering across the many-hued fronts professed loyalty to everything from "Sooners" to "Palo Duro State Park."

While they changed to their practice gear, he fitted half a dozen old balls into a rubber-tired rack and, whistling a tune to himself, rolled it onto the court. Alice, whom he had brought with him from home, watched his busy preparations, her plumed tail swinging. Lee liked his job, liked the people with whom he worked. To his surprise he was learning to like the town.

Except for Frances Bonner, his entire starting six—Pat Thompson, Candy Brown, Portia Stovall, Ginger Selman, and Susan Grove—had returned. A strong team was the prospect.

"I wanted to talk to you a minute about our goals," Lee began after seating them in lower bleacher seats. "First of all, Mr. Bannister has promised us new suits."

"Yea!" they yelled, springing to their feet and waving their arms.

"Not warmups," he reminded, "just suits. Shirts of red and black Jacquard knit. Black tackle twill, block numbers trimmed in white. Just like you picked out."

"Yea!"

"Black nylon trunks."

"Yippee!"

"Long Jacquard knit socks, same color as the shirts."

"Yeow!" They had waited a long time for this news.

"Something else." He pulled a piece of chalk out of his trouser pocket and began rolling it between both hands. Eyes big, they listened intently. "You know our goals as well as I—we have to sell girls basketball in Middleton. There are people in this town who would like to see it eliminated. First, we have to win. We have to build a product our crowds will want to see."

He paused, looking at them challengingly. "But I haven't mentioned our number one goal. What's the biggest thing we could possibly do in girls basketball this year?"

"Win the state!"

Their soprano cries rang out almost as one. An excited glow warmed Lee. Beulah had won the state championship last season, but in addition to its powerful team, Beulah's whole community supported its girls program enthusiastically—big crowds, fine equipment, a proud tradition. Middleton had none of these. To win the state championship in spite of them was a formidable aim, but they were at least all together on it and without a shred of prompting from him.

As he talked, he heard a gnawing sound as if a mouse were chewing on something nearby. The girls heard it too. When it distracted their attention, Lee stopped. The noise seemed to come from directly underneath the rollaway bleachers.

There he found Alice eating old twists of chewing gum off the bottoms of the seats. Lee called her to him. "Lie down." She flopped down on the floor behind him, and he resumed talking.

Again their faces became wreathed in smiles, and he seemed to be losing their attention. Lee spun around. Again the culprit was Alice.

With her head between her front paws, but her rear hoisted so high that she seemed to be lying down in front and standing up behind, the dog was listening carefully to every word he said.

"That's the kind of attention I want from you," Lee told the squad.

When he went outside to put her in his car, the fog was lifting in tints of lilac and pale yellow, disappearing in small patches as the sun burned through.

After the Monday practice, Bonnie Bradshaw, a substitute guard, lingered behind the others. A sophomore, she wore her brunette hair elevated in a bun and tied with a yellow ribbon.

"Mr. Driskill," she began, "I have a problem."

"You do?" Curious, Lee opened the drawer to his desk and extracted two sticks of gum.

She looked at him shyly but trustingly. "I had a first date last night with Bo Warren. He tried to kiss me good-night, but I wouldn't let him. Was that all right?"

Lee stifled an inclination to smile. He knew she was sincere, but he also had Bo Warren in a history class, and he felt an obligation to the boy, too.

"If he tried to kiss you on a first date you must have given him some encouragement. Maybe he thought he was supposed to. What went on in the car before he brought you home?"

Bonnie looked as indignant as if he had slapped her in the face. "Nothing," she insisted flatly. "He didn't even have a car. We walked."

She seemed genuinely worried. "Mr. Driskill, I've another date with him Saturday night. He says he'll have a car this time. I know he'll try to kiss me again." Her violet eyes flashed with sudden inspiration. "I know what I'll do. I'll have Mom leave the porch light on, and maybe he'll be afraid to try to kiss me."

Lee handed her one of the sticks of chewing gum. "After two or three dates, most boys probably expect a little warmth in return for spending their money and furnishing the transportation. Of course, the minute a boy switches to fiery kissing, or catch-as-catch-can wrestling, or anything else off-color, you've got to stop him. Fast. Boys aren't idiots. If you discourage them, they'll behave. If they don't—find you another boy."

She looked at him unwaveringly, drinking it all in. "That's not as easy as it sounds, Mr. Driskill."

"I know it. And some nights you may have to stay home without a date. But not forever. Pat and Candy do lots of double-dating together. I think double-dating is fine. Why don't you talk to them? Why don't you talk to your mother about it, too?"

Bonnie's face glowed with gratitude. "Thanks, Mr. Driskill, I will."

Watching her as she strode away, Lee shook his head. Why had she come to him first?

When he put the question to Jean at home that night, Jean laughed. "I think I know. In almost every school there's at least one person that young people feel they can trust and communicate with. It may be the Spanish teacher, the English prof, the lady librarian, or the custodian. They have confidence in that person. He probably doesn't have a degree in psychology or counseling, but he likes young people and they like him. In Middleton, that person must be the girls basketball coach."

Lee stared incredulously at his wife. Where did she get all her infallible knowledge? She seldom set foot inside the school except to see a basketball game.

As they sat down to dinner, Jean said, "I hear Frances Bonner and her husband are having a hard time."

Lee looked up, listening keenly. "That so?" The name of the boy that they had seen with Frances at the drive-in and whom she had married was Johnny Ice. The school board had expelled her instantly, afraid that her marriage might produce an imitative wave of half a dozen more. The boy, only sixteen, had dropped out of the sophomore class at Folsom to take a part-time job at a filling station, but he had since lost it.

Jean got up to refill the biscuit plate. "They're living now with the boy's parents on a small farm near Broomfield."

Lee said, "That's only fifteen miles from here. I think we ought to go and see her."

Jean came back in and passed him the biscuits, neatly folded in aluminum foil to keep them hot. "Frances is pregnant. Her parents won't help them, although Dell Morgan says Mr. Bonner offered to take the baby after it was born and bring it up. He told Frances it would be better for the baby to be with him and Mrs. Bonner than with Frances. Frances turned him down real fast. She told him, 'You had me for sixteen years. I hope nobody else has to go through that!' "

Upset, Lee buttered his biscuit so violently that he smeared butter all over his thumb. "That boy!" He shook his head. "I know they're both too young, but that boy is even greener than Frances. He doesn't know yet who he is or where his legs are."

Jean looked thoughtfully at the fork in her hand. "I think married couples of their age must be the loneliest people on earth. Their marriages undergo strains that other marriages aren't subject to. They lose all their teen-age friends, and they can't make adult friends. Usually they are thrown back on their own parents, and of course Frances won't go near hers."

Lee tried to swallow his anger and the salad, too. "I think it's criminal to expel them. That keeps them from completing their education. Frances is a good student, but she won't have much chance for intellectual development out there on that shinnery farm. It's in high school that kids begin to find out how their minds work and how to thrash out things with other kids their own age."

At Monday's practice, he discussed Frances with the basketball squad. They listened to him silently, compassion in their faces.

With the back of her hand, Pat Thompson brushed the hair out of her eyes. "I feel bad about it. Because of her parents, Frances was a sort of loner, but I think we contributed to that by not bringing her into our group outside basketball. If we stay together off the court as well as on it, these things shouldn't happen."

"Let's give her a baby shower," proposed Liz Blair.

After a flurry of busy planning, they drove to Broomfield the following Saturday. Jean went, too.

"When Frances came to the door, she looked lonesome and discouraged," Jean told Lee that night. "But when Candy called out 'Surprise!' and Frances saw who had come and what they had brought her—bottle warmer, baby dresses, an overall set, crib sheets, and a silver cup and silver feeding spoon—she cheered up quickly. We stayed an hour."

With so many experienced players returning, Lee worked less on fundamentals and more on the new ball freeze he had decided to introduce. They had lost the Floyd City game last season because when they were slightly ahead in the score and their best guards had fouled out, they had no plan by which their forwards could maintain possession of the ball, keeping it away from the vulnerable half of the court.

All through late October they practiced the new device in secret. Lee designed the Middleton freeze around Pat Thompson, who dribbled and passed well and was deadly accurate at free throwing—qualities the new strategy demanded. Lee stationed Candy and Portia, his other two forwards, as far away from Pat as the dimensions permitted, both on the left sideline, Portia in the extreme corner, Candy even with the free throw line. Thus Pat had most of the court to herself and no one girl could take the dribble away from her.

If Middleton wished to score off its freeze, as well as to kill time, Pat might try to jump around her guard for a lay-up. If either Portia's or Candy's guard deserted to help stop Pat's drive, Pat would pass to the open girl under the goal, and she would score. The team called this maneuver "Choc Malt" and later shortened it to "Choc."

If time-consuming ball possession was Middleton's

motive, whichever forward got the open shot would refuse it, dribbling beneath the enemy goal and returning the ball to Pat, who would retreat to the center and start the whole maddening process over again. This phase of the freeze the players nicknamed "Frosty," in deference to Ginger who had to give up her beloved frosted root beers from September to March.

"How do you like it?" Lee asked Ginger one week before the Glendora game, first on the schedule.

Ginger cocked her black head on one side. "Coach, want me to give you the straight-skinny?"

Lee nodded.

"Not very well. Because I don't get to play much. I just stand and watch our forwards." She grinned. "Actually I see where it might help a lot."

He turned to Pat. "What do you think?"

"It looks cool. Only why should we turn down a set-up shot when we're running Frosty?"

"To cool off the opposition offense," Lee explained. "Their forwards won't like standing idle for long periods. When they finally do get the ball, they may be too eager, too aggressive, and lose their fine touch. Also, to keep the ball away from our guard end if our guards are in foul trouble. And to maintain possession so we can take the last shot of the quarter."

Pat nodded understandingly.

Rains had pelted the red soil, succoring the cotton. The farmers and their families had more money to spend. The gymnasium was one half full when Glendora invaded to launch the season. With Middleton leading by thirty points and four minutes left to play, Lee signaled his forwards into "Choc."

The freeze chilled Glendora which expected attack rather than restraint. Despite two goofs that Lee corrected during time-outs, the Tornadoes built their margin steadily higher. Twice Pat sped around her guard and, beset by Portia's opponent, slipped side passes to Portia who cashed one field goal and rimmed the other.

"Nice pass, Pat! Should have had it!" Portia called shrilly.

Fouled three times by Glendora's desperation tactics, Pat ringed five of six free throws; and when Lee waved the Middleton team into "Frosty" and the forwards began crisscrossing beneath the goal, ignoring the shot and dribbling back to the middle to renew the keep-away tactics, the crowd saw humor in Glendora's confusion and cheered. Not wishing to embarrass the opponents, Lee quickly withdrew all his starters. The second team finished the game, using the normal offense.

When Lee walked to his office afterward to leave his scorebook, he found Gus Brawley and John Bannister there ahead of him.

As usual, Brawley was scowling, and his unshorn hair looked like a frayed rope as it tumbled from beneath his black hat. Bannister, who had stopped to drink from a nearby water fountain, looked as if he would rather be anywhere else.

As Lee walked up, Brawley frowned at Bannister and beckoned commandingly to him. Bannister stopped drinking and hurried over. Lee watched, fascinated. The school board president had only to raise his finger, and the superintendent always came running. With Bannister at his side, Brawley turned very deliberately to Lee. Tonight he wore a suit of brown tweed, and on the third finger of his right hand a gold ring set with a large emerald.

"Mr. Driskill, we don't want any more of that disgraceful stalling that your team did at the end of their game tonight. That's a dull way to play basketball. It violates the object of the game. The official rules state plainly that the purpose of each team is to throw the ball into the basket, yet your team turned down shot after shot when they were wide open with no guard near them."

Lee stared at him, flabbergasted.

"Mr. Brawley, the rules do not say that a player has to shoot every time she dribbles beneath the basket. The decision of when to shoot is left entirely to the offensive players and is not restricted by the rules."

Brawley's black eyes glittered. "Mr. Driskill, in order to finance girls basketball in Middleton we have to have good crowds. And crowds don't like stalling. Crowds come to see scoring. That's what they pay their money for."

Lee looked at him incredulously. The man's interference had reached a new plateau of effrontery when he tried to dictate a team's style of play.

Lee said, "I think you're mistaken there, too. Crowds come to see their teams win. We want to win fairly, but our aim is to win. I think we'll have a better chance of winning if we use our ball freeze. We didn't need it tonight, but we might in the next game."

In the gesture Lee had come to know so well, Brawley's shaggy eyebrows began to knit together menacingly and his broad, dimpled chin to lift. He was not accustomed to being argued with in Middleton, either in the high school or anyplace else. "Mr. Driskill. There's not going to be any next game with Middleton stalling in it. Tell me this. Why doesn't your team play like Mr. Hooper's boys? Our boys team doesn't sit on the ball. They go down the floor so fast they almost ignite it. They always try to score. And so do their opponents. And our crowds love it."

Lee felt his lips go thin. "That's fine. But there's nothing in girls rules that says we have to play like our opponent. If I'm a boxer and have quick feet and a good left jab, why should I jump in and slug with an opponent who is good at it? If I'm fighting a tiger, would you expect me to bite and claw like the tiger?" He saw that Saul Myerson, the editor, had joined them and was listening intently.

Brawley purred smoothly, "Why is it, Mr. Driskill, that when your team plays, our gymnasium is practically empty, but when Mr. Hooper's team plays, it's nearly always full?"

A blind anger rose in Lee, and he moved a step closer. "I'll tell you why. Because girls basketball here has been so kicked around that nobody thinks it's any good or will take the trouble to go see it and find out for themselves." He looked at Brawley with leveled eyes. "Noon practice, sack lunches from home after a game, ragged uniforms, low budget, constant interference from an unfriendly school board that is trying to take over girls basketball here as it tries to take over everything else in the school system."

Brawley's face took on a look of brutal authority.

"Mr. Driskill, our school board will be told of your crude criticism of it. Meanwhile, there will be no more stalling by a Middleton team in this or any other gymnasium. Do you understand? Now I want your promise on it."

Lee shook his head. "I'm not promising you anything. As long as I'm the coach, I'll use the plays I think will get the job done. We'll continue to use the freeze. I don't want you meddling in any phase of my program."

Brawley stood very still, studying Lee intently. Then he reached into his vest pocket and produced a celluloid toothpick with which he began to dig at the popcorn in his teeth. His voice again grew soft and sinister. "All right, Mr. Driskill. I see you're going to be difficult again. I know how to reach difficult people. I've always known how to reach them."

He spun around, presenting his beefy back, and walked off to see the boys game, his right shoulder drooping. Shaken and indecisive, John Bannister followed him.

Myerson came up, flexing the crook in his right hand, his sharp eyes surveying Lee with admiration. "That's telling him. He's needed telling off like that for a long time. He has a big following here, mainly people from his church, the biggest in town. Threatened you, didn't he? He'll try to follow through, too, if I know Gus Brawley. He doesn't like me either, because I keep urging my readers to attend his school board meetings. He's king in this town. Wish there was some way we could force him to abdicate."

Lee unlocked his office door and went inside. Myerson followed. "You're doing a good job with your squad. I'd like to help you."

Lee tossed his scorebook on the desk. "Mr. Myerson, our girls appreciate your covering their games same as you do the boys games. All young people like to be appreciated. These girls aren't muscle molls. They're the finest and most popular girls in school. They're leaders in everything—church work, dramatics, homemaking, pep club, glee club. They make good grades. They're unselfish, too. Pat Thompson worked all summer with underprivileged children, little tots. She got paid for that. Then she came back in the afternoon on her own time and taught them how to swim. She didn't get paid for that. They put basketball ahead of everything while it's in season. They want to be the best. They think nothing is too good and no ambition too lofty for their school."

Myerson took off his gold-rimmed spectacles and began to polish them on his clean shirt front. "I see what you mean. I'm in your corner from now on."

The Tornadoes needed plenty of corner help—especially smelling salts—the following morning, but for a different reason.

Bannister sent for Lee. When Lee walked into Bannister's office, he expected anything, even dismissal. The superintendent closed the door behind him and sat down heavily. His face was pale and drawn, as if he didn't like what he had to do.

"You've lost your new uniforms," he said.

Lee felt the fury rising in him. He licked his lips. "What do you mean?"

"I mean that Mr. Braw—the school board—has

withdrawn permission to buy them. I just telephoned the factory, canceling the whole order."

Lee felt as if someone had flattened him with a sandbag. He couldn't speak.

Bannister looked at him appealingly. "Lee, if you'd only apologize and agree not to use that stall, I'm sure he—I mean they—would give you back your uniforms and let me reactivate the order."

Lee set his teeth and stared at him accusingly. "But you promised them to us. I've already told the girls."

Bannister looked cornered and uncomfortable. "I'm sorry. There's nothing I can do about it."

Lee sat there, breathing deeply to steady himself. His angry gaze never left Bannister's face. "This is the only basketball team I've ever been around that has to play in uniforms held together by safety pins and is coached by the president of the school board."

Bannister bowed his head but didn't speak. Lee got up and walked out.

That noon, he told the girls about it. Pain and shock came into their faces, but they took it well.

"I wish I could think of some way we could earn the money ourselves to buy the uniforms," he added. "I'm fed up with waiting for the school board to do it for us."

For a moment they just sat there. Then Pat Thompson's head lifted proudly, and her gray eyes sparkled. "Mr. Driskill, we could pull cotton. A lot of our parents farm cotton. Most of us know how to plant it, hoe it, and pull it. Some of us can pull four or five hundred pounds a day."

Ginger's eyes lighted as if deep fires burned behind

them. "There would be almost a dozen of us. Help is scarce on the farms. My dad says he can't hire hands anywhere this year."

Doris Crossett's blue eyes gleamed thoughtfully. "We've got lots of time. School lets out soon for the cotton harvest. Frost comes late this year. The second pulling will last through Thanksgiving."

Pat looked at Candy. "You can snap bolls, can't you, Candy?"

"You bet," Candy gushed, "I've been snapping them ever since I've been big enough to pull the sack." Her charming laugh rang out.

Pat looked around at them challengingly. "Why don't we all hire out together? It would be lots more fun that way." Quickly, they organized the venture, making it sound exciting.

Lee rubbed his hands together. "Count me in, too." He wasn't about to let them carry the whole load.

Pat's eyes measured him shrewdly. "How many pounds a day can you pull, Mr. Driskill?"

Lee laughed. "I never pulled an ounce of cotton in my life. I come from the northwest part of the state where wheat's the main crop. But I can learn."

They worked in jeans and slim-jims. At the end of three days, they had eighty dollars. But uniforms for twelve girls cost four hundred dollars. Laboring clumsily alongside them, Lee was surprised at their industry and endurance.

"They go at it the same way they play basketball, as if they were killing snakes," he told Jean the first night. "They sure don't quit. Some of the town girls, like Sadie, Susan, and Bonnie, didn't do so well. They'd never worked a day in the fields. But they hung in there pretty good. Hand me a clean pair of shorts, will you, hon? My knees are sore. I've been walking on them all day."

In his front page column that week, Saul Myerson scored the school board for not properly equipping a girls team that hadn't lost a game. But when Lee drove to town to thank him, Myerson looked pale and agitated as he fed envelopes into a small job press.

"The girls and I appreciate it," Lee told him. "Say, you don't look so good. What's the matter?"

With one hand, Myerson reached across Lee and flipped off a switch. The gears of the press ground slowly to a halt. "Brawley!"

Lee blinked. "Brawley? What's he done now?"

"Canceled all his advertising in my paper. Bottling works, sporting goods store, ladies ready-to-wear—the whole shooting match. That column's going to cost me two hundred dollars a month."

Shocked, Lee licked the dryness from his lips and whistled under his breath. "That's quite a lick. I'm sure sorry if we brought any of this down on you, Saul."

The editor doubled his crooked fingers into a fist and winked bleakly. "You didn't. I brought it on myself. But I'm not taking it lying down. I know how to hurt that so-and-so. School board election comes in March. I'm gonna file. If I can beat the man they run, Gus is gonna have me on his board. And at all their meetings. I wonder how he'd like that!"

On the sixth morning of the cotton harvest, when the uniform fund had grown to $190, Pete Reif and

Bob Cochrane of Bill Hooper's Middleton High School boys team came to the field with Sadie York and Pat Thompson. They had on overalls and carried leather gloves.

Pat walked up to Lee. "Mr. Driskill, Pete and Bob want to help us pull today. What do you think?"

Pete grinned bashfully. "We'd like to help you get the new uniforms. We've been helping our dads pull at home, but they let us off today so we could help the girls. They'll let us off again Saturday, so you could count on us then, too." Both were farm boys and not afraid of work.

Lee pulled on his gloves. "I think it's fine. We need all the help we can get."

The next day five other boys who dated girl players joined the pulling brigade, and when the cotton harvest ended and classes resumed, the fund topped $275, and the girls searched for other means of adding to the revenue.

On the first morning of classes, John Bannister sent for Lee and closed the door behind him.

"How much money have you raised with this cotton pulling?" Concern and annoyance lined the superintendent's face as he walked behind his desk and sat down.

Lee told him.

Bannister bit his lip. "Why don't you give it back to the girls, and we'll order the new uniforms in the morning."

Scenting victory, Lee masked his elation. He thought he knew what had happened. The whole town had heard about the cotton pulling and thought it was fine until they learned why the team did it. Then criticism of Bannister and the school board swelled in a flood tide.

Lee sank into a chair and grew wary. "How does the school board stand on this?"

"They'll go along."

Lee's mouth hardened. They had gone along once before, then rescinded their action. "Is this a guess on your part, John, or do you have positive knowledge that they mean it this time?"

Pain entered Bannister's face. "They voted to last night."

Recognizing his bargaining power, Lee decided to push it to the hilt. "Why don't you buy us the uniforms—shirts, trunks, and stockings—and we'll use our cotton money to buy a dozen new warmups? They'll cost $240 more. We have that much now. We've a good chance to go to the state tournament this year, but if we had to wear those raunchy old warmups, we'd be the worst-dressed team there."

Bannister shook his head stubbornly. "The board doesn't want any more of this cotton pulling to buy school equipment of any kind."

Lee's eyes narrowed shrewdly. "Then what will you do about the warmups?"

Bannister swallowed wearily. "We'll buy them for you, too."

"Is that a board action?"

Bannister leaned back, sitting stiffly erect. "I'm sure I can persuade them."

Lee eyed him cautiously, determined to settle all phases of the issue while he had their feet to the fire.

"If you, or the board, will put that on public record—say an announcement in the *Mirror*—declaring that you are buying both uniforms and warmups immediately so they'll be available soon, I think the girls will go for it."

And that was how it was done.

The incident helped attendance. The entire community heard how the all-victorious Tornadoes won their uniforms. Saul Myerson chronicled their feats in the *Mirror*, and spectators began to flock earlier to the gymnasium to see them play. When they tipped off against Cottonwood, the crowd came at the half. When they thrashed Austin Creek, 67–44, the gymnasium had filled comfortably midway of the second quarter. When they whirled past Yoakum, the spectators came at the start of the second quarter, peering up eagerly on the west wall to find out the score before settling back in their seats.

"There's nothing like a few wins to unzip the wallets," as Ginger put it.

The Tornadoes organized their own campaign to gain spectators, Lee learned from Saul Myerson. Whenever they went to town for any reason, the girls made it a point to call upon the merchants and businessmen in twos and threes and invite them to attend the games. "You coming out tonight to see us play?" they would ask. It was hard to say "no" to girls as pretty and successful as these.

The whole team played so well that they won their first nine games decisively. "I think we can step with almost anybody this year," Lee told Jean. "I know we could if we had another tough guard." He swallowed miserably. Every time he thought about that, he thought about Frances. But Frances' basketball days were gone with the wind that whipped the red sand across the flats.

On the night the Tornadoes defeated Ziller, notching their tenth consecutive victory, Lee learned that Frances' marriage was tottering.

Chapter 9

Iodine and Jacquard Knit

"Frances is washing pots and pans in a creamery at Manville," Hugh Morgan divulged over hot coffee and doughnuts at his home after the game, "but her young husband isn't doing anything. All he wants to do is race that souped-up jalopy. Frances told Mary that every time Johnny Ice gets hold of a dollar he blows it on that gear-jammer."

Lee felt his insides tensing up again. "Soon as she has her baby, maybe we can get her back in school."

Morgan shook his head. "It'll be tough. I know of no written rule here that would bar her. But our school board is afraid that a married girl might somehow corrupt the unmarried ones, give them information not otherwise available. In other states, courts have even backed boards of education that expelled such students."

Exasperation flooded through Lee as he stirred sugar into his coffee. "I don't see why married high school students should be expelled or segregated any more than married people out of school need to be segregated from the general population."

Morgan nodded in sympathy. "I agree. But high school sophomores are far too young for marriage. What's needed is to stop these impulse marriages. You can elope nowadays in a waiting auto. Duke Carney, a principal over at Mayhew, told me last year that he had a marriage coming up in his eighth grade."

"Some young marriages work," Lee insisted. "Some sixteen-year-old boys are more mature than college boys. Some twelve-year-old girls are more mature than their mothers. There surely must be some young people who sincerely want a family and children."

Morgan got up and filled Lee's cup from the pot. "School boards know, and the statistics bear them out, that teen-age kids who marry have the highest divorce rate of all. Like three-legged racehorses, they're bad risks. They don't know anything about budgets or credit, or how to support themselves, or how to take care of a baby. They're one step away from government welfare. I think it's wrong to expel them, but I think it's important to prevent such marriages before one starts an epidemic. That's why school boards deal so harshly with them." And that was the way they left it.

On the morning after the team defeated Crockett by

eight points at Crockett, using "Choc," their ball freeze, to protect and expand a slight lead in the fourth period, Lee got to school early and stood outside, enjoying the fresh air and sunshine.

"Mr. Driskill." Bonnie Bradshaw, who had just arrived from home, came up to him, face beaming. "Mr. Driskill," she confided, "look at Jimmy Leonard, my new boy friend."

Following her eyes, Lee looked and saw a tallish sophomore who played linebacker on the football team. He was wearing a red jacket with a black "M" on it and kept lifting his blond head to stare searchingly at a group of girls standing before the main entrance.

Bonnie giggled happily. "Jimmy's looking for me." Lee looked again. Sure enough, he was.

In her excitement, she dropped a book. Stooping, Lee picked it up. "Jimmy doesn't try to kiss me goodnight," the girl said dreamily. "When he tells me goodnight, he stands out in the front yard and I stand on the front porch."

Lee laughed quietly to himself. He thought, the day will soon come when you'll want him to kiss you goodnight. As he handed her the book, he soliloquized, Jimmy's a wise kid not to become too involved. He ought to be quarterbacking that football team instead of being wasted as linebacker.

Frances Ice's baby was born early in December. A week later Jean drove to Broomfield to see them.

"It's a boy, and Frances is crazy about it," Jean reported upon her return. "She spent only one day in the hospital. I don't think they can afford even that. They're still staying at the boy's parents'."

"How's the father taking it?" Lee asked, lowering his newspaper.

Jean's face clouded. "He was there with her, but he didn't seem happy or excited. He moped around the house looking stunned and mad. Later, when we were alone, Frances told me why. The boy had to sell his hot rod to pay the doctor."

"Serves him right," Lee muttered grimly. "He's afoot, and he doesn't like it." Many a teen-aged husband, he knew, first came to grips with the raw reality of life when he had to part with a beloved speed buggy to pay for an infant he had fathered.

Jean went on, "Frances told me that she was afraid he was going to leave her and the baby rather than give up his car. But he hasn't yet."

Dropping the newspaper, Lee growled, "If that young goon leaves Frances now . . . ."

"He hasn't left her," Jean reminded him. "And why do you call him a goon? This is all new to him, too. No wonder he finds it difficult to support a wife and child when he can't even support himself."

"I doubt if he's trying to get a job," Lee fumed. Unable to read, he got up and put on his coat. "Want to take a walk?"

"All right," she replied. "Wait until I put on my flat shoes."

Taking Alice, they hiked to the cotton gin and back before Lee felt calm enough to sleep. He was also concerned about something else. The next game posed a most serious challenge.

For a whole year Lee and his squad had kept the sting of the Floyd City defeat stored in the backs of their minds. The boisterous behavior of the Floyd City crowd that employed the goat-getting techniques of spectators at professional sports, the odious officiating and the formidability of Lorrie Sue, the amazonian guard, haunted the Middleton team like a wild, disordered dream.

"I've scheduled this year's game at Floyd City again, instead of here," Lee had told his squad in October. "On their home floor, they throw out more challenges in more directions than any other six teams we play. They're just what we need before the tournaments."

He looked teasingly at Pat Thompson. "Try not to let Lorrie Sue fall on you, Pat. If she does, we'll have to pick you up with a blotter."

Pat grinned. The whole squad knew that Lorrie Sue was the only guard Pat had ever played against whom she couldn't drive around.

This time the Tornadoes were expecting all the annoying distractions. When the handfuls of gravel, flung by small boys running alongside the Middleton bus, smashed against the windows the girls just looked grim and tolerant. When Lee walked out on the court and the Floyd City students punctuated each step he took with a chanted "Hut! Hut! Hut!" it didn't disconcert him. But most of the abuse was directed at Pat Thompson.

Every time she put up a shot in practice, the crowd grunted "Oomph!" in unison the instant the ball left her fingers. If she hit the shot, the crowd murmured a long-drawn-out "Ah!" If she missed, they sighed "Oh!" And again the same deep voice rang out from the balcony, "Wait until Lorrie Sue gets hold of you, Thompson!"

There was a change in the introduction ceremony. All over the hall the lights were extinguished, and a green spotlight was flashed on each player introduced. A chorus of boos greeted Pat when she dribbled out, and a rush of anger blazed through Lee. They hated her ponytail and thought she was cocky. But Pat didn't seem to mind. Rubbing rosin on her hands, she threw back her shoulders fearlessly, and her gray eyes flicked coolly over the packed galleries.

When Floyd City's starters were introduced, one by one, and Lorrie Sue sprinted out last, all 180 pounds of her, the crowd roared and the student cheering section flung her name in worshipful salvos against the opposite wall: "Lorrie Sue! Lorrie Sue! Lorrie Sue!" In a copy of the *Floyd City Clarion* they found in the hall, they read that the Floyd City girls had won eighteen consecutive games on their home floor.

When the lights came on again, Lee Driskill saw something that made his heart leap in fear. One of the officials had appeared during the blackout. A swarthy little man, he wore low sideburns. He was the same one who had called two technical fouls on Lee in the other game and had seemed reluctant ever to penalize the rough illegalities of Lorrie Sue.

The ball went up. Lorrie Sue snatched it out of the air and fired from her ear at a forward breaking behind Sadie. The collision spilled both girls, but the swarthy little official's call went against Floyd City. Pat, ignoring the crowd's "Oomph!" cashed the free toss.

Floyd City missed a shot. Ginger rebounded and, dribbling to the division line, gave off to Portia. Floyd City sank back into that zone with Lorrie Sue, her lower lip thrust out ferociously, crouched in the center. Pat cut behind a screen and tried a shot, but with a herculean effort, Lorrie Sue hurled herself into the air and slapped the shot back into Pat's face.

A bellow of delight broke from the Floyd City crowd, but before they could still their roaring, Pat, quick as lightning, snatched up the ball and bounced to Portia streaking in from the corner. Goal! Lee half rose, feeling a warmth around his heart. His team was ready.

Lee studied Floyd City's zone carefully. They still depended upon Lorrie Sue to do it all. He wigwagged Middleton into its regular offense against a zone, one back and two in, and they played keep-away, compelling Lorrie Sue to jump back and forth, and passing under her or behind her for short set shots. Middleton led by five at the quarter, by eight at the half, by thirteen at the end of the third quarter. With Pat cutting them to tatters with "Choc," the Floyd City crowd saw the handwriting on the wall.

Resigned to losing the game, the audience centered all its noisy attention on the Lorrie Sue–Pat Thompson duel. In the head-on conflict between them, Lorrie Sue, seldom whistled down by the officials, seemed to have the better of it. Lee felt the anger thicken in his chest. It was almost like playing without any officials at all, and Pat wasn't accustomed to that.

Actually Pat was jumping around Lorrie Sue so fast that her head and shoulders were well in advance of the Floyd City guard, as the rules stipulated. But each time a big dark shadow crashed into her from the side or rear, jolting her so roughly that, hard put to control the ball, Pat would pull up and circle back while the crowd booed her roundly.

With five minutes to play, Ginger crossed her hands, calling time. In the Middleton huddle she stamped her feet and her dark eyes flamed. "Mr. Driskill, this is the roughest thing I ever saw. These officials are so afraid of the crowd that they're letting Lorrie Sue clobber Pat. They don't call anything. I'm getting tired of it. We've got Floyd City whipped, but we've never whipped Lorrie Sue."

Pat raked a strand of brown hair out of her eyes and frowned up at Lee. "What shall I do, Mr. Driskill?"

Lee looked at her, a fury of anger shaking him to the core. They had to protect themselves, and he could think of only one way.

"Pat, she's all bluff. You can't go around her with these officials. You've got to go through her. Draw the charging foul if you must. She's having all the fun."

Pat rocked back, looking at him with surprise as if to say, "I don't know about this." Then, obedience strong within her, she nodded.

Play resumed. When Pat got the ball, she faked a set shot, drew Lorrie Sue to her, and started her drive around the Floyd City guard. Although Pat had established a straight-line path, as the rules provided, Lorrie Sue came up savagely from the side. But this time Pat didn't give ground. She dropped her shoulder and kept boring in. They collided. Pat was spilled roughly on the court while the crowd guffawed with joy. When Pat stopped spinning, she was sitting on the floor near the Middleton bench.

She looked up coolly at Lee. "Who do you think is going to give out first, she or I?"

Flipping over on her stomach, she put her hands on the floor, whipped both feet under her like a gymnast, and sprang standing to her feet. To Lee's amazement, the official thrust both arms high into the air, fists closed, thumbs up.

"Held ball!" he ruled.

The game went on. Two minutes before the end, Pat dribbled past the Middleton bench.

"Want me to try it again?" she asked challengingly.

So proud of her he couldn't speak, Lee nodded.

With her own guards cheering her on, Pat tried again. Gray eyes flashing, she lowered her shoulder, and with all the speed in her gaunt, beautiful body, she drove straight at Lorrie Sue's meaty left hip. And to everybody's astonishment Lorrie Sue stepped aside, declining the contact. Astonished, Pat both walked with the ball and threw it over the backboard. And the jeers came down like hail.

With the light of discovery dawning in her face, Pat stood under the goal, hands on hips, looking at Lee and nodding her ponytail up and down as if to say, "You were right."

Lee's arteries tingled with triumph. Pat had just learned the one immutable law of sport, that in every confrontation between two spirited opponents, somebody will eventually grow discouraged and quit. You whip her, or she whips you. It's that simple.

Three more times, Middleton worked the ball to Pat. Each time Pat faked her pass or shot and, dropping her shoulder like a blade, dribbled straight at Lorrie Sue. Each time the hefty Floyd City guard gave ground, letting her go by without contesting her, and Pat laid the ball softly against the bank for two points. Their booing fading to a murmur, the Floyd City crowd threw up their hands unhappily. Picking up their wraps, they headed for the exits.

When the game ended, Pat and Lorrie Sue embraced near the Middleton bench. Lee stood proudly, waiting to hand Pat her warmups. Lorrie Sue told Pat, "This is the last time we'll play against each other, and I'm glad. I don't want to get hit that hard in the ribs any more."

"I enjoyed our games," Pat replied quietly. "You're the finest guard I ever played against."

A stranger walked up to Lee, a natty little man in a stylish gray topcoat. "You the Middleton coach? I'm Tex Schulte. I coach the Quinlan College Queens. Ever hear of us? We fly all over the United States to play our games." His staccato voice sounded like that of a radio sportscaster. He spewed out his words, but he didn't waste them.

Lee shook hands. "You bet we've heard of you." Everybody connected with girls basketball knew about oilman Tex Schulte and his Quinlan Queens. A team of older girls, they had won several National Federation championships. They had played in Mexico and Canada and also against the Soviet Union's touring team. The Queens got their choice of the best girl players in the nation. A bid from them was the finest honor that could come to a girl athlete.

Schulte's roving black eyes clung to the Middleton girls walking off the court. "That ponytail forward of yours. She a senior?"

Lee shook his head. "Nope. Just a junior."

Disappointment clouded Tex Schulte's features. "I'll be frank," he said, drawing on a pair of brown alligator gloves. "We're always looking for new players. I flew here tonight to scout this Lorrie Lou, or whatever her name is. But your doll's better. She's got courage. Tonight she took on this whole crowd and Lorrie Lou, too, and whipped 'em all."

Lee grinned. "Thank you. We think Pat's some girl."

Schulte pulled off one glove and slapped it nervously into the palm of his other hand. "I'm chairman of the financial board at Quinlan College as well as coach. We give full scholarships to the girls we want. Does your doll want to go to college?"

"Yes. Pat wants to be an elementary school teacher, I think. She likes to work with children."

Schulte listened carefully. "Our school doesn't turn out teachers, but it's a strong liberal arts college. We're getting two new buildings next fall. The faculty's good. It's a nice college. Methodist."

Lee dropped his scorebook into his small valise and snapped the lid shut. "Methodist? That's Pat's church. You could identify with her on that, all right. She's president of their Youth Federation here. Would you like to meet her?"

Schulte's eyes began to dart about restlessly. "Yes, I would. But I can't tonight. Got to fly back, and my pilot's hurrying me. There's a front coming in, and he wants to get out ahead of it. Tell you what I'll do." Rummaging in an inside shirt pocket, he produced a small leather notebook. "May I have her name and that of her parents? I'd like to get in touch with them later."

He clicked the lead down in a small gold pencil that

appeared in his pudgy right hand. Lee supplied the information. With a final handshake, Tex Schulte and his pilot walked briskly out of the building. Watching them, Lee felt proud. He was glad that Schulte shared his high opinion of Pat.

On the Tuesday morning following the Floyd City game, Lee went past Hugh Morgan's office to use the telephone. As he walked through the door, he saw Morgan standing back against the wall, his face flushed.

"Mr. Morgan"—Lee recognized the arrogant, abusive voice instantly—"You have admitted taking a school printing order to a local publishing house without permission from anyone—superintendent or Board of Education. Is that correct?"

Morgan nodded. "That's right, Mr. Brawley. We had no more pass-out slips, and Mr. Bannister was in Kansas City attending a national meeting. Somebody had to do it. It was only an eight-dollar job, and the *Mirror* has the only print shop in town." He looked pale and tense.

Brawley's big, misshapen shoulders that so reminded Lee of a cobra's hood shifted as if he were about to strike. "Mr. Morgan, please credit me with enough intelligence not to swallow a stupid excuse like that. You could have printed some temporary slips on the ditto machine in Mr. Bannister's office. You could have asked me. I was available. I'm always available . . . ."

Lee turned and walked out, nauseated by the repetition of a scene already offensive to him. He knew why Brawley had attacked Morgan over an eight-dollar pass-out-slip order. Brawley disliked Saul Myerson and was determined to keep on punishing him financially for his criticism of the board in the *Mirror.*

Brawley's was the first criticism Lee had ever heard of Morgan. The principal, Lee knew, did his job superbly.

Later that morning Lee found Morgan, a lanky, woebegone figure who had lost a lot of his cheerfulness. "Brawley told me that the school board now had one strike against me. I don't know what that means. I suppose he was threatening me."

Reaching out a long arm, he grasped his Thermos bottle and nervously unscrewed the lid. Over cups of hot coffee, they talked about school boards in general.

"Most boards of education do a good job in spite of the criticism and abuse the job brings them," the principal summed it up. "But this Middleton board jumps down your throat for any trifle. They want to control everything."

Vexation came into Morgan's usually placid face, and he clutched the handle of his cup. "There are lots of potentially fine board members in this town who won't run for election because they're afraid it might hurt their business, and indeed it might. Many of the parents feel that if they ruffle the waters it will somehow be taken out on their kids. In Middleton, they've even let the Parent–Teachers Association die because Brawley and his followers don't like parents taking issue with them on anything. Brawley cracks all the whips in town. He has the whole community whipped down."

In the final game of the district tournament, Middleton was cracking the whip over Mesa. In the third quarter, a ball rolled free on the court. Candy Brown and a Mesa girl raced side by side for it. Just as Candy's quick hands grabbed the ball, the Mesa girl dived for it, hooking Candy across the right knee. Candy went down and didn't get up.

Lee sprinted from the bench, reaching her first. He saw the look of both pain and surprise showing on Candy's face. "What happened?" she asked.

Carefully Lee straightened her leg. "She threw a football block on you. It was an accident but it was rough."

He helped her to the bench. Seated there, Candy flexed the knee a little. Standing, she gently put her weight on it.

Lee frowned anxiously. "We'll let Doc Leisure look at it. I think he's somewhere in the crowd. Here he comes now."

"I don't think it's injured seriously," the doctor said after he examined it. "I think she can play on it. I'll put a heavy elastic brace on it. After the season's over, we'll send her to Seymour City and let a specialist look at it."

Two days later, Candy moved almost as well as ever. And when the squad worked out at noon, much of the grade-school population brought their dinner pails to the court to watch admiringly. All eyes were on the big elastic brace Candy wore.

Next day, Lee saw something that made him chuckle. When Candy came on the court wearing her brace, Lee called her to his side. "Look there, at that little black-haired pixie standing by the rail. In the red sweater."

Candy looked. The little girl wore an elastic brace on her knee, too. Before the practice ended, they saw two other feminine small fry sporting elastic bandages on their knees.

"You're famous, Candy," Lee told her, "or maybe I should say your knee is famous."

Grinning, Candy walked across the court to shoot her fifty free throws.

In the same edition of the *Mirror* that chronicled Middleton's conclusive defeat of Fair Valley, Saul Myerson announced that he would be a candidate for the Board of Education at the annual election in March.

"Although some of our board members are public-spirited and well-intentioned people, too often the board meets without representation of the public at large, holds discussions in secret, makes decisions that are never announced, and does not tell the community how its elected representatives voted," wrote Myerson boldly. "It hires and fires people, spends tens of thousands of dollars, and nobody knows what is going on.

"Above all, there is a serious breakdown in communication. Apparently our board keeps no written minutes of its actions, or at least this information is denied the *Mirror* when it seeks it for publication. If I am elected, the *Mirror* will print what goes on at our school board meetings so that the entire Middleton community will be informed."

Jean spoke soberly of his candidacy that night at dinner. "Mr. Brawley won't like it. Mr. Daniels said this morning that he heard Mr. Brawley was going to run Fred Ferguson, the treasurer of his church, against Mr. Myerson and back him with the full power of the church membership."

On Saturday, after the Middleton girls won their seventeenth straight game, Lee went with Jean to the supermarket. He was pushing the grocery cart when a familiar voice called from the dairy counter, "Mr. Driskill. Mr. Driskill," and Frances Ice, also pushing a cart, swung toward them.

Lee saw that her vehicle contained only a few pitiful necessities—a carton of milk, a loaf of bread, three scrawny potatoes, and what looked like a small twist of salt pork wrapped in butcher's paper. But the girl seemed happy.

"Where's Johnny?" Lee couldn't help asking.

"Home minding the baby," Frances replied. "And putting iodine on his hands."

"Iodine on his hands?" queried Jean. "What's the matter with his hands?"

"Blisters."

"Blisters?" Surprised, Lee looked at Jean, then back at Frances. "How'd he get them?"

"Digging graves." Frances' chin raised proudly. "At the cemetery."

Lee did his best to hide his astonishment. "That's hard work. The grave-digging machine must have broken down. I'll bet he had to use a pick. That ground is hard out there."

Frances nodded. "And on Sunday he works in a parking lot." Blinking, Lee wondered what had happened to change the boy.

Frances seemed to read his thoughts. With a look so pathetically honest that it went straight to his heart, she said, "Mr. Driskill, you taught us in basketball to try hard and not quit when things went bad. I've been trying hard to make Johnny like me well enough not to leave me and the baby. I've been trying to dress up a little, keep our room neat, keep fresh flowers on the table, and cook the things he likes. Mr. Morgan came to see [illegible] too. He took Johnny out in the kitchen and talked to him about going to church and going to work. He helped Johnny get this job at the cemetery."

The girl seemed hungry for some outside appreciation of her husband. Lee said heartily, "Well, looks like you married a worker, Frances."

Her chin raised proudly. "We're leaving our in-laws next month. Johnny thinks he's found us a place in the country." With one hand, she reached down shyly and turned the carton of milk until it sat flush in the corner of the cart's wire compartment. "I'm working, too. I'm selling pots and pans."

She looked at Lee pleadingly. "Mr. Driskill, now that the baby has been born, do you think they might let me come back to school? I want to graduate with my class. I know I can catch up. I've been studying every night at home."

Lee spoke frankly. "The main obstacle is the school board."

She nodded. "That's what Mr. Morgan told me. He said he'd do all he could." Resignation in her face, she dropped her eyes. "I'm afraid we didn't help him any. Johnny and I are finding out that it's who married you that counts. It's better to be married at home, or in a church, or in a minister's home. Not by a justice of the peace."

Lee liked her frankness. It took courage to speak so candidly.

"I know it'll cost more to go to school but . . . ." Determination in her face, she looked up at him appealingly. "If they'll let me come back I'll put on steam and sell more pots and pans."

Lee laughed. "If anybody could, I'll bet it would be you."

"Say, Mr. Driskill." Frances' eyes beamed with pride. "That basketball team of yours! Everybody's talking about how well it's playing. I sure hope you win the state."

"If we had you, we would win it," Lee said loyally.

She smiled shyly, obviously pleased. "You don't need me any more. It was awfully nice of the team to come to Broomfield and give us that baby shower. None of the other girls in school have come except Mary Morgan. The whole town's mad at us, I guess."

She looked at the clock on the wall, and Lee saw that she didn't own a wristwatch. "I have to go. It's almost time to feed the baby." She started toward the cash register to pay for her items.

"Hold on a minute, will you?" Lee hurried to the meat counter and then to the dairy counter. He returned with two steaks and a quart of ice cream, paid for them, and dropped them in her sack.

"For yours and Johnny's supper," he explained. "This will be Jean's and my shower—for the mama and the daddy."

Frances' eyes became as lustrous as the glass pendants dangling from the chandelier over the cash register. "Oh, thank you. You shouldn't have done that."

Jean added, "We're anxious to see your baby. We'll drive over some night—as soon as the basketball season is over."

Together, they watched her move off with her springy stride, her bright head up as she pushed the grocery cart lightly in front of her. Lee stared after her thoughtfully, impressed with her growing maturity.

On the day before the final game of the regional tournament, to be held at Middleton, a brown semi-trailer backed slowly down the concrete ramp behind the high school. The driver, a tall fellow in a dark khaki uniform, came to the door of Lee's office and looked inquiringly at him. "You the girls basketball coach?"

Lee nodded. "Sure am. Name's Lee Driskill."

"I have several big boxes for you out in the truck. Where do you want 'em unloaded?"

Lee stared at the driver for a moment, then he remembered. The new basketball uniforms! "Right here."

He helped the driver carry in the boxes and opened one of them. Lifting out the fresh garments and running his fingers along their satiny smoothness, Lee felt no special elation. They had waited so long and gone through so much getting the uniforms that their arrival seemed almost anticlimactic.

But he enjoyed the excitement in the eyes of his players as the news spread over the school. In twos and threes, they ran downstairs, feet echoing on the concrete, and burst into his office with wide-eyed eagerness. Soon the room was full of chattering girls.

They persuaded Ginger, the captain, to model one of the new suits and when Lee saw how well the red and black Jacquard knit stockings blended with the black nylon trunks, and how sharply the black numbers trimmed in white stood out on the backs of the shirts, he tried to imagine the emotional excitement twelve girls would feel the first time they ran out on the court wearing the new regalia.

That night, each uniform was lovingly taken home so that fifteen mothers could hurriedly make the necessary alterations before the squad wore them the following night.

With the Middleton gymnasium three-fourths full, Binford came onto the court first, for the final game of the regional tournament, drawing a roar from its cheering section.

But where were the Tornadoes? A buzz of surprise and uneasiness passed over the Middleton crowd. The Tornadoes' cheerleaders, disappointed because Binford was making all the noise and having all the fun, kept casting worried glances at the team's locker-room door. What was keeping them?

When the officials appeared in their striped shirts and the Binford team, followed by a lusty cheer, ran off the court to its dressing room for the pre-game ritual, Lee could wait no longer. He knew that the delay was somehow connected with the new uniforms. Hurrying to the Middleton locker room, he rapped smartly on the door. The game started in three minutes, and his team hadn't even warmed up.

The door opened. In it stood Marge Stanfield, the student manager, her mouth agape. "Come in, Mr. Driskill," she quavered.

Lee suspected she had been stalling while the girls primped in their new uniforms, striving to get every detail perfect. He walked angrily past her into the room and looked about him.

Pale and contrite, they sat on benches and chairs, braced for a scolding. Reading their young faces, Lee realized they wished to please him in everything, but being feminine, they could no more help taking an unreasonable period of time to adjust their new fittings than chickadees could keep from preening themselves on a gate post.

Planting his feet solidly, Lee stared long and hard at Ginger, the captain. Binford was tough. Binford had won eight straight. He must somehow shock them out of their state of ecstasy or the achievement of a whole season would go up in smoke.

"I don't want to hurry you since you seem so reluctant to go out where the action is," he began, his voice crackling with sarcasm, "but if you ladies are finally ready for the grand entrance, perhaps we should promenade onto the floor." He paused and threw a scathing look at each of his six starters. They all blinked back at him, their eyes growing wider and wider.

The room became so quiet that a flake of plaster that dropped off the ceiling was plainly heard by everybody. Still glaring at them, Lee thrust his hands into the side pockets of the black flannel blazer they had given him and which he always wore during games. His voice became softer without losing any of its edge.

"Or maybe you could forget what you're wearing and atone for this silly delay by following our game plan and playing a real fine first half. Then it might be easier for me to tolerate your presence when you come back to the dressing room between halves. My remarks to you then might be more pleasant. But I'm going to let the score determine that."

He nodded at Ginger. The team stood with their heads bowed. Lee walked to the door and opened it. "It's too late for your regular warm-up. I want each of you starters to get a ball and do a couple of wind-sprints, wide open, up and down the court, dribbling as fast as you can move. Okay! Dig out!"

"Yea, team!" they yelled in queer, muffled tones. Hands linked, they raced onto the court in their new gear. A gigantic roar greeted them.

"Mr. Driskill." Lee saw that Marge, his manager, seemed determined to speak to him despite her fear. "Look around. At the walls," she said. "They only have one mirror."

Lee looked. She was right. There was only one. One mirror for fifteen girls on the first night they wore their new uniforms.

He sighed, trying to get hold of himself. He must be fair about this. He must not forget how important it was to girls to look nice. He thought of how these particular girls had got down on their knees and pulled cotton bolls to pay for their new attire and how they had waited two whole years for this intoxicating moment. Could they still play basketball in spite of it?

Afterward he wondered why he had ever doubted them, or their fierce pride. Once the ball went up at center they became the same gutsy team that always fought as if somebody were trying to push them off a raft into a river full of crocodiles. They blew half a dozen shots in the first five minutes, probably because they had taken no shooting practice, but they caught Binford in the middle of the first quarter and led by eight at the half.

Between halves, Lee sent them out early for the shooting practice they had missed before the game. They had no trouble staying on that raft. It was Binford that was fed to the crocodiles.

The state tournament was next.

Chapter 10

Doctor Godshalk

Eight schools, each champion of a different geographic region, converged on Seymour City for the state tournament.

Ridge, the northeastern region champion, was Middleton's first opponent, and with Pat Thompson scoring thirty-three points, the Tornadoes won by sixteen. Padgett, the southeastern region champion, challenged in the semifinal, and Middleton won that by nine with nearly a hundred followers present.

On Saturday night the Tornadoes, with a seasonal record of 24–0, found themselves only one victory away from the goal they had set when practice began in October. Is it really true that we're here? Lee kept asking himself. His team had come so incredibly far from that first intolerable year.

Beulah, the defending champion from the northwest section of the state, was the other finalist, and as Lee climbed to the top of the bleachers to scout them in their first two tournament games, he doubted if they could be beaten. Could the Tornadoes cope with Beulah's best, forward Debbie Dillon? Big and tomboyish, with sandy blonde hair, she walked on her toes in a kind of strut, and she had whipped every guard she had met. Lee shook his head gloomily. Deadly with her hook shot, left and right, she would funnel in the goals over Ginger.

But guard play was Beulah's speciality. Joe Buckingham, the Beulah coach, built great three-girl defenses. Frowning, Lee studied them carefully but saw no weakness. Buckingham's guards, bigger than most, not only maneuvered well for rebounds, but they covered opposition forwards like a coat of calcimine. Their best was Vera Schultz, a German girl, who had two golden braids tied above her head and full red lips. Lee knew they would put her on Pat.

With nervous fascination, he watched Joe Buckingham during Beulah's semifinal romp over Nardin. A short, stocky man, Buckingham sat hunched over, coolly directing his team as he guzzled drink after drink from the case of pint-sized bottles of water lying between his feet. Lee had already met and lost to him once, in the finals of the Beulah tournament the year before.

With seven thousand fans watching in the Seymour City arena, the championship game became a tense dogfight. To Lee's consternation, Beulah also owned a maddening ball freeze. Midway in the last quarter the contest settled into a competition to see which team could establish any sort of lead so that its freeze could be turned on and the opponent be denied possession of the ball.

Squirming on the bench, a towel in his hands, Lee discovered that he had underestimated his own team. Unawed by Beulah's reputation, the Tornadoes fought with nerve and heart and vigor. With four minutes to play and the score tied, Pat came up fast to set a screen on Portia's guard, and Candy bounced a quick pass to Portia who dribbled to the goal and banked the shot left-handed. And a moment later, when Debbie Dillon missed one of her hook shots and Ginger Selman pulled down the rebound, Lee's heart pumped joyfully. Now was the time to apply the chill. He stood, crossing his hands for time out.

"Frosty," he ordered when they huddled around him, elation in their perspiring faces as they sensed their opportunity. "Handle it carefully. They'll probably foul you purposely trying to get the ball, but you know what to do."

With the crowd howling, play resumed. Middleton, ahead by two, gave the ball to Pat. Pat began her delaying tactics. Down the right sideline and back, across the middle and back, she dribbled warily, hounded by Vera Schultz.

The crowd murmured in surprise and wonder. Beulah, the champion, had fallen behind late in the game, a situation almost too extraordinary to be believed. Vera Schultz kept lunging at Pat, trying to slap the ball away, but Pat, watching her coolly, protected the dribble with her body and her quick hands, defying every effort of her opponent.

Lee felt a leaping sensation in his chest, not quite believing. Out of the corner of his eye he stole a look at the Beulah bench. No panic there. Joe Buckingham, grim and defiant, hoisted one of his pint bottles and drained it without taking his fierce eyes off the action.

Lee pulled a short breath and sponged his face with the towel in his hand. Take care of that ball, Pat! Handle it! Handle it until the cover comes off, but don't let Beulah have it. This is what we've worked for so hard. Now we're about to get it. Don't muff it! He kept stealing anxious looks at the big electric clock dangling from the ceiling in the court's center and saw the yellow figures changing with irritating slowness: 2:43, 2:42, 2:41.

When the clock showed 1:30, Joe Buckingham stood, kicking the water bottles from around his feet. He ran down the sideline where Pat was still nursing the dribble despite all the efforts of Vera Schultz.

"Double team! Double team!" he shouted hoarsely. Instantly his guards knew what to do. Two of them suddenly charged Pat, trapping her along the sideline. Pat hook-passed to Portia, and the third Beulah guard hooked Portia's wrist while giving the impression she was trying for the ball. The nearest official whistled the foul.

Portia sucked in a long breath, glued her eyes to the hoop, and sent the ball one-handed. It struck the back rim too hard and caromed off, Vera Schultz rebounding. A glad roar broke from the Beulah section. Lee ground his left fist into his right palm. They had needed that point. They had needed the rebound, too! Middleton still led by two, but now Beulah had the ball.

Then it happened. Ginger fouled Debbie Dillon in the act of shooting. With ice water in her veins, the Beulah girl toed the line, took one determined look at the goal, and calmly threaded it twice, tying the score. The crowd's mad roar shook the building to its stone foundations.

The two teams fought evenly through one overtime period. Debbie Dillon banked home one of her left-handed hooks to give Beulah the lead. With five seconds left, Pat Thompson put everything into one dribbling dash around Vera Schultz and tied the score. The two teams rested for a moment, the orange-and-black-clad Beulahians surrounding Joe Buckingham, the red and black huddle engulfing Lee. Another two-minute extra period would be played.

In the Middleton huddle, Lee tried to stay cool. "Pat will jump center for us when the period starts." He turned to Pat. Trim and stiff-backed, she wore her fighting look—gray eyes alert, reddish-brown head cocked slightly on one side—as she listened.

"Tip it to your right, to Portia." It never occurred to him that Pat might not get that tip. His eyes swept all their faces. "We'll use 'Frosty' and play for the last shot. You know what to do. Stay loose and relaxed. Handle the ball carefully. No wild passes. No wild shots. Take your time. And you guards. Just do your job. Try not to foul."

The buzzer's harsh squawk called both teams to the climax. The two huddles leaned forward for the big handshakes, their muffled "Yea, teams" barely discernible above the crowd's din. Both teams ran to their positions on the court. Lee settled back on the bench, clenching the towel. Jump, Pat! Jump clear out of your socks! Pat and Debbie Dillon faced each other in the center circle, and an official spun the ball high between them.

The ball came off Pat's fingers into Portia's hands. Lee settled back thankfully. All right, Tornadoes! That's it! Go to work!

Pat, beset by two guards, lined the ball to Candy. Candy faked a drive, dribbled to her left, returned the pass to Pat. Again Beulah attacked Pat fiercely with two guards. Pat bounce-passed expertly between them. Now Portia had the ball. She faked a shot, dribbled once, bounced back to Pat near the center line. With leveled passes and Pat's skillful dribbling, the Tornadoes probed the outer fringes of Joe Buckingham's defense, feinting to go in but always returning the ball to Pat in the back court.

The clock kept running. Middleton's forwards kept moving and deploying. The crowd, nervously biting its fingernails, kept pleading with its favorites to score or to hold. The pressure was on Beulah. Everyone knew that Middleton would delay until time almost ran out and then put up a shot.

With twenty seconds left, Pat's dribbling sorties became bolder and Beulah's guarding more desperate. At fifteen seconds, Pat drove to her right across court, and suddenly Lee saw that Beulah had overloaded that side, leaving Candy open.

He half rose. "Candy's open! Give it to Candy!" he

shouted. But Pat had already flipped the overhead pass to Candy who caught the ball in stride and drove dribbling to the goal. It was an easy shot, and she had no opposition. Candy went up on her left leg to lay the ball up right-handed. But the ball never left her hand.

Instead her leg collapsed, and Candy tumbled out of bounds and into the spectators, massed five and six deep behind the goal. When Lee reached her, she lay fluttering on the floor in a forlorn little heap, like a young wren felled by a slingshot.

She looked up at him beseechingly, her doll face stiff with pain, her enormous eyes filled with tears. "I'm sorry, Mr. Driskill. My knee went out when I planted my foot to shoot. I know I would have made it."

"Don't worry about it," he told her.

He turned slowly, an expression of shocked disbelief on his face, and summoned several boys from the Middleton boys team. Carefully, they picked Candy up and carried her to the dressing room. For one agonized moment, Lee stared after them, wanting to go with his wounded athlete.

Then Jean, calm and composed, appeared at his elbow. Instantly she sensed what was needed. "I'll go with her, Lee," she said and followed Candy.

Twelve seconds remained. It was Beulah's ball out of bounds, since Candy had obviously traveled with it when she had her accident. Beulah needed only five seconds to work the ball across the center line, and Debbie Dillon beat the buzzer with a right-handed hook that banked through so cleanly that the white net tossing behind it looked like river spray flung high onto a muddy shore. Beulah had won. The crowd broke into thunder and swarmed out onto the court.

For a moment Lee stood rigid, his throat tight, his face wooden, unable to accept what he had seen. He felt only a sick bitterness. They had lost the state by a twisted knee, lost it at precisely the same second they were winning it. Wretchedly it occurred to him that it might be years before another Middleton team had a chance like this. Portia graduated. So did Ginger, Sadie, and Susan, his three starting guards. He had nobody coming up to replace them.

Buckingham, the Beulah coach, walked up, a bottle half full of water in his left hand, a sympathetic look in his wide-set black eyes.

"Driskill, I don't like to win 'em this way," he began. "You've got a darned fine team!"

To Lee, the words meant nothing. Hot with anger, he wanted to retort that tonight it was a better team than Beulah's and that only an untimely kiss by the goddess of rare bad luck had deprived it of the victory. But he controlled himself. Buckingham seemed like a real gentleman. He hadn't spouted a lot of platitudes.

Lee shook hands. "Thank you," he mumbled.

Like all coaches, he abhorred having to congratulate an opponent right after a game, when both were still hot and excited. The less said, the better. He liked the way his girls did it. A tearful smile, a quick hug, a friendly remark, a desire to know your opponent better afterward—and let it go at that. Turning away, he headed for the dressing room to try to comfort his team.

Two days later, Lee drove Candy and her mother to Seymour City to see Dr. Will Godshalk, the noted orthopedic surgeon who had done thousands of successful operations on the limbs of athletes. They arrived at his waiting room at one o'clock in the afternoon. It was filled with people wearing casts or holding crutches. Presently, they were ushered into a small treatment room, containing a chair and an examining table.

Finally, Lee heard the doctor approaching. He was whistling under his breath as he came down the hall—a cheerful, tuneless whistling that he seemed to make up as he walked along. He stopped when he reached their door and entered, a wrinkled little man wearing a white scrub coat and gold-rimmed spectacles. He shut the door and regarded them with alert brown eyes.

"Well, young lady," he said, looking at Candy. "Why don't you sit up there," he motioned toward a small examining table, "and let's have a look at that knee. How'd you hurt it? Bucking off tackle or sweeping right end?"

Candy went into her noiseless laugh, pressing the heel of her hand against her nose, and looking as if it were all a great joke on her. "I was dribbling. As I set my foot to shoot, my knee went out."

She told him about the first injury. Listening thoughtfully, he gently manipulated the limb with both hands. He ordered X rays taken. That accomplished, he squinted at the negatives, then dropped them on the desk.

He leaned back and looked at Candy. "You have a bruised knee cartilage. You won't need an operation if you're willing not to be active. You can do all the things girls ordinarily do—work, ride, dance. And you won't limp. But you couldn't do anything strenuous. You couldn't play basketball again."

Candy's eyes grew rounder. "Not play basketball anymore?" She looked at him as if he'd asked her not to breathe anymore.

"It's your choice, young lady."

Candy turned to Lee. "If Mr. Driskill will come over with me the day I'm to come to the hospital for the operation, I think I'll get it done."

Surprised, Lee sat up straighter in his chair. She had made up her mind, blam! "I'll sure try to make it," he said. The operation was scheduled for the following Tuesday. That meant Candy would be admitted to the hospital on Monday.

Back in Middleton, he checked his calendar and discovered that he had previously accepted an invitation to speak at a coaching clinic in Winthrop on Monday. He disliked canceling it because he knew they wouldn't have time to get another speaker. He telephoned to Candy's mother.

"That's all right, Mr. Driskill," she assured him when he explained the situation to her. "Don't worry about it. Candy's father can't go because he's to be a witness in county court that day. But I'll be going with Candy. She'll be all right. I'll explain it all to her."

Lee took Jean and Alice with him when he started in the car for the coaching clinic on Monday. All the way over he kept thinking about Candy and her mother checking in alone at the big hospital in Seymour City.

It would all be so strange and different. It was Jean who thought of a possible solution.

"They have you talking last on the program," she said. "Why don't you ask them to switch your talk ahead of the other two? Then we could drive to Seymour City in time to be with Candy and her mother at the hospital tonight. My Aunt Bessie lives in Seymour City. She has a big house. We could stay all night with her. Then you could be with Candy when she goes into the operating room in the morning."

That was the way they did it. Arriving at Seymour City at dusk, they drove to the hospital and found Candy's room. They peeped in. She lay on her side in a small heap in the only bed in the room. Her mother sat stiff and silent in a hard-backed chair nearby. Both looked lonely and unhappy.

Jean opened the door wider, and Lee pushed through it, carrying a big pot of yellow mums he had purchased. Through the fragrant blossoms, he saw Candy's enormous brown eyes widening. She began to giggle, grinning from ear to ear.

"I didn't think you were going to get here."

They sat and visited with her for an hour. Lee teased her about her boy friends. He pointed to the new set of bois d'arc crutches standing in a corner. "You've always been able to lick every boy you ever went with. How're you going to swing on 'em wearing those things?" Candy's charming laughter reverberated through the hall.

A nurse came in to give her a hypo. Lee and Jean rose. "I'll be here in the morning before they take you to the operating room," he promised.

The next morning Lee was there when they slid Candy's small body onto a stretcher with rubber-tired wheels. He pushed it down the hall to the elevator while Mrs. Brown and the nurse walked alongside.

As he wheeled her into the elevator, Candy's face seemed to whiten beneath her tan. She looked entreatingly at the nurse. "Can my coach go up, too?" she asked. The nurse shook her head.

Candy swiveled her head around to face Lee. "You be right here when I wake up." Lee nodded soberly, feeling sorrier for her by the moment. The door closed and they heard the elevator whir quietly as it ascended.

An hour later, Dr. Godshalk found them in the hospital waiting room.

"Everything's fine," he assured them. "I took out cartilage on one side. The knee will be as strong as ever after it heals and she exercises it. She's in the recovery room. They'll bring her down in a few minutes."

Lee blew out his breath in thankful exultation. Mrs. Brown thanked the surgeon. While they waited, Lee went to the hospital restaurant and brought back two cups of hot coffee.

Soon the elevator doors rolled smoothly open and a stretcher, pushed by a male orderly, appeared. On it lay Candy, covered to her chin by a sheet. Lee walked to meet them. It didn't look like Candy. All her splendid energy was gone. With a tired little sigh, she fluttered her eyelids open.

Then she saw Lee and reached out feebly with one hand. Lee took it and held it all the way to her room, walking beside the cart. She peered up at him accusingly. Her voice was as hushed as a dying breeze. "I thought you said it wouldn't hurt."

She needs bucking up, he thought, frowning. Later, he walked outside to a telephone booth, dialed the high school at Middleton, and asked the school secretary to call Pat Thompson out of the chemistry lab. He didn't have long to wait. Through the receiver, he could hear Pat's quick feet approaching.

"Pat? This is Lee Driskill. Candy's fine. The operation's over. She just came out of the recovery room. Why don't you get Ginger, Portia, Sadie—any of the girls you can find—and call Candy in her room?" He gave them the number.

When he walked back into Candy's hospital room, Candy's resonant laughter pealed out merrily as she exchanged girl talk with them over the long distance.

On the day Candy's father brought her home, Saul Myerson defeated Fred Ferguson handily in the school board election and began a five-year term on the Middleton Board of Education.

Three days after the board's first meeting, Lee encountered the editor in front of the bank. "How'd it go?" he asked.

Myerson's deep probing eyes fixed Lee with a clear look. "Brawley wasn't there. He took off last week on his annual fishing trip to Lower California. The others surprised me by electing me clerk. They told me that since I beefed so much about them not keeping written minutes, that would be my responsibility from now on. So I'm keeping them. And they'll be in the next issue of the paper." An expression of mischief lit his brooding eyes. "Give the people light, and they'll find their own way— with the help of the *Mirror*."

The following week the *Mirror* chronicled a sobering news item, the resignation of Superintendent John Bannister. Physicians had advised the superintendent that his duties were too arduous for his health. Bannister and his family departed on a two-week vacation to southern Texas, leaving Hugh Morgan, the principal, in charge.

Three days later, Lee was hurrying to his world history class when a girl's voice stopped him in the hall. "Good morning, Mr. Driskill."

Lee spun around. Frances Ice stood by the water fountain, several books under her arm and a smile on her face. "Mr. Morgan said I could come back to school and take three subjects."

Lee stared in surprise. "I think that's great." Admiration for Hugh Morgan's courage swept through him. It took nerve to reinstate Frances with Gus Brawley and the school board opposed to it. The jangle of electric bells made them separate.

Later, Lee encountered Morgan in the hall. "There's no good reason in the world for keeping that girl out of school," the tall principal defended his action. "By going to summer school and taking extra work next year, she can graduate with her class. She's a good student. She can do the work easily."

Lee nodded. The explanation made sense to him. But it didn't make sense to the school board.

A week later, Lee had settled himself in the living

room with the evening newspaper when the telephone rang. In his stocking feet, he padded to the kitchen and took down the instrument. "Hello."

"Lee?" Hugh Morgan came on the line, his voice strangely urgent. "You going to be home for a minute? I want to come by and talk to you."

"Come on over. Bring Dell if you want. I'll put on the coffeepot."

The pot had just begun to bubble when a car's headlights turned into the driveway. Morgan knocked, and Lee saw that he was alone. He showed him in and took his coat. "Sit down. Be right with you." Something was wrong. The principal looked pale and distraught. Jean came in from the kitchen to pour the coffee.

"What's the matter, Hugh?" Lee asked.

The principal clasped his hands and stared nervously at the rug. "I think I've just been fired."

Shocked, Lee almost dropped his coffee. "Fired? By whom?"

"By Brawley."

"Brawley? I thought he was still in Mexico."

Morgan shook his head. "He got back last night and came by the school late this afternoon to see me. He was mad because I had reinstated Frances. He told me I was guilty of flagrant insubordination and that they had a way of dealing with my kind. He said the board had just passed a rule that a school administrator and his wife can't teach in the same system and that Dell's contract as teacher at Wilson Elementary would not be renewed. He said the board had voted to take my salary bonus away from me, too. He said they weren't firing me, but they would demote me to the principalship of one of the elementary schools and get a new principal for the high school."

Lee licked his lips, forcing himself to release the tension growing within him. "If they took this action in a meeting, Saul Myerson must have been there. Do you mind if I phone him? Right now?" Wearily, Morgan nodded his consent.

Myerson hit the ceiling. "This is the first I've heard about it. Sounds like they've held a rump meeting and forgot to notify me. The whole town's going to read about this—in the *Mirror.* I'm going to ask my readers what the school board is trying to hide. I'll do it, God willing and the creek doesn't rise."

And he did. But the action stood. Brawley called an emergency meeting of the board, inviting Myerson. There the action became official despite the protestations of Myerson and some of the parents.

Two weeks later Morgan landed a job as principal at Crockett, a bigger school. Sharp and efficient, he had no difficulty placing himself. Oddly, the Middleton board did not expel Frances, probably because she made fine grades. But they did stipulate that she would arrive and leave directly before and after classes so that she would have no contact with the other students. The town settled down.

And Lee decided to settle down in it. He and Jean purchased a six-room brick home three blocks from the school. A man isn't free unless he owns something and has self-pride, he told himself.

"I like the people here," Lee summarized it as they drove to the realty office to sign the papers. "And I like the country. The fishing and quail hunting are fabulous."

He planted a mimosa tree in front of the house and a peach and a cherry tree in back and watered them faithfully. Jean set out flowers and shrubs. They both liked Middleton. They had even learned to tolerate the shortgrass weather.

Its pattern rarely varied. Day and night, the wind blew and blew. After five or six days of this, clouds would darken the sky, producing lightning and thunder. A shower that the natives called a "cotton rain" would spatter the wet earth, enough to invigorate the cotton. Then came a pretty day with the sunshine drying the soil. Then the wind would rise again, and the dust would fly. But it was home.

One thing was lacking. Jean looked at Lee, the longing plain in her face. "If we could just speed up the adoption people . . . ."

A month passed. Candy Brown's knee seemed to heal so slowly that Lee despaired of her being ready for the start of spring practice. But she was elected Future Farmers of America queen. One week after she discarded the bois d'arc crutches, she was crowned before the whole student body in the school auditorium. It was a formal ceremony with flowers and orchestra music. Candy and her girl attendants wore evening gowns. Bill Ethington, the boy who crowned her, stood tense and bashful in a black tuxedo.

Candy approached the coronation stairway with such clumsy stiffness that Lee in the audience turned to Jean with alarm. "Lord, Jean. I'm afraid she's going to fall. Why doesn't that stupid boy help her?"

Grasping the arm of the coronation chair, Candy pulled herself up the two steps. Slowly the service unwound to its conclusion. Poised and radiant, Candy obviously enjoyed it, and all the starry-eyed girls present seemed to enjoy it, too. But Bill Ethington was obviously flustered. Although all the boys present regarded his performance with envy and open laughter, he managed to place the crown on Candy's brunette head and to kiss her. But afterward, he didn't take her arm and assist her down the red-carpeted coronation stairway. Squirming and gnawing his lips, Lee wanted to shout, Help her, you idiot!

Candy was equal to the moment. Smiling, she slowly negotiated the stairs. The spectators along both aisles held out their hands to catch her if she fell, but she was successful. Lee blew out his breath with relief.

All summer, Candy worked on that knee. She did faithfully all the exercises prescribed by Doctor Godshalk, mainly lifting her foot with weights attached to it and swinging her leg back and forth while seated on a table. In late afternoon Pat would come by for her, and they would go to the athletic field. In the scorching heat, they would run around and around the football rectangle. Usually they took Bonnie Bradshaw and the other new sophomores with them. Browned by the sun, they soon developed the stamina and leg tone so necessary to basketball.

"If we do our running this summer, we'll have more time for practice this fall," Lee told Pat, the new captain.

With Pat and Candy the only returning starters, they would need it. It looked like a long, difficult season.

Chapter 11

Roll a Round Pie

The first day of practice launching Lee's fourth year at Middleton dawned sunny and mild. It was a Saturday morning in October. The wind, hidden back in the hills, became so hushed that when Lee walked with Alice to the gymnasium he could hear the meadowlarks whistling pensively from the buffalo grass and smell the tart fragrance of the sage.

An hour remained before practice. Wanting to enjoy the stimulating air, Lee turned away from the school, located at the edge of town, and walked into the country. He had gone a mile when a breeze freshened gently out of the north, cooling his cheek. The tall range grass began to whisper and to bend. A reddish haze appeared on the northern horizon, softening the outline of the sand hills along the river.

"Looks like a dust storm," Lee muttered. Whistling to his dog, he began walking back toward the school.

The speed of these phenomena, which the inhabitants nonchalantly called "local dust," never ceased to amaze him. The wind rose, flattening the cotton stalks with a noisy swish. Last year's tumbleweeds bowled through the furrows, lodging against the barbed-wire fence. Plumes of sand lifted off the river, darkening the sky. The gale picked up everything—sand, dust, small pebbles—until Lee found it painful to keep open his eyes.

With a sudden show of comradeship, Alice walked directly behind him. When they reached the school, Lee cast a look over his shoulder and saw that the sun was now a pale disk ringed by a milky halo. The morning that had dawned so pleasantly was now completely dirty and wild.

The girls paid no attention to it; they had lived with blowing dust all their lives. They came dressed like boys, wearing blue jeans, sweat shirts, and loafers without socks. Here and there, someone wore a letter jacket for warmth. Most of them had their hair tied up in a scarf.

This workout, and the others that followed, swirled with the ferocity of a scheduled game. Lee was grateful for the enthusiasm of Pat and Candy, his seniors. Practicing with burning effort is a most important spur in any sport. After watching Pat and Candy hustle and work, the new players exerted themselves, too. They would have been ashamed not to.

"Way to go, troops!" Pat would call encouragingly. "We're going to win the state this year, sure."

Although Lee knew they lacked the defensive guns to achieve that high distinction, he was grateful to his captain anyhow. They would go as far as they could.

Melba Johnson, a Negro sophomore who practiced in orange socks and whose long legs seemed to start below her chin, had come up from junior high to replace the graduated Portia. Middleton's forward trio of Pat, Candy, and Melba looked so formidable in early drills that Lee gave them extra responsibility. With so much talent concentrated at one end of the court, Lee taught his forwards to press fiercely. When they lost the ball from a missed shot or lost rebound, they assaulted the opposition guards so hotly with two-on-one guarding or pick-off tactics that they often recovered the ball before the opponents could work it across the division line.

"We need to guard at both ends of the floor," Lee told his forwards. "We need to do it worse than ever this year."

The reason was obvious. With all three guards from the previous season graduated, Dorothy Crossett, a substitute, was the only guard with game experience. They would need more points than ever to win. When Lee looked for guards, he looked for stable, tenacious people with pride. If in addition a girl possessed a slight streak of obstinacy, that was all the better.

He went to work with what he had, mostly sophomores small and green. There was Freda Hofmann, a friendly German girl with blonde pigtails and prominent teeth; she knew all about hard work on the farm and was not backward about putting it out on the court. Another was Bonnie Barr, a little brunette lass with a Roman nose and black gambler's eyes. Her father had been the town bootlegger, and her home life was hard, but when anybody mentioned basketball, her eyes lit up like neon signs. And there was Holly Blinn. A shy girl, Holly had a great mop of honey-colored hair and braces on her teeth. "The orthodontist says I can take 'em off the first of the year," she proudly told Lee.

On the first day that Holly reported, Lee looked at her, his forehead wrinkling. She looked familiar. "Aren't you Trudy Blinn's sister?" he asked. He would never forget Trudy Blinn or her mother.

"Yes, sir."

Lee eyed her curiously. He didn't want another desertion. "I formed the opinion some time ago that your mother frowned on basketball and favored participation in the band. What instrument do you play?"

"None, sir," Holly replied. "I am what they call tone deaf. I can't stay on pitch. Besides, I'm clumsy. Everytime the bandmaster raises his baton, I lead off on the wrong foot."

Lee grinned. "Bully for you. I don't care which foot you lead off on here, just as long as you lead off fast."

From his squad of sixteen he knew that he was continuing to draw many of the most popular and highly respected girls in the school. Pat Thompson had told him why: "We have a fabulous time on trips, and I guess the other girls hear us talking about it. It's exciting just to stay overnight away from home. We always stay at nice motels and meet a lot of people. It's fun to visit with your opponents, too."

On weekends, Ginger Selman and Sadie York, home from college, occasionally joined them in the scrimmages.

Wishing to toughen his small guards, Lee devised two new contact drills designed to teach them not to flinch in heavy traffic. Outside, the wind howled and the sand obscured the sky. Inside the gym, the Tornadoes tackled the drills with shrill whoops.

Two guards would face him, five feet apart. He would bounce the ball between them. Serious as owls, they would wrestle for it, diving and plunging like boys in a free-for-all. Or, standing behind them, Lee would tell them to face the goal. Then he would throw the ball against the backboard and have them contend for it when it came down. After each stalemate, two more girls would step out and resume the individual jousting with the entire squad clapping and cheering as they watched. They also worked endlessly at bringing the ball out of the hole beneath the defensive goal while being jostled roughly by teammates simulating opponents.

"We don't have any brutes on our squad," Lee told them frankly. "So you guards must be hungry and mean. A basketball team is just as tough as its guards. In a six-girl game, if four of you can whip your opponent, discourage her physically and mentally, we ought to win the game."

But Middleton lost three of its first six contests largely because of its inexperienced guards.

In the dressing room after the Mesa defeat, Pat Thompson sat bent over in mingled fatigue and disappointment. Lee walked past and stopped. He knew how strongly Pat had counted on their winning the state championship. "What's the matter, Pat? Tired?"

She looked up at him, her gray eyes narrowing with deep determination. "Mr. Driskill, we're wounded but we're not dead," she said seriously.

In John Bannister's place as superintendent, the school board had hired Dale Spainhower, a meek little man with the eyes of a water spaniel and hands as soft as a woman's. Like all the people Gus Brawley selected to command his various enterprises, the new superintendent's foremost aim in life was to please his superior. When Brawley came to the school for any purpose, Spainhower would silently follow him around, hands clasped deferentially together as if he considered it a privilege just to be in the presence of this strong-willed man who had done so much for the school and for the town. Spainhower seldom made decisions by himself. "I'll check with Mr. Brawley," he countered every question. Horace Hawkins, the new principal, was equally incapable. But they gave Lee no trouble.

Middleton's little guards ran into steady trouble when they encountered the opposition's tall forwards as the Tornadoes defeated Folsom, Sand Point, and Brighton but bowed to Beeville and Hondo.

In the Hondo game Lee tried switching Candy, then Melba, to guard and bringing in Ann Hitchcock, a junior reserve, to play forward. This strengthened the defense but weakened the offense. Even with Pat, Candy, and Melba intact at forward, all the games were high score. And on the nights when the forwards weren't hitting, defeat came.

It was at Crockett that Lee discovered that big crowds frightened Bonnie Barr. Traveling together in a bus, both the Middleton boys and girls played and a large contingent of fans followed them, helping to fill the Crockett gymnasium. After Bonnie double-dribbled twice and fired a wild pitch into the spectators, Lee withdrew her and motioned for her to sit beside him.

"What's the matter?" he asked.

Teeth chattering, she looked at him, terror in her face. "Coach, it's not their team I fear. That crowd wants to slobberknock us."

Lee stared at her sternly. "Unless you learn to forget the crowd and keep your eye on the ball, I can't use you, Bonnie. Your errors would kill us."

He let her think about that for five minutes. When he sent her back in, she got with the situation. It was a close game until Kay Duffy, Crockett's best forward, fouled out and walked disconsolately to the sideline. Middleton also lost Holly Blinn on fouls but won, 67–64.

But always, in spite of the team's successes, Lee felt the shadow of Gus Brawley's dislike hovering over him. The firing of Hugh Morgan had disheartened him profoundly. When will he try to "reach" me next time, he wondered. Shrugging resignedly, he resolved to talk with Saul Myerson about it.

On the following Saturday Lee decided to forget his

troubles and go quail hunting in the Kafir corn area east of town. Everything went fine at first. Alice pointed unerringly, and Lee's pump gun knocked ten birds out of the sky. But when he started home, he discovered that one of his tires was flat and he had no jack. Bob Burnsides, his neighbor, had forgotten to return it after he borrowed it the night before.

Tired and annoyed, Lee stood, eyes sweeping over the countryside. There wasn't a house in sight save for a small clapboard shack in the distance. Although a windmill spun behind it, it looked deserted.

As he walked half a mile through oak and sumac to reach it, his nostrils caught the pleasant odor of wood smoke, and his hopes rose. An ancient sedan whose original red paint had faded to a dingy pink stood in the yard. Chrysanthemums, yellow and ball-shaped, bloomed cheerfully from a southside window box. An old pillow had been thrust into a broken window to keep out the cold. Lee went to the door and knocked.

A light tread of approaching feet sounded from within. The door swung open and revealed a girl with an oval face, a tallish girl who wore a brown dress that had been darned in several places. Her long hair, black as gun metal, cascaded down her back. Lee recognized her and swept off his hunting hat.

"Frances," he blurted out. "I didn't know you lived here."

"Why, it's Mr. Driskill." Pleasure shone in her face. Turning, she spoke to someone behind her. "Johnny, look who's here." She stepped back. "What a coincidence. We were just coming into town to talk to you. Won't you come in?"

Lee stepped inside. It was plain that they weren't enjoying quality living. There were no kitchen faucets or sink, only a blue enamel wash pan on a small stand and beside it a bucket of water with a dipper floating in it. No pictures graced the walls, although a miniature of Jesus had been nailed above the woodbox. A log fire crackled and snapped in a wood-burning stove where a small aluminum teakettle sang merrily.

Johnny, the young husband, sat near the stove, gently rocking a cradle. He kept peeping into it solicitously and mumbling something tender and reassuring as if he could comfort the infant by the friendly tone of his voice. He peered up shyly at Lee. "Hello," he said but did not rise.

"Hi, Johnny," Lee spoke. The boy was slight of build, and his hair and eyebrows were as white as gypsum.

Frances shook her head and grinned. "Johnny has talked more to that baby in the last three months than he did to me all the time he was courting me." She motioned to a chair. "Won't you sit down, Mr. Driskill? It's been pretty today, hasn't it?"

Lee sat down. There was a pile of schoolbooks on the window ledge, a pencil dividing the pages of the top one. "How's school going?" he asked.

"Oh, all right. Got one B. The rest are A's, I think. I take the baby to school with me and leave him in the nursery. How do you like our house?"

Lee looked around. "It's small, but it's just your size."

"It sure is," she said honestly. "We own two knives, two forks, two cooking kettles, one skillet, and three spoons. But it beats that apartment. This is more like a home." With her long hands she reached back and smoothed the hair behind her ears. "Nothing seemed very permanent until we got off to ourselves."

She looked proudly at her husband. "Johnny's working full time at an auto repair shop in Middleton. Mr. Boggs, the owner, says Johnny can handle a set of wrenches like a surgeon handling a scalpel. In another year, he may sell Johnny a small interest in the business and put him in charge while he starts another shop someplace else."

Lee plucked a sandbur off the top of his boot sock. Again he felt grudging admiration for this boy whom he had earlier decided to dislike.

The teakettle's singing became a noisy hiss. Frances rose and picked up the water pail which was almost empty. "We have a cow now, and the milk comes in handy for the baby. Excuse me a minute while I get a bucket of water. We keep water boiling so I can sterilize his bottles."

The boy rose and came quickly to her side. "I'll get it, Fran," he said, taking the bucket from her. She sat back down while Johnny went out the back door carrying the pail.

With one hand, she smoothed her skirt over her knees. "I think Johnny and I are going to stay together," she told Lee straightforwardly. "I don't think my parents or his thought we'd last more than a week, but we have. Moving out here by ourselves helped. Having a baby helped, too. We didn't want our parents thinking we were sorry we had it."

A bemused smile lit her face. "My great-grandmother who lives in Texas told me when I was ten years old that a girl wasn't ready for marriage until she could roll a round pie and milk a cow dry. I can do both now."

Again her eyes, frank and open, swept his. "Mr. Driskill, I have my own axiom about early marriages. I think dishwashing keeps the wedding ring bright." To Lee's surprise, she held out her left hand, revealing a small, narrow band of gold.

Lee bent over, looking at it, impressed by the new wisdom in her. "It's lovely," he praised.

"Johnny bought it," she explained proudly. "He's paying two dollars a month on it."

The baby began to whimper, and she arose to attend to him. Lee looked at the baby, listening to the suckling noises he made with his tiny lips. He envied Frances and Johnny. He and Jean had always wanted a baby. For years they had tried to adopt a boy, but the adoption people moved with exasperating slowness.

The young husband returned with the bucket of fresh water and poured some into the teakettle, silencing its hissing.

Frances looked at Lee. "You look hot. Can I get you a drink?"

"I'd like one," he confessed.

She brought him a glass of the fresh windmill water her husband had just brought in. Lee drank it to the last drop and sat holding the empty tumbler.

"I was coming into town to talk to you," Frances began, "but now that you're here, this might be a better time." She looked once at Johnny, then her eyes swung back to Lee. Now they were wide, appealing eyes. "Mr. Driskill, do you think it would be possible for me to come out for basketball?"

Surprised, Lee twirled the tumbler in his hand, pondering her question. He hadn't expected that a girl with a baby would want to play basketball again. How well could she play after a two-year absence from the game? They certainly needed a guard her size to patrol the opponents' big post forward.

Before he could answer, she added practically, "Do you think the girls would accept me?"

"Let's take your first question first," he replied. "I'd have to check with the school administration." He knew that Brawley and the school board probably would oppose her association with the other girl students. Lee also wondered how serious Frances herself was.

He licked his lips, looking at her. "Remember when you were a sophomore, how we put our basketball team ahead of everything?" he asked. "We've never tried putting it ahead of a husband and a small baby. Could you attend all the meetings, come to the practices on time? What if the baby got sick the night before a game?"

Frances looked fondly at the baby in the crib. "Mr. Driskill, he's never been sick in his life."

Lee frowned. He doubted if she understood the seriousness of what she asked. "How about your physical condition? We're already two thirds the way through our schedule. You haven't even done a calisthenics drill with us."

She looked at him earnestly. Obviously this meant a lot to her. "Don't worry about my being in shape, Mr. Driskill. I've been running the four-mile section around this place every day for a month, just like you started us doing year before last." She smiled. "And I stayed on the road. I didn't cut across the field."

She looked past him out the back door. "I guess you didn't see the backboard and goal Johnny built for me against the barn. Johnny used to play high school basketball at Folsom. He and I have been playing against each other, one on one, every day since we moved here—except when it rains. He takes the ball about even with the stock tank and tries to work it into the goal with me guarding him. If he misses the shot, I rebound and try to dribble it back past him to the middle."

She looked mischievously at her young husband, "Tell him what happened yesterday."

Johnny's blush ran rosy red down his neck. "Aw, Fran." With a great show of becoming interested in something else, he opened a small knife and began stripping loose plaster off the woodbox.

Frances giggled under her breath. "He didn't score a single goal over me yesterday. I just don't like to be scored on. I blocked three of his shots. He says I foul worse than any boy he ever played against." She shot another roguish glance at her husband. "There aren't any referees out here in the boonies."

Lee set the tumbler on the table. He felt a pang of pity for them both. That barnyard basketball was probably their only recreation. They needed to see more people, have more fun. After all, each of them was only seventeen.

The longing look came back into Frances' face. "Mr. Driskill, I enjoyed basketball more than anything else I ever did in school. I played only one year in high school and one in junior high." She spread her hands helplessly and her face clouded. "As you know, I never enjoyed living at home. That's why basketball and school always seemed so great to me. I want to help my team. I think I'm needed. Basketball is something I can do for my school in return for all it has done for me."

"Why haven't you spoken to me sooner?" Lee asked. "We have just one more month to play."

She seemed very definite about it. "Because I wanted to find out if I could still play. Also, I didn't think the team needed me until Johnny and I saw you lose to Mesa a month ago. We took the baby to that game. In the last half, the noise frightened him, and I carried him out into the lobby. I didn't want to see any more anyhow. I still hate to see my team get beat."

Lee looked at her thoughtfully. "I'll do some checking tomorrow."

He left them six quail and helped Johnny clean them. Johnny drove him back to his car and helped him change the tire. As Lee drove home with Alice beside him on the front seat, he remembered Johnny Ice's attention to his new son. Babies were engrossing subjects. They had engrossed women for thousands of years and judging from what he had seen today they could engross a man, too.

Before practice that afternoon, Lee told his squad about Frances wanting to return to the team. "The school board will probably oppose it. I'm not sure how Mr. Spainhower will feel about it. How do you feel?"

Candy Brown pulled up the elastic brace on her knee. "I think it would be peachy to have her back. I remember her as a very thoughtful person, one who was always considerate of others."

The sophomores on the squad didn't know Frances very well. They didn't talk a lot anyhow; they just listened. Pat and Candy were the leaders. They all wanted to vote right then, but Lee wouldn't permit it.

"I want each of you to go home tonight and talk this over with your mothers and fathers," he said. "Not your brothers or sisters or anybody else—just your parents. Ask them how they'd feel about having a married girl on our ball club."

When they came to practice next day, Lee brought up the question and put Pat, the captain, in charge. He walked out into the lobby while they talked. In five minutes Pat called him. "Mr. Driskill, we want Frances on our ball club."

"Does this reflect the feelings of your parents?" Lee asked. They all nodded their heads vigorously.

"Okay. I'll talk to Mr. Spainhower in the morning."

Chapter 12

The Windmill

Next morning Lee laid the whole matter before Spainhower. The superintendent looked uneasy. "I'll have to check with the school board," he said.

Lee frowned. The "school board" had departed for the western coast of Mexico on his annual fishing expedition. Lee stroked his chin thoughtfully. They might do better with Brawley gone.

"Why don't we examine the Board of Education *Policy Manual* and see if there's a rule against it?" Lee proposed, producing his copy.

Scanning it from cover to cover, they found no rule of any category regarding married students. "This girl is a fine student," Lee pointed out, "she will probably be the salutatorian of her class. It seems to me that she's eligible right now unless the board has passed a rule forbidding it."

Spainhower blinked nervously. "Just the same, I feel we should have the board's permission," he said lamely. "I'll call an emergency meeting and ask for an expression of their wishes." It was obvious that he didn't want to make a judgment that might upset Brawley.

After school, Lee called on Saul Myerson, alerting him about the board meeting.

"Hmmm," Myerson muttered. "I've got an idea. Won't hurt to try it." His gnarled right hand reached for the telephone.

He dialed Dorothy Thompson and Millie Brown, the mothers of Pat and Candy, explaining frankly what was at stake. "We need to change the minds of two school board members, Ray Kiley and Joe McGuire, or Frances won't get to play," the editor told them. "Wives sometimes exert a strong influence on husbands. I know Joe McGuire's wife, Bertha, likes girls basketball. She played guard at Rocky fifteen years ago, and she was a good one. In that family, she's the one who puts the shorts in the suitcase. She makes the decisions. She and Jane Kiley might put some starch in their husbands' backs. Could you possibly talk to them, right away, about why it's important that the school board let Frances play?"

Next morning, Pat, Candy, and Dorothy Crossett came up to Lee before his world history class.

"Mr. Driskill," Pat said, "what would you think about Candy and Dort and I going with our mothers to talk to Mrs. McGuire and Mrs. Kiley? Maybe it would help if they heard from us directly how our team feels about Frances."

Lee nodded. "Sounds great to me."

To his surprise, Joe McGuire did sheepishly swing over to their side, joining Myerson. But Ray Kiley, who was superintendent of Brawley's church, refused. The vote to let Frances play was deadlocked two to two, and the board took no action. That marked the first split in history of a Brawley-dominated school board. As Myerson pointed out, it represented progress.

Brand's voice crackled like burning twigs. "Gus doesn't want this. We don't want it either. There's no rule in our records covering it, and until we get one I suppose the decision is up to the superintendent." He looked sternly at Spainhower, in whose weak face panic blossomed. "And Mr. Spainhower knows how Gus feels."

"I think we ought to wait until Mr. Brawley returns," Spainhower said, squirming.

"It's not fair to the girl or to the team to wait until a school board member returns from a fishing trip to Mexico," Lee interposed mildly. Myerson had invited him to the meeting. "The basketball season might be over then. If this girl's ever going to play, she should play right now."

Brand glared at him. "Your team hasn't been doing as well this year, has it? That's mainly why you want her to play, isn't it?"

With an effort, Lee curbed his anger. "That's one reason," he admitted. "But this was Frances' idea, not mine." He told them about the quail hunt, about Frances' distance running, and about the one-goal scrimmages on the barnyard court. "If a girl is willing to put out all that work, I want her to have her chance. Our team wants her, too. And the parents of our team want her."

Myerson looked blandly at Brand. "George, our girls team has a better record than our boys team. Our girls stand 12–6, our boys 9–8." Brand flushed and fell silent.

Lee followed Spainhower out of the meeting. "Mr. Spainhower, there's nothing in the Board of Education *Policy Manual* forbidding her to play. The school board today took no action forbidding her to play. She's a fine girl making all A's and B's in the classroom. Until the Board of Education rules that she can't play, why don't you certify her eligibility? She has just one month of basketball left in her whole life."

Spainhower's water-spaniel eyes began to blink nervously. He looked cornered. "There's merit in what you say. I'll have Miss Rogers certify her. But I don't think she should even practice on school property until this is all cleared up. That's as far as I am prepared to go at this time."

Lee frowned. "In the name of heaven, if you're certifying her, why can't she practice with us on school property? She's already going to class with us every day on school property."

Spainhower's womanly hands began to flutter. "Because Mr. Brawley might not like it," he replied wretchedly.

Disgusted, Lee walked out.

Myerson waited for him outside. The editor's brown eyes glinted. "At least, I'll bet we've broken Gus from ever taking another Mexican fishing trip in February. He'd better stay home and mind his store."

With a vague hope for some miracle that would permit Frances to join them at the tournaments, Lee included her in the workouts. Spainhower had forbidden her to practice on school property, but the weather was balmy. Lee switched their workouts to Pat's outdoor goal. Frances brought her baby, and Dorothy Thompson minded him. Occasionally they practiced on Frances' barnyard layout. The mothers of the players helped with the transportation and the baby-sitting. The girls worked hard at half-court scrimmage with Frances guarding Pat Thompson and Bonnie Barr riding patrol on Candy Brown.

"Frances looked rusty against Pat but she didn't let it bug her," Lee told Jean at dinner. "She's worked herself into good physical shape. Even if she doesn't get to play, she's helping us a lot. Every day Pat has to move faster and faster to score on her."

Later, Lee lay reading on the divan. The telephone rang. He walked into the kitchen to answer it. "Hello."

"Coach Driskill? This is Tex Schulte, coach of the Quinlan Queens. You still got that forward? That battling doll with the red ponytail? Good! You play Cottonwood there tomorrow night, don't you? I'd like to fly out and see her play. Okay? I'll phone her parents. How's your record? Oh? It'll get better. See you tomorrow then."

Pleased that they wanted to scout Pat, Lee hung up.

Next morning the news of Tex Schulte's coming

spread all over town. Lee heard it at the café, at the drugstore, and at the *Middleton Mirror* where he found Saul Myerson wearing a green eyeshade and scanning a damp proof.

"Frank Thompson has been up and down the street telling everybody," Saul disclosed. "The Quinlan coach called him last night, too. Frank and Dorothy Thompson are having a little party for him after the game."

At school Lee saw Frank Thompson drive up in his green pickup with Pat in the front seat beside him. As Pat got out carrying her books, Lee walked up. "Say, that's nice about Tex Schulte flying in tonight to see Pat play against Cottonwood."

Pat's face tightened unhappily. "I wish he'd wait until our season's over. I want to keep my mind on Cottonwood."

"Hoo haw!" scoffed Frank Thompson. "You can take Cottonwood by yourself."

Pat flushed and changed the subject. "How is Mrs. Driskill?" she asked Lee. "It seems weeks since I've seen her. You'll bring her to our home tonight after the game, won't you?"

Lee nodded and carried her books for her inside the foyer. Still disturbed, Pat shook her head. "Daddy brags too much. All our fathers boast, but I think mine outdoes the others."

Lee laughed. "A little boasting is normal in all fathers. Yours just happens to believe that you could make the Boston Celtics." He handed her the books. "A little publicity won't spoil you, Pat."

Pat spun the dial on her locker. "I'm afraid the other girls on the team might not like it. I wish Mr. Schulte was coming to scout Candy instead of me."

"Candy's too little for college basketball," Lee pointed out logically. "Besides, you know Candy. She thinks you could make the Celtics, too. She'll be happier about this than anybody."

The Cottonwood game wasn't difficult. Pat could have scored fifty points, but instead she became a most circumspect team player, refusing shot after shot to feed passes to Candy and Melba. Afterward, she changed to her cheerleading garb and led the student cheering section. Then with her staff of cheerleaders, she walked over to a group of her favorite people, the elementary school children, and directed them in two yells. Faces glowing, the youngsters performed so loudly and enthusiastically that the adult spectators gave them a fine hand. "Bye, Pat!" a dozen of the kids called shrilly as Pat and her staff returned to the high school section. It was plain they adored her.

Later, when Lee picked up Jean in the car, she frowned. "I thought that in the game Pat deliberately played as if she wanted Mr. Schulte to turn her down on that scholarship."

But at the Thompson home, Pat seemed to go out of her way to be courteous to the coach of the Quinlan Queens.

"We're honored that you came to visit us. May I take your coat?" she greeted him at the door after first introducing him to her parents and to Jean.

"May I offer you some hot coffee?" she asked pleasantly a minute later. "And some of Mom's chocolate cake?"

Although she had played hard in the game, Pat moved lightly as thistle down about the room. Lee saw Tex Schulte watching her with interest.

Frank, Pat's father, kept trying to steer the Quinlan coach away from the other guests and into the kitchen where they could talk about the scholarship. With stamina gained from auctioneering, he pushed Schulte hard.

"Hoo haw!" he barked. "Where else you gonna get a forward like her?"

Schulte smiled politely. "I'll talk it over with our business manager," Lee heard him say. And that's as far as he would commit himself.

Pat seemed oblivious to their sparring. "It's lovely outdoors. Looks like you'll have a beautiful moonlight night to fly home," she said graciously as she held Tex Schulte's coat at the door. "Thank you for coming all this distance to see us. We're shooting for the state tournament at Seymour City. Maybe you can come and see our team play."

Lee glanced at her with admiration. Pat always kept the big goal in mind. He sighed and looked for Jean. With their personnel, they'd be lucky to win the district.

"I want you to be at the dressing room half an hour early tonight," Lee told his squad the day of the Glendora game. "I want to diagram their offense again and the defense we'll use against it." There was never enough time to do everything.

Freda, the German girl who played guard with her long blonde braids flying, thrust one hand into the air. "Mr. Driskill, I can't come at five thirty. I have to work."

Taken aback, Lee looked at her. "Work? What in the world do you work at the night of a basketball game?"

Freda seemed surprised that he even thought it important. "I have to wash down our house. Outdoors. With a broom and a bucket of soapsuds." She saw his puzzled expression. "Mr. Driskill, I've always done some kind of work before I play basketball." She assured him, "On Tuesday night before our games, I iron. It never makes me tired. I'm used to it."

Leaning back against his desk, Lee thought to himself that nationality and family custom had no effect on fatigue and let it go at that. Freda played well in the victory over Glendora.

As Middleton's sophomore guards gained experience, the Tornadoes swept both district tournament games. Lee was pleased. "In the basketball wars, you don't stand still," he told Jean. "You fall back, or you get stronger. We're growing stronger. But I'm still afraid we're not strong enough to play with the quality clubs. We need Frances to guard their tall forwards."

The two teams that the newspapers rhapsodized about—Anderson, located in the southeast mountain area, and Beulah, the defending champion—were both all-victorious. Debbie Dillon, Beulah's big, tomboyish forward, was averaging thirty-three points per game and overwhelming all defenses.

Three days of practice remained before the regional tournament. Then the weather turned nasty. A cold wave swept down from the north, and the freezing wind locked the farm ponds with ice and drove the livestock to shelter. Outdoor practice was impossible.

"We have no warm place to work if we include Frances, and I want to include her." Lee worried as he spread his napkin at Sunday dinner.

Jean passed the roast chicken stuffed with sage dressing. "Why don't you phone Hugh Morgan at Crockett?" she suggested. "That's only an hour's drive from here. Their season is over. Maybe he'd let you practice at night in their gymnasium."

Morgan did better than that. Thoroughly sympathetic to Lee's problem, he not only arranged for Middleton to practice in the Crockett gym on Monday, Tuesday, and Wednesday nights, but he persuaded some of the Crockett players to join the workouts and scrimmage them. Each night the mothers of the Middleton players went along as drivers and chaperones while Johnny Ice sat at home with the baby.

On Tuesday morning, Miss Rogers summoned Lee to the telephone. "It's Mr. Brand, and he sounds mad," she confided, twisting her hands fearfully.

Lee took the call in the superintendent's office.

"Mr. Driskill," the banker began in high excited tones, "I've just learned that you've been including the Ice girl in your practices at the Thompson farm and at Crockett. This is purely a device to get around Mr. Spainhower's order forbidding her to practice on school property. It violates the wishes of the school board. We want you to stop it at once. She can't practice with you anywhere, understand?"

Lee planted both feet obstinately. "Why not?"

"Because we say so. You don't seem to understand

that the school board sets the policy here. If we permit this loose association, we encourage other teen-agers to run off and get married, too. People are talking. They don't want this. The school board doesn't want it."

Lee scowled. He tightened his grip on the telephone. "Mr. Brand, as long as we don't practice on school property, I honestly don't think any school official has jurisdiction over what we do. The mothers of our players see nothing wrong with this procedure. Some of them go with us to Crockett. The Crockett school authorities gave us permission to practice there."

Brand's voice became woman-shrill. "I'll bet Hugh Morgan gave you the permission. I'll bet he's behind this."

Lee bit his underlip, trying to keep his voice calm. "Mr. Brand, you're simply mistaken. It was my wife's idea, not Morgan's. We had to have a warm place to work. I intend to keep on including Frances in our practices. She's a fine girl and a fine student. Her marriage is succeeding. Our players and their parents like her and want her."

Brand began to sputter. "You're getting bolder and bolder. You're trying to set the policy on this matter instead of letting the school board do it. You wait until Gus gets back from Mexico. Then we'll have a majority. Then we'll deal with this situation." He slammed down the receiver.

Lee stared thoughtfully at the instrument in his hand. They'll deal with me, too, if I take a wrong step, he told himself grimly. He hung up the phone and thanked Miss Rogers for its use.

Meanwhile he had to deal with something else, his

opponents in the coming regional tournament. Especially Beeville whose record was 21–2. We've gone about as far as we can go, he reasoned. The minute we lose, our season is over, and there won't be any problem with the school board about Frances Ice. Then he saw again the deep longing in the girl's face, the hunger for one last fling of schoolgirl pleasure before she discarded her basketball shoes forever and became a mother full time. Sighing, he walked back to his office. It was up to the team to keep her hopes alive.

With the Middleton forwards pressing the Beeville guards relentlessly, the Tornadoes fought Beeville evenly all the way. Middleton's superior organization was the difference. With the score tied, the Tornadoes went into "Frosty" and nursed the ball until the last three seconds. Then Candy passed to Melba, who banked in a jumper while going to her left. The crowd erupted into thunder.

Lee stood transfixed, watching his team celebrate. The Tornado substitutes exploded off the bench. Joined by the Tornadoes on the court, they grabbed Melba at about the free throw line, burying her under a glad pile. Lee couldn't see her leave the court, but he could follow the progress of the jubilant knot of bodies that escorted her. He swabbed his hot face with a towel. Once more, Middleton was going to the state tournament.

As he entered the dressing room to talk to the team, Bonnie Barr called out jovially, "Coach, we have a new name for our defense."

"You do? What?"

Bonnie's black eyes shone proudly. "The Posse. Because we spend all our time chasing the bad guys." The squad roared.

Later, Pat Thompson confronted Lee. Her wet reddish-brown hair glistened eerily in the lights, and there were points of fire in her stone-gray eyes. "Mr. Driskill, we want Frances on our team at the state tournament. We can win it with her. What can we do to help you get her?"

What they did, the whole team, was to go in a body Sunday afternoon to see Dale Spainhower. Until the board itself by a majority vote set a policy, the decision lay with the superintendent.

On Sunday night, the fathers took turns telephoning Mr. Spainhower. From Frank Thompson, the voluble auctioneer, to popular Dr. York, whose younger daughter Nellie was a freshman substitute, they laid their case before him, buttressing it with logic and noise. On Monday, the mothers called en masse on Mr. Spainhower at the school. Bertha McGuire, the wife of board member Joe McGuire, was their spokeswoman. When the meeting ended, it was a nervous Mr. Spainhower who escorted the ladies from his office. Bewilderment showed in his water-spaniel eyes, and his soft hands trembled indecisively.

At four o'clock on Tuesday afternoon, Mr. Spainhower sent for Lee. "Shut the door, please, Mr. Driskill," he said, his voice sinking to a distracted whisper.

Lee closed the door and sat down.

Harassed and upset, the superintendent stared miserably at the wall. Pitying him, Lee crossed his legs and waited. He thought he saw something furtive in the man's weak face, the twitching of a facial muscle, a quick shift of the eyes.

Then Mr. Spainhower found his voice. "Mr. Driskill, I want no part in making this decision. I won't rule on it either way. I'd have too many people mad at me. I'm leaving it all up to you. You can play her if you want to. There's no rule against your playing her. I'm not giving you permission to play her. I'm simply giving you the authority to decide. It's your decision. I'm washing my hands of the matter."

Thunderstruck, Lee stared at him. Although it was irregular, the superintendent had capitulated. Frances could play. They had won. Kneading his knuckles into his hand, Lee felt a surge of triumph. He'd play her, all right. But first he must drive to her home and tell her.

He thanked Mr. Spainhower and hurried out, his feet scarcely touching the floor.

As he swung down the hall, he heard a patter of footsteps behind him. Miss Rogers overtook him. Fear in her face, she wrung her thin hands. "Mr. Driskill, may I talk to you a minute?"

She walked to the stairway with him, then halted.

"Mr. Driskill, I simply must warn you about something," she began, her voice low and tremulous. "Just before Mr. Spainhower talked to you, he talked to Mr. Brawley on long distance. He found him at a fishing cabin in Lower California. Mr. Spainhower didn't ask me to place the call, like he usually does. He placed it himself. But I didn't eavesdrop. The speaker phone was turned on, and I couldn't help overhearing one thing Mr. Brawley said. It concerns you."

She looked timorously around her, then resumed. "Mr. Spainhower told Mr. Brawley about the pressure he'd had on the Frances Ice matter. Mr. Brawley told him to give you the power of deciding it. He said he was sure you'd play her, and then the board would have grounds for discharging you when he returned. He said he'd been trying to reach you—whatever that means—for a long time. He told Mr. Spainhower that you and Hugh Morgan were troublemakers. That they had got Mr. Morgan and now they were going to get you. I hope you'll be awfully careful, Mr. Driskill."

Stunned, Lee could only stare at her. So that was how it was. They were after him, not Frances. They meant to let him hang himself. If Miss Rogers hadn't overheard the telephone conversation, they would have done it, too. He looked once at his hands, flexing them. They wouldn't trap him as they had Hugh Morgan.

Keeping his voice steady, Lee thanked Miss Rogers and turned to go. He sucked in a deep breath and felt his mouth go taut with disappointment. He felt deeply distressed about Frances. Now he must tell her she wasn't going to play.

The brevity of Frances' stay on the sports scene reminded Lee of that haunting line from the English poet Housman, which likened the fame won by a young athlete who died soon after winning a race for his town to "the garland briefer than a girl's." That fit all girls, Lee reflected, athletes or not. Their time in the sun was short indeed. And Frances Ice's time was shortest of all.

She and Johnny had no phone. Lee climbed into his

car and drove east, his mind in a whirl. He thought of all the hard work this deeply lonely girl had done preparing herself for this final participation. And now her dream had flown like a wayward leaf in this dusty, windy land. She would be disappointed, but she'd get over it. He would like to see the look on Brawley's face when Mr. Spainhower told him that Lee hadn't taken the bait and they had no grounds for firing him. He'd be mad enough to do murder.

Soon Lee saw the small clapboard shack in the distance. This time it didn't look deserted. A spiral of gray smoke twisted out of the mud chimney. The windmill whirred busily.

He steered into the driveway, braked to a stop, looked around. The broken window had been repaired. A freshly plowed garden plot at the side of the house was ready for spring planting. The ancient sedan was gone but a baby's sleepy wail rose above the rush of the wind, and Lee knew Frances was there.

And then he saw something familiar fluttering from the windmill brace, something he had checked out to her the day before so she would have plenty of time to launder it had the decision been favorable. It was a black Jacquard-knit shirt, on the back of which was inscribed a large black 55. The rest of the uniform hung there, too—the striped stockings, the black nylon trunks, the red woolen warmups with the word MIDDLETON printed in black letters on the front. The whipping of the garments in the wind could be heard above the screaking of the blades. Inside the house, Lee could hear Frances singing. It was the gay, lilting song of a girl sealed away in some happy dream.

Lee's heart twisted. He knew what the dream was. And now he had to shatter it.

Or did he? He felt a slow rage at the forces arrayed against her, and at the frustrations she had suffered all her life. Hands shaking, be balanced it this way and that. He was tired of the endless bickering with the school board. And now, because of the authority granted him, he had it within his power to emancipate her, to restore her to honor and acceptance in the school and the community.

Abruptly he decided to do it. It would cost him his job, but he put all that behind him. He had made up his mind. Drawing a long breath, he turned the key in his starter and drove back to town.

In the garage where Johnny Ice worked, he found the young father under a green coupe with its hood raised. Only Johnny's feet, shoes half-soled and ankles bare, stuck out. Lee knelt so that the boy could hear him. "Johnny. It's Lee Driskill."

Johnny turned on his side and crawled halfway out. "Oh, hello, Mr. Driskill." A smudge of grease coated his nose.

"Tell Frances she's going to the state tournament with us and she's going to play. We'll come by for her at noon tomorrow."

Johnny raised one oily hand and, with the back of it, tried to wipe the grease off his nose. "I'll tell her," he said.

Chapter 13

●

The Heroics of Frances Ice

At Seymour City, the state capital and tournament site, Lee parked the bus at the motel and watched the girls alight.

They looked very stylish in their new blazers and skirts of tan wool. The Middleton Quarterback Club had purchased the blazers and the material for the skirts, which the mothers had selected and sewn. Pat and Dorothy Thompson had stayed up most of one night helping Frances with her skirt, and when the girls strolled in twos and threes through the motel lobby, Frances looked as attractive as the others.

Lee followed them in and registered.

With the state high school athletic association paying all expenses, their accommodations were plush. Lee had always been amused and impressed at how girls from a small town lived it up on a trip to the city.

Their first act was to inspect their rooms—the soft thickness of the wall-to-wall royal blue carpeting ("I'm going to sleep on the floor instead of the bed," Ann Hitchcock vowed), the central heating system, the color television with its choice of four channels, and the mirrors. Girls needed lots of mirrors, Lee had learned.

Bonnie Barr pulled back the drapes, sank into a soft chair, and stared out the window at the deserted swimming pool in the plaza. "Wonder what the poor folks are doing tonight?" she drawled lazily.

At lunch Lee watched them carefully lift the silver by their plates and unfold the blue linen napkins. No detail escaped their scrutiny. They noticed the sweet smell of the burning apple logs in the fireplace. They observed how the furniture matched the paneling. They commented on the cleanliness of everything. Humble and appreciative, they seemed to be storing up information that they would someday use in their own homes. And Lee knew that on the way back to Middleton they would come, one by one, past his seat in the bus and thank him sincerely for everything.

Best of all, he liked to watch them eat. Their appetites rivaled those of boys. Most of them had grown up in the country where hard work abounded and food was plentiful.

"Careful!" Lee teased them. "You might eat yourselves out of the tournament. If you lose tonight, I'm going to feed you liver and onions." He knew they abhorred liver and onions. "If you win you can have anything on the menu within reach of our budget." He knew what that choice would be. Hamburgers and French fries. And not to save money on the budget, either.

"They're sure polite and courteous," the motel manager complimented him at the cash register when he paid for their first meal. "A bunch of real nice young ladies."

Lee laughed, pocketing his wallet. "Thank you. They're ladies, all right—until they get on that basketball court." But privately, he thought they were as cute as the dickens, and it tore his heart to think this would be his last trip with them.

Dellaplane, the first-round opponent, brought a 24–2 record into the competition. Lee didn't send Frances into action until late in the first quarter when Holly Blinn was assessed her third of three quick fouls.

Frances had her troubles, too. After weeks of rebounding off wooden outdoor backboards, she was baffled by the glass boards at Seymour City. The ball came off the glass with more hop, bounding over her head or shoulder before she could get her hands up. Twice she drop-kicked loose balls, giving possession to Dellaplane. Another time Dellaplane double-teamed her and Frances pivoted into the nearer opponent, fouling her.

"Never mind, Fran! Buckle down!" Candy called shrilly from the middle line.

"All right, Fran! All right!" Pat sang out in her far-carrying cheerleader's voice. "Nobody hurt. It'll come back to you."

But it didn't, and twice Lee withdrew Frances for short rests, motioning for her to sit beside him while he talked to her. He wasn't too surprised. After all, it was her first game in two years.

Thrusting her head and arms through her warm-up tops, she looked at him honestly, "I'm not doing very well, am I?"

"You'll do better as soon as you get used to those live backboards and that springy floor," Lee soothed. "Your defense is fine. Your timing is off but it'll come back. You just need to play more and get used to the equipment. Be ready, now. In a minute, I'm going to send you back in."

Inwardly he was worried. Unless they rallied, this would be her last game ever. And not a very satisfying one either.

In the third quarter, the Dellaplane girls, recruited from the coal-mining area, spurted into a six-point lead. Bursting with tension, Middleton's sophomore guards ran with the ball, double-dribbled, and heaved pass after pass into the crowd.

But at the start of the fourth quarter, the Tornadoes' forward power began to curl like a whip around Dellaplane. Candy Brown faked a shot and passed to Pat who swung around her guard and laid the ball up. Then Candy faked to Pat and dropped the ball off to Melba sweeping in from the opposite side. Goal! All three Middleton forwards ran together, embracing one another happily. Melba's white teeth flashed in her dark face. "Beautiful, Candy. Beautiful!"

Alarmed, Dellaplane's guards began to foul. Pat put four straight free throws through the ring, and Middleton forged ahead by three. Lee's hand tightened with satisfaction on the towel.

Then Dellaplane rallied. Twice her forwards pressed Middleton's little guards, preventing them from advancing the ball to the middle line in the required ten seconds. With a minute to play and Middleton leading by one, Lee switched Pat Thompson to guard.

"When you get in trouble, pass the ball to Pat," he instructed his guards. "She'll take it to the middle." To Pat he said, "Just get the ball to the middle line. Then call time and I'll substitute you back to forward."

Pat did more than that. When Dellaplane missed a long shot, she went up for the rebound and had no trouble dribbling through the Dellaplane press to the division stripe. Then she called time, and Lee moved her back to forward. The Tornadoes went into "Choc," and when Melba banked a lay-up just before the final buzzer, Lee felt his lips flatten exultantly on his teeth. They had won. But Pat had had to play in both ends of the court to pull it off.

After the girls showered and dressed, Lee found Bonnie Barr. "Bonnie, what happened to your posse? The bad guys kept riding off into the sunset for goal after goal."

Bonnie looked ruefully down at her shoes and shook her black head. "I guess we didn't change horses often enough. This is fast company up here, Coach."

It became even faster in the semifinals. Rawlins, a team from the northeastern ranch country, had won twenty-four games and lost one. Their only tall player was Ruth Oberlander, a wire-thin six-footer who looked as if she would hate to miss a goal even in shooting practice. The rest were small and quick, and Lee hoped his guards could cope with them. But Ruth Oberlander presented a challenge.

Settling himself on the bench, Lee studied her anxiously. Proud and aloof, her dark eyes glowed as if deep fires burned behind them. When Frances walked out to guard her, the Rawlins girl didn't even notice her. Her eye was on the ball in the referee's hand; she looked at it as if it belonged to her by divine right and the sooner she got it the better. Only Frances had the height to guard her.

Middleton scored first when Pat, faking her drive, suddenly applied the brakes, shoes whining, and forked in a fifteen-foot jumper. The crowd's glad roar shook the walls, and Lee knew that hundreds of Middleton fans were there. Then the ball went to Ruth Oberlander, and she showed what she could do. With one shake of her proud head, she drew Frances only inches out of position, but that was all the room she needed. Quick as a flash, she whipped around Frances and banked the goal.

Pat long-strided around her guard to score. Ruth Oberlander jumped high into the air to hit a ten-footer. That became the first-half pattern. First Thompson would score; then Oberlander. Clutching his towel, Lee alternately felt joy and pain. The two fine forwards seldom missed, and the game devolved into a shooting duel between them.

As he watched, Lee had to admire Frances Ice. Despite the trimming she was taking, she kept her poise. On the few occasions the Oberlander girl missed, Frances fenced her away from the rebound by spotting the ball, leaping for it, and holding it away from her body with elbows out, so that her opponent couldn't tie her up. All through the first half, Frances seemed to be studying every move the Rawlins star made. She was rarely fooled twice by the same maneuver.

In the second quarter, Lee brought her to the bench for a short rest. He stared at her keenly, afraid she might be tiring, but her breathing wasn't labored, and her green eyes blazed defiantly.

"How many goals has she made over me?" Frances asked as she pulled on her warm-up jacket without taking her eyes off the action on the court.

"Oh, five or six."

Frances set her jaw firmly, her eyes darkening. "Mr. Driskill, she's good. But I think I've about got her figured out. She's not going to make that many over me in the last half."

The remark thrilled Lee. He crumpled his towel and lifted his shoulders. She really thinks she can do it, he told himself. At the half the scoreboard revealed a tie—24 to 24. As the teams came back on the court for the final fourteen minutes, the public-address man intoned, "You're seeing two great forwards here tonight. Pat Thompson of Middleton has scored eighteen points. Ruth Oberlander of Rawlins has scored nineteen." Frances, busy rubbing rosin on her hands, heard. Frowning, she raised her head in determination, every tendon in her throat showing.

Middleton began the third quarter in a spasm of frustration. Pat outjumped Ruth Oberlander at center, and half a minute later drove around a Rawlins guard but missed a running one-hander. Candy, a swift little tiger, beat everybody to the rebound and sprang high to finger the ball against the bank, but it crawled fiendishly around the ring and dropped off. Pat slapped it back out to Melba who set herself and arched a shot deep from the corner, but it too missed.

Lee frowned and gulped. Why didn't the darned ball drop? When Rawlins finally worked the ball to Ruth Oberlander, a long rolling murmur of elation broke from the Rawlins supporters.

But bafflement became Rawlins' lot, too. Frances pressed Ruth Oberlander hard all the way into the scoring zone, disputing every bounce of the ball and talking to her constantly. Ruth finally got off a shot over Frances' flailing arms but it rimmed the hoop. When Frances, knees flexed, elbows high, pounced on the rebound, Lee clutched his towel and felt light-headed with relief. For the first time, Frances seemed onto her game.

Melba's short jump shot behind Pat's screen moved Middleton in front by two. Rawlins fed the ball to Ruth Oberlander, but again Frances attacked her, hounding her all the way into the scoring zone. Then the crowd bawled with surprise. With an incredibly rapid movement, Frances slapped the ball underhanded out of Ruth's hands, beat her to the recovery, dribbled safely to the line and, stretching her long neck to look for an open forward, gave it off to Candy Brown. Pat took a bounce pass from Melba and, losing her guard with a fast pivot, lifted the ball into the hoop. Lee felt his hands tighten jubilantly on the towel. Middleton led by four.

A look of pique crossed Ruth Oberlander's face as she took the center throw at the division line. Frances was waiting for her there, talking to her softly and melting cleanly into her steps. Ruth tried a shot, but Frances' hand came up so fast into her face that she hurried it slightly and missed. As they struggled for the rebound, Ruth Oberlander fouled Frances, and the official ran with the ball to the other end of the floor. There Pat, waiting at the line, pulled a long breath and drilled the free throw.

Lee fought down his joy and made himself take notice of the details. Rawlins called time out. While their coach tried to repair the breach in his offense, Lee substituted Holly Blinn for Freda, who had broken a shoelace. He huddled his own team.

"All right!" he told them over their multiple handshake. "Stay after 'em!" He looked proudly at Frances. "Keep pressing her. She doesn't like to be pressed."

Frances kept pressing, and Middleton's forwards kept hitting. With a minute and a half left to play, the Tornadoes led by nine, and Lee knew that his team had made the state finals in two consecutive seasons. He stood, signaling the substitutes to peel off their warmups. Murder! he told himself. With a forward like Pat and a guard like Frances, we can play against anyone.

It was then that disaster struck. Pat, dauntless despite two hard games, drove around her guard. In trying to stop her, the Rawlins girl's knee caught Pat's left leg low in the thigh. Pat didn't fall, but when she tried to walk to the foul line to shoot the free throw, she nearly lost her balance. The official called time.

Lee ran out onto the court. He saw the knot swelling and stared at it in stunned disbelief. He put his hand on it and felt Pat flinch with pain. The muscle was hard as concrete. He knew then that they had lost the state championship, lost it before the finals were played. Bitterly he stood and faced the sideline.

Bill Hooper, coach of the Middleton boys, hurried onto the floor. "Can I help?"

Pat put an arm around each of their necks, and they assisted her to the bench.

Lee knelt in front of her, his face stiff with shock. "How does it feel?"

Pat sighed disgustedly, long lashes hiding her gray eyes. "Sore."

They helped her to the training room where Ted Donovan, the state university trainer, waited for them, an ice bag in one hand. He had seen the accident and was ready. He motioned to a table covered with black leather. "Sit there, please."

Lee and Bill Hooper lifted Pat to a sitting position, and Donovan examined the leg carefully. "Pretty bad charley horse," he muttered. With a piece of gauze he fastened the ice bag to the swollen thigh, wrapping it securely.

Lee looked at him, his mind refusing to accept what he had seen. Voice rough, he asked, "How about the finals tomorrow night? Can she play?"

He knew the answer before Donovan spoke. "Coach, she may be able to hobble around a little. But she won't have full movement of that leg for several days."

With pleading eyes, Pat searched Lee's face as if appealing to him to do something. Lee felt their impact, but all he could do was to clench his fists and look back at her with helpless compassion. She was their bread-and-butter player. In the state championship finals, she would need both legs.

Bitterly he turned and walked a few steps off. In spite of all his hard work and planning, everything was flying wild. He wanted to lose his temper, turn on somebody, ball his fist, and swing from his heels in a wild protest against the bad breaks life was dealing him. Finally his self-control returned.

During the next two hours, Pat lived in the arena training room. They tried everything that might help—ice massage, infrared treatment through a wet towel, ultrasound. Her father even purchased a swimsuit for her so that she could wear it and soak her thigh in the whirlpool bath, but nothing seemed to help in the short time available.

The next morning Pat put on her uniform, and Lee drove her and her father to the empty arena. After more treatment, she tried out the leg, protected by a football thigh pad. Limping badly, she couldn't make any quick moves. Lee's heart plummeted. That took away their best weapon, her drive around the guard. She couldn't shoot her jump shot, either. She couldn't lay the ball up right-handed. She couldn't press. She couldn't center jump. But she could set shoot and hit free throws. When Lee asked her to dribble, and she moved up court in a wretched little hippety-hop, his heart plunged again.

Lee borrowed a pair of basketball shoes; he laced them on. "All right, Pat," he said, "let's see if you can keep me from taking the ball away from you."

Pat leaned over and began to bounce the ball,

watching him warily. He made a rush to her right side, trying to bat the ball away from her. A fighting look came into her gray eyes, and she backed up. Still keeping her body between him and the ball, she bounced it behind her back.

He attacked her left side, but she pivoted in the other direction. Changing hands and dribbling by feel, she maneuvered away from him despite her limp. All over one end of the court they contended, and although Pat moved like a crippled rabbit, her quick hands defied Lee's efforts to touch the ball. But when he darted behind her, giving her an uncontested path to the goal, she couldn't move fast enough to go in before he caught her. All her splendid speed was gone.

"Did your leg hurt?" he asked as he sat down and began changing back to his street shoes.

"Not much," Pat deprecated, "only when I tried to drive." Her eyes suddenly became grave. "Mr. Driskill, you're going to let me play, aren't you?"

Lee picked up the borrowed shoes and stood. They all wanted to play. Whether they had a bruised knee cartilage, a new baby, or a bump as big as a walnut on their thigh. He eyed her thoughtfully. "You can't guard, and you can't rebound. But I've been thinking we might try to run our high-low post offense with you in back court instead of Candy. We'd play Candy in your high post position. That way, you wouldn't have to drive. You'd do mostly passing. We might combine this with something else you can still do in spite of your leg."

Pat looked at him shrewdly, her head canted a little on one side. "Mr. Driskill, you must mean 'Frosty.'"

He nodded grimly. "It's a gamble but it might throw

them off their game. We've got to make them play at our tempo, and our tempo is going to be slow as molasses."

Lee brought the whole team back that afternoon to practice the new alignment.

When Middleton came into the arena that night to play Beulah for the championship, the place was jammed with people. On their way to the dressing room, the Tornadoes had to walk in single file down one sideline in plain view of everybody. As they detoured around the feet of the spectators, squeezed side by side around the court, a few scattered boos greeted them. But Lee had told them what to do. "Pay no attention to the crowd. Just smile and keep your eyes on the dressing-room door." The Middleton team kept walking and smiling. And then something happened—something spontaneous and heartwarming. High in the packed balcony a woman stood and began clapping her hands. "Yea, Middleton!" she called in a clear soprano that carried all over the premises.

Slowly the applause began to spread. All around the arena hundreds stood, and their cheering swelled into a deep, full-throated roar, punctuated by shrill screams and the measured stamp of hundreds of feet. And it didn't stop. Lee looked around, surprised. Everybody knew about Pat's injury, but many from Middleton must have come anyhow. Loyal to their team, they aimed to support it despite its diminished chances.

Lee blinked, feeling singularly proud and moved. They had achieved part of their goal, at least. They had established the sport in their community.

Before they had come onto the court, Crystal Gates, his student manager, had approached him at the arena door. "Mr. Driskill," she said excitedly, "forty-two junior high girls have signed to come out for our spring basketball training." That's fine, he had told her. And then he added bitterly to himself, but I won't be there to coach them.

At the scoring table, Joe Buckingham waited for him. The Beulah coach carried his personal carton of pint bottles filled with drinking water.

"Is this a six-pint game or an eight-pint game?" Lee asked as they shook hands.

When Pat dribbled at a limp into the spotlight, last of all the Middleton starters to be introduced, a murmur of admiration ran through the crowd, and they gave her the biggest ovation of all.

From the Beulah cheering section a yell pealed out:

> "Hi there Middleton, how do you do?
> Your team looks swell, so do you.
> So let's shake hands, let the game begin.
> Good luck to you, may the better team win."

On the Middleton bench, Lee scowled and sat down. He didn't agree with the phrase "Your team looks swell." His team would look lots better if Pat Thompson were at full mobility. He picked up a towel and sat brooding. They'll still have to beat us, he told himself doggedly.

He raised his eyes to the court, hardly recognizing Vera Schultz, Beulah's all-state guard. Instead of doing her hair in golden braids tied above her head, she now wore it cut straight around and fringed across her forehead. She and Pat exchanged friendly back slaps and then settled down to the serious business of becoming deadly enemies. On the other side of the division line Debbie Dillon, Beulah's blonde ace, shot a curious look at Frances Ice standing beside her.

All around the center circle the resolute members of both teams crowded each other gently for position. Beulah had crushed Anderson in the other semifinal. The crowd murmured with excitement as an official walked to the middle with the ball. Then Melba and Debbie Dillon crouched, and the ball spun high between them.

Debbie tipped to a Beulah forward who promptly gave the ball back to her. Debbie dribbled toward the goal. Instantly Frances began to press her, yelling at her and stabbing upward at the ball. The Beulah star, who had overpowered all the guards she had played against the last two seasons, regarded Frances coolly and disdainfully, then decided to punish her, to take her down a notch.

Suddenly, Debbie cut her eyes to the left, faked a pass in that direction, and drove to the right with all the speed in her brown legs. But Frances, her feet flashing, ignored the feint and exploded with her into the hole, roughly brushing her and cutting her off. After three bounces Debbie pulled up and circled back, passing off to a teammate.

Beulah began weaving off its screening attack, and this time the play went to the other side. They set the screen against Frances, and Debbie broke around the block, dribbling left-handed. But Frances, straightening to her full height, squeezed through the hole with her, blending so quickly into Debbie's footsteps that the Beulah girl had no direct route to the goal. Lee curled his fingers around the towel, feeling a surge of exhilaration.

"Way to go, Frances!" Pat's shrill voice rang from the middle line. But a third Beulah screen worked, pinching off Bonnie Barr, and a Beulah forward with her hair tied saucily in a green ribbon took the open path to the basket. Beulah led 2 to 0.

Lee bent forward, cupping his hands. "Fight over the top of those screens, Bonnie!" he yelled crossly. "Help each other out there!"

Pat, wearing her football thigh pad, had the ball. She began her hippety-hop dribble, moving down the right sideline, then back to the middle, then laterally to the left. It was "Frosty," Middleton's ball freeze, and the crowd watched breathlessly, surprised to see delaying tactics come so soon.

Lee shot a tiny look of triumph down the sideline at Joe Buckingham, Beulah's coach, wondering how he'd take it. Buckingham sat still as stone, his black eyes calmly evaluating the situation. The six bottles of water between his feet were still untouched.

Lee frowned, tugging at the knot in his tie. Buckingham knew that Pat was disabled, but he didn't know how badly. Buckingham would soon find out. More than any coach he had ever met, Lee feared and respected this one.

"Cut out the stalling, Middleton!" an iron-lunged fan bawled. "Give us some action!"

Lee laced his fingers around one knee, smiling. It felt good to be running the game. It was a feeling of authority, as if he had all those Beulah players by the hand and the crowd, too. When we move, they move.

After the big electric clock ticked off a full minute, Joe Buckingham shouted something at Vera Schultz, and the Beulah guard began to attack Pat more vigorously. And when Pat fended her off, pivoting away from her and keeping the dribble in spite of her clumsy gait, the crowd began to applaud with salvos of handclapping, as if sympathizing with the underdog team and its crippled, indomitable forward.

Lee swabbed his chin exultantly with the towel. He wished Gus Brawley were here to see the excitement and drama of this freeze. It was odd how adversity could sometimes become an advantage.

After two minutes of "Frosty," Lee wigwagged his forwards into the high-low post. Candy, a typhoon of speed, broke around her guard, calling for the ball. Pat, the rearmost player, bounced it to her. Melba had moved to the opposite corner, taking her guard with her, and Candy scooted all the way to the basket, scoring left-handed off the bank.

Lee pounded his fist triumphantly into his palm, and a long, pealing yell broke from the crowd. Beulah 2, Middleton 2.

At Beulah's end of the court, Debbie Dillon took the ball into the scoring zone, harassed every foot of the way by Frances Ice. After nearly two minutes of standing and watching the Middleton ball freeze, the Beulah forwards went eagerly to work. They set a screen and broke a left-handed forward around it, but with Freda covering tightly, the shot caromed off the ring. Debbie Dillon rebounded and swung around the opposite side, but Frances, her quick feet flashing, clogged the dribbling lane, and Debbie couldn't turn the corner. However, when the green-ribboned forward tried a set shot, Bonnie hooked her arm. The Beulah girl sank both free throws.

With Beulah leading 6–4 and one minute left in the quarter, Lee waved the Tornadoes into "Frosty." Playing for the last shot, they controlled the ball until only three seconds remained. The crowd strained to its feet to watch. Melba took the shot, a jumper from inside the corner, but it missed, and with a moan of disappointment the crowd sat down. It was then that Lee saw Joe Buckingham reach for his first bottle of water.

In the second quarter, the game's deliberate tempo stayed much the same. Lee thought he read the crowd's mood correctly. Leaning forward in their seats, the spectators buzzed as they watched with curious fascination the Middleton freezing tactics that compelled Beulah to play its style of game, denying it the momentum it might have achieved from a normal exchange of the ball.

With three minutes left in the first half, Debbie Dillon hit her first field goal over Frances, a left-handed hook, and a glad roar burst from the Beulah contingent. They had waited a long time for that shot. But thereafter, Frances attached herself to the Beulah ace like a policewoman escorting a prisoner to see the sergeant, and as Lee crossed and uncrossed his legs, pride swelled in his throat.

When Candy's free throw tied the score just before the half ended, Lee shouted to Pat, "Run 'Frosty' when we get the ball," and Pat nodded. He wanted them to freeze it until the end of the period and take the last shot.

But it was Buckingham's freeze the crowd saw

instead, and Beulah took the last shot. The green-ribboned forward delivered it from the top of a leap fifteen feet in front of the basket. The ball struck inside the ring and rebounded several times against the front and back arcs as if trying to escape. But the ring held it prisoner. Beulah led 11–9 at the half.

In the last half, Debbie Dillon again outjumped Melba, and Beulah corralled the tip. With a flash of temper, Lee drove his right fist into his left palm. Because of Pat's disability, they hadn't got a tip all night. In a low-score game like this, every possession was as precious as diamonds.

Beulah scored first on a new outside screen Buckingham had devised between halves. Watching it, Lee shifted on the hard seat and gave Buckingham credit. He had changed Debbie Dillon from shooter to feeder. They first set it against Freda, blocking her out so solidly that the left-handed forward who took Debbie Dillon's pass sped to the goal without being touched.

Lee stood. He felt his lips flatten against his teeth. "Fight through that screen, Freda! Be more aggressive! Help her, Frances!" A moment later Candy walked with the ball, giving possession to Beulah.

This time Beulah worked the outside screen against Bonnie, on the opposite side. Again Debbie Dillon flipped the feeding pass, and this time Green Ribbon had little opposition as she lifted the ball against the glass.

A profound gloom settled over the Middleton supporters. The Beulah adherents sprang to their feet and roared with joy, whistling shrilly through their teeth and stomping the bleacher floors. The champions led,

15–9. At last, the game was going down its logical groove. Lee called time out.

Tight-lipped, he rubbed his face with shaking hands, feeling as if he'd come to the edge of a cliff. A six-point deficit in a game like this could be fatal. Would they ever get it back? He relaxed, forcing himself to think calmly. He mustn't let them see him downhearted.

Eyes pleading, they looked at him trustingly in the huddle. Stooping, he diagramed the new Beulah play on the floor with chalk from his pocket. "They're trying to win it with their other two forwards," he told them. He turned to Frances. "They've made a feeder out of the Dillon girl. Next time they try it, check off her, and fill the forward's route."

He stood and looked at them entreatingly. "You can beat them. There's still half the game left. No sweat. Plenty of time to catch them."

Pat's stormy eyes swept them proudly. "Where's your fight?" she challenged. "We didn't come all the way down here to lose."

Candy frowned and squared her small shoulders. "You bet we didn't!" she seconded. "Let's try harder."

They set up the high-low post. Pat, in back court, slapped the ball twice and passed to Candy. Cutting and deploying carefully, they ran every option in their series, but Beulah defended perfectly. Each time a Middleton sortie was stopped, the Beulah fans roared triumphantly. Then Vera Schultz, unaccustomed to guarding so far away from the goal, dropped six feet off of Pat, failing to follow her into the back court.

For the first time in the game, Pat found herself

unguarded. Thirty feet from the goal, she balanced herself, sighted the ring, and thrusting upward off her right leg, flipped a long shot off her fingers. The ball rose, soared in a graceful parabola, and fell, drilling the hoop dead center. The crowd's glad roar reverberated off the walls in wild acclaim for Middleton's crippled standout.

Then Beulah changed its tactics. Debbie Dillon began to dribble alone in back court, passing off to her forwards and making no effort to work the ball in. Occasionally she would bluff a drive down the middle with Frances festooned to her, but she always turned back. A cheer, growing progressively louder, broke from the Beulah adherents. Leading 15–11, Beulah had moved skillfully into its own ball freeze. Now Joe Buckingham was running the game, and it was Lee's turn to squirm. His guards looked at him for instructions, but he shook his head. Plenty of time left. Beulah held the ball out until the end of the third quarter, maneuvering for the last shot.

Debbie Dillon took it, jumping to her full height to try an eight-footer squarely in front of the goal.

Bam! Starting her leap half a count after Debbie's, Frances Ice sprang high, swinging one long arm and blocking the ball cleanly. It spurted harmlessly across the end line as the buzzer sounded. Settling himself, Lee sighed with relief. Pat was crippled, but Frances had kept them in the game with defensive heroics that bordered on the fantastic.

Seven minutes left! The fourth quarter started like all the others, Debbie Dillon outjumping Melba, who was shorter. But this time Frances deflected the tip, and with a clumsy leap Pat intercepted her with sure hands. Lee gasped and felt the blood pounding happily in his temples. And when, after a minute and a half of "Frosty," Melba threaded the hoop from her favorite corner angle, he felt his heart leap joyfully. Two points back!

The pressure on each player was tremendous. A Beulah forward missed a free throw, and Frances pounced on the rebound. Melba double-dribbled and looked heartsick as she handed the ball to the nearest official. But half a moment later a Beulah guard wild-pitched into the crowd, restoring possession to the Tornadoes. Middleton set up its high-low post, and Pat lanced her passes in and out. Then Candy, checked beneath the goal, passed back out to Pat. Unguarded for an instant, Pat set herself and fired another long shot.

With superhuman effort, Vera Schultz flung herself on Pat, deflecting the shot but nicking Pat's wrist. An official's whistle trilled. "Foul!" he ruled. "Two shots."

Pat hobbled to the foul line. She looked once at Lee. He thrust out his lips in a confident manner, nodded his head vigorously and, with the thumb and forefinger of his right hand, described a tiny circle. *Put it up there high and easy*, his gesture told her. *Stick 'em both in there. You can do it. No problem.*

Better than anyone else, he'd rather Pat try the pressure-laden tosses, even on one leg. He looked around and saw his reserves on the bench hiding their faces in their arms, too agitated to watch the shots.

Pat faced the backboard. She placed her feet, balanced herself, pulled a short breath, looked up, got the ring in her sights, and arched the ball. *Swish*! The official waited for the crowd's crashing roar to subside before tossing it back to her for the second shot. Again Pat set herself, gulped a short breath, raised her eyes, and fired. *Swish*!

Tie score! Three minutes to play. Beulah's ball. Standing, Lee felt a choking lump in his throat. He marveled at the courage of his team. And he marveled at how absolutely and unquestioningly they accepted everything he told them. When they had fallen behind by six, he had told them they could win, and they had believed him.

Joe Buckingham motioned for time and, hidden from sight by his players, outlined his strategy. Lee knew what it would be. Ball freeze. Hold the ball out and play for the last shot. If they missed it, get the tip at the start of the overtime period and repeat the process.

Lee faced his team. Their eyes glowed with a steely confidence. "Candy, go to guard for Freda. I want you and Frances and Bonnie to press them closely. We won't give them the last shot. Watch the clock. If they still have the ball with thirty seconds left, foul them. Do it cleanly, but do it. We'll put them on the free throw line, see if they can hit. If they miss, we'll rebound and go for the last shot ourselves. If they make it, it's still our ball and we'll still go for the last shot. We'll have thirty seconds to work for it. Got it?"

Beulah began its freeze. With a low murmur of excitement, the crowd edged forward in its seats. The Middleton guards advanced warily on their opponents, creeping closer and closer. Lee shot a look at the Beulah bench and saw Joe Buckingham drain the last of his water bottles and sit back, calm and unruffled.

Back and forth Beulah's forwards whipped their

passes, feinting to go inside but always retreating. Frances tried for an interception, missed by a foot, hurried back. Candy flung herself headlong for a Beulah pass and, missing, careened ten feet on her shoulder but scrambled back.

Sitting stiffly erect, Lee watched the clock. When its hand neared the thirty-five second mark, Middleton's guards tried again, and this time they succeeded. While Candy hotly attacked the forward in the green hair ribbon from the front, windmilling her arms and yelling, Bonnie Barr slipped in behind her and stole the dribble. Lee leaped to his feet in wonder and delight, signaling time out.

In the huddle, he felt proud and humble. Their eyes shone, gazing steadily at him, beaming with faith. "High and low post," he told them above the uproar. "Unless a better shot comes, I want Melba to take the last one, a jumper."

He looked at them imploringly. "No turnovers. Stay calm. Outcool 'em. You have the advantage now. If they foul you to put you on the line, try to hit the free throw. You guards may have to play some more. If you do, try not to foul them." Squinting at him from behind the sweat patterns on their faces, they did their handshake and ran back to their stations on the court.

Play started. Lee took a deep, steadying breath and watched. Pat began her jerky dribble. Buckingham had switched guards, putting a junior on Pat and moving Vera Schultz to the high post opposite Melba. Cautiously Middleton worked the ball in and out, probing the Beulah defense for a flaw. But Beulah didn't goof. Joe Buckingham's death watch scotched every Middleton thrust.

On the clock, the yellow numerals jumped like a tumbler doing stationary somersaults—21, 20, 19, 18. Lee twisted the towel helplessly in his hands. He thought, they're going for an extra period so they'll get the tip and the ball and the last shot. They're not going to foul us. They're not going to give us a good shot, either. We'll have to take a bad one.

With four seconds to go, Melba took it. Off-balance and hounded by Vera Schultz, she almost made it. But not quite. With the crowd screaming piercingly and continuously, the ball dropped off the hoop into a forest of Beulah hands.

But a sprite in Middleton red and black darted through them, propelled herself upward and, with a quick flick of her small wrists, fingered the ball against the bank and into the ring. Candy Brown! Then came the final squawk of the buzzer and pandemonium.

Lee jumped to his feet and ran onto the court. His team, starters and substitutes, struck him in a landslide of sweaty bodies, hugging him, kissing him on both cheeks, screaming and crying wildly and happily. They tried to pick him up so they could chair him around the court, but the whole mass of them became unbalanced and toppled over in a heap.

Lee's eyesight grew dim and his hearing faded. Afterward, he discovered that his shirt pocket was torn; two buttons were gone from his blazer; and his tie was dangling down the back of his neck instead of the front where it belonged. But thinking about it later, he decided that he wouldn't have missed it for all the coffee in Brazil.

He would need a libation of strong black coffee at school the following Monday.

Chapter 14

●

The Alligator-Skin Briefcase

At Lee's final study-hall period Monday, Miss Rogers came to his desk, wringing her hands.

"Mr. Brawley is back from Mexico and wants to see you," she said breathlessly. "He's in Mr. Bannister's office—I mean Mr. Morgan's—I mean Mr. Spainhower's office. Mr. Brand is with him."

Aware of her agitation, Lee kept his voice calm. He had been expecting this. He glanced at his watch. "Tell them I'm in charge of study hall and can't leave now. I'll see them at the end of the period." His team's success wouldn't deter them, he knew. They had fired Hugh Morgan only two weeks after he had been voted High School Principal of the Year by his association.

Miss Rogers was back in half a minute, her face flooded with fear. "Mr. Brawley says to come now. I'm to watch study hall for you."

Resentment welled in Lee. He rose, clipping his mechanical pencil to his shirt pocket. Not wishing to frighten her further, he concealed his anger and left.

In the hall he walked through groups of milling students who greeted him cordially. "Hello, Mr. Driskill." "Congratulations, Mr. Driskill." "Hello, sir."

The students had wanted to honor the squad in assembly. Pat Thompson and Frances Ice had been voted to the first all-state team and Candy Brown to the second. But Horace Hawkins, the principal, told everybody that the Board of Education had forbidden a victory celebration for the present.

As Lee walked into the superintendent's office, he saw Spainhower cowering against the wall, his weak hands fluttering apprehensively. The superintendent had no place to sit because George Brand had appropriated his swivel chair. Gus Brawley stood in the middle of the room, expensively dressed in a coffee-brown suit, brown suede shoes, and a muffler of yellow plaid. Probably as a result of his fishing trip, his face and hands were as tan as saddle leather. When Lee came in, Brawley moved behind him, closing and locking the door.

Then Brawley walked back to Spainhower's desk, sat on the edge and, folding his arms across his chest, looked at Lee coldly. "Mr. Driskill," he began, speaking deliberately. "Before you leave this room, I want you to write out your resignation as girls basketball coach and history teacher of Middleton High School, effective at the end of this school year."

Lee pushed his hands into his pockets. Coolly he asked, "What are the board's charges against me?"

Brawley glared at him as if asking the question was a gross impertinence. "Mr. Driskill, you've flouted the authority of this board since the first year you arrived in Middleton. Although you've been warned several times, you've persisted in this flagrant defiance, baiting us and mocking us. This board has finally grown tired of your abuse and has decided to defend itself against you."

Lee grinned crookedly. He was tired of polite talk. "That was beautifully done, Mr. Brawley. You did it so well that you almost believe it yourself. But you named no specific action of mine that has brought all this on. Surely you can think of one."

A controlled hostility came into Brawley's face. His big nose began to lift, and his thatchlike brows to knit together. "Don't be lippy, Mr. Driskill. We know how to reach lippy people."

Lee chuckled mirthlessly. "I'll say you do. You've reached me pretty well. You've just fired me. You say the Board of Education has taken this action. Does Mr. Myerson or Mr. McGuire or Mr. Kiley know about it?" Lee nodded toward the banker sitting sullenly in the superintendent's chair. "Have you even bothered to tell George Brand yet?"

Brawley began to puff and swell like an adder getting ready to strike. Enjoying it, Lee looked him in the eye and kept talking. "Why do you keep saying that the Board of Education did this or that? Everybody in town knows you're the Board of Education in Middleton. You come close to running everything else in this town, too—everything except the girls basketball team—and I won't let you run that. And that's why you're firing me."

Brawley's hooded eyes took on a shrewd cunning look. When he spoke, his voice was soft, intimate, almost reassuring. "Mr. Driskill, the Board of Education isn't discharging you. You're going to resign only the coaching and the high school teaching. Then we'll find something else for you to do—like teaching a room in our elementary school. Of course, you'd lose your coaching bonus. Your salary would be reduced. But the board is not discharging you."

Feeling a queer bitter amusement, Lee stared at him, trying to get it straight in his mind. They could do this without having to give him the public hearing that the state law required when a teacher was discharged. That was how they had got Hugh Morgan. Not by firing him, but by threatening to demote him, to cut his salary and shame him before the entire town until he left of his own volition and sought other employment.

The school board president was watching Lee like a hawk. "You asked a minute ago for a reason. All right, Mr. Driskill. You know the reason as well as I. Your arbitrary action of playing that married girl in the state tournament after our superintendent"—he nodded toward Spainhower—"had not given you permission, and after board member George Brand"—he nodded toward the banker—"warned you that it violated the wishes of a majority of the board left the board no alternative but to discipline you."

Brawley reached behind him and pulled open a drawer of Spainhower's desk. "If you don't resign, we'll strip you anyhow. But a resignation is quieter and cleaner." He extracted a blank sheet of bond stationery that bore at the top the printed letterhead of the Middleton schools. He laid it on the desk between himself and Lee, releasing it with an upward flourish of his hand.

Lee studied him, feeling no consternation. He knew he had lost his coaching job, but he wasn't signing anything. In spite of all their obstruction, he had coached their team to the state championship. They could never take that away from him or the girls.

Brawley went on, purring smoothly. "And don't get conceited about winning that tournament last week at Seymour City. You used an ineligible player." His black eyes glittered triumphantly. "We'll expect Mr. Spainhower to write four letters tomorrow. One will go to the commissioner of the state high school athletic association, the others to the superintendents at Dellaplane, Rawlins, and Beulah high schools. Each letter will say that Middleton is forfeiting all three games it won in the state tournament, and forfeiting the state championship, too."

Fury flamed in Lee, and his hands came clawing out of his pockets. He felt as if someone had kicked him in the groin. Then he remembered, and he struggled to regain mastery over his emotions, but he knew that he had failed.

Brawley's eyes were like black ice. They probed Lee's face with the most rigid keenness, searching for evidences of what Brawley enjoyed most in life, watching an opponent's writhings and sufferings after he had shocked him into an emotional funk.

Without a word to any of them, Lee unbolted the

door and walked out. The halls were silent, and through the second-story windows he saw the last of the students disappearing toward home in the big red buses. He drove to the Ford agency and found Jean. They sat together in the front seat and he told her about it.

"No use to feel all torn up," she comforted, reaching over and patting his hand. "Everybody in the state knows you're a good coach. You can catch on at half a dozen schools."

Lee's jaw tightened. "I don't want to leave this one. I wish there was some way to beat him. This school has been putting up with his tyranny for a long time."

He knew that Jean was more hurt than she let on. They would have to sell the house and give up the yard.

Next morning before dawn, Lee sat up and swung his bare feet to the floor. Careful not to waken Jean, he stood and with an angry effort stretched. Gazing out the window, he saw that it was going to be a nice day, and then he remembered that there was something wrong with it, and his hands shook as he drew on his trousers.

This was the day they were going to take the state championship away from his team. He shaved, dried his face, finished dressing, got in his car, and headed for town. The sun peeked suddenly over the red hills, stabbing the scene with long streamers of light.

As he drove, he looked around. He had grown fond of this country, the gentle hills barred in white gypsum, the reddish tips of the willows growing around the ponds, the small concrete farm homes with the sandy land plowed right up to the houses as if the owners were reluctant to lose a foot of profit, the shortgrass shimmering in the distance. It was a country and a job worth fighting for.

In Middleton's business section the wind shook the streetlights, rattled the shopwindows, and flung the town's flagpole rope and chain noisily against the steel staff. In the sun's flat rays the varnished sign looked a little weatherworn, but it was still there: Stooky & Son, Attorneys-at-Law.

When Lee pushed against the glass door, it opened. He took one step inside and knew that he had found his man. An aroma of fresh-perked coffee drifted from the back room, and he heard something bubbling in a pot. Despite his nervous stomach the smell excited his taste buds.

"Mr. Stooky?" he called tentatively.

"Sam Stooky here." From behind the partition the same harsh, discordant voice jangled like bells out of tune. "Be with you in a minute."

Soon the lawyer appeared bearing a bright pewter mug filled with hot coffee. His backswept gray hair was whiter and thinner, but his blue eyes sparkled keenly.

"Well! It's the girls basketball coach." He set the mug on an old walnut table and came forward, extending a big hand. "How about a congratulatory cup of coffee?" he asked as he and Lee shook hands.

It was nice to be recognized after four years. Stooky fetched a second cup. They sat down. Lee tried a swallow of the hot beverage but scarcely tasted it.

The lawyer pushed a white sugar bowl with a spoon in it toward Lee. "What can I do for you, young man?"

Full of his mission, Lee talked for fifteen minutes, describing one by one his disagreements with Gus Brawley and the school board, including the one in the superintendent's office the previous afternoon.

"Hmmmm!" Sam Stooky growled amiably. "I'd have to say Gus is a pretty good judge of coaching talent. If I remember correctly the occasion of your previous visit, he forced you to take the girls coaching position against your will. And now that you've won the state championship and made him look good, he decides he's made a horrendous mistake." His blue eyes twinkled. "Sounds like he's crazy as popcorn on a hot stove."

Lee leaned forward, his insides tensing. He knew he had the jitters again. "I want to stop them from forfeiting our state championship," he said earnestly. "It isn't fair. My team has worked too hard and gone through too much. I'd like you to represent me. But you'd have to work fast."

The lawyer reached down into a wire wastebasket and came up with a discarded envelope that bore an address and canceled postmark. Fascinated, Lee watched. Stooky reached across the table for a letter opener with a bone handle and slit the used envelope down both sides, spreading it out on the table, blank side up. He reached in his shirt pocket for a mechanical pencil and looked quizzically at Lee. "Now about that young lady—Frances Ice—who used to be Frances—let's see—Bonner, wasn't it? When did you first ask permission for her to play basketball? And when was it first denied you and by whom? You talk, and I'll take notes."

Two mugs of coffee later, Sam Stooky stood. Although the envelope was only half covered with scribbling, he seemed satisfied. "I'll be glad to represent you. And I'll go right to work on it. Seems to me I've heard of another case like this several years ago. The attorney general's office in the state capital opens at nine o'clock. I have a friend there. I'll telephone him first. Why don't you phone me at noon, and I'll tell you where we stand?"

Lee rose, feeling a little better. He had to return home and drive Jean to work. A slight scratching drew his attention to an old iron stove that stood cold and unused in the corner. Its door was open. Through it, the big yellow cat with the extravagantly whiskered cheeks leaped softly to the floor. It stretched comfortably, thrusting out each padded foot in turn.

A raspy chuckle escaped Sam Stooky. "You remember Buck, don't you? He sleeps in the old stove now. He's sort of a third partner. Young Sam and I considered sending him off to the university for a refresher course in jurisprudence, but Buck didn't want to go. He's a shortgrass cat. I guess he doesn't like all those student demonstrations. Besides, there wouldn't be any stove for him to sleep in over there."

"Mmmrrow," Buck meowed hoarsely, and padded into the rear room and out the door.

Old Sam laughed. "Ever since he ate Flossie White's canary, he thinks he can sing."

At the *Mirror* office Lee found Saul Myerson bending over a hand press. When Lee told him what had happened, the editor took it coolly. Reaching behind him, he untied his shop apron. "So they've held another rump meeting and forgot to invite me. Probably a chili dinner at Brawley's or an ice cream supper at George Brand's mansion. But I can see why they didn't want me at this one. So they're going to forfeit your championship? And reward you by dropping you to janitor? We'll fight 'em! Got any plans?"

Lee told him what he had done.

Saul reached for his hat. "Good! Glad you got Sam Stooky. He's reliable. I can raise the money the legal action costs right here on Main Street."

At noon Lee dialed the lawyer's telephone number. The elder Stooky came on the line. Lee fought down his excitement. He had a lot riding on this call.

"Mr. Driskill? Stooky speaking. I talked to the attorney general's office. As a personal favor, they looked up the law for us on this. Found something interesting." Lee felt a flash of hope. "I've asked them to wire me the information. We should have it in an hour. I'll go myself to the Western Union office and get it. We'll confront them with it this afternoon and see what happens. Can you be at my office at, say, about three thirty?"

Mystified, Lee felt his throat tighten. Confront them with it? Was that all they were going to do? How did Stooky expect to stop Brawley in eight and one half hours when nobody else had stopped him in twenty years?

Lee was there at three twenty-five. Saul Myerson walked up, wearing his old green topcoat and carrying the battered, black portable typewriter case. "I'm going along. I have two good reasons. The school board's involved and I'm still on the board. Also, this is one rump session the *Mirror* aims to cover." He looked shrewdly at Lee, his brown eyes crinkling. "Give the people light and they'll find their own way—with the help of the *Mirror*."

They walked in and met Sam Stooky's son, who wore long, slanting sideburns and a gray tweed suit. He shook hands with Myerson, then took his pipe out of his mouth and greeted Lee Driskill. "I'm proud to meet you. Congratulations on what your team did at Seymour City. The whole town's excited."

Old Sam was all business. He slipped quickly into the gray topcoat that his son held for him. Young Sam looked at him, grinning. "All set, Dad? Sheriff on his way?"

Old Sam picked up a worn briefcase of brown alligator skin, which had a hole so big in one corner that it looked as if the alligator had bitten himself. In his harsh, clanging voice he said, "Sheriff ought to be there now. So had the prisoner."

He turned courteously to Lee. "Shall we go, Mr. Driskill?" He led the way out the back door to his car, parked in an alley.

In the hall outside the superintendent's office, groups of stern-faced students silently eyed them. Heads turned, and boys and girls whispered among themselves as they passed. Lee saw some of his players standing in a sober, anxious group.

Bonnie Bradshaw stepped forward. "Mr. Driskill, we just heard. Losing the championship is bad, but losing you would be awful."

Melba's smoky eyes flamed. "I'm mad enough to march on Brawley and Brand by myself. I've got my sign all ready to paint."

Lee grinned. "Thank you. I guess we'll find out something after this meeting. I'll see you in the morning."

Pat shook her head positively. "No sir, Mr. Driskill. We want to know today. We'll wait right here until you come out."

In the superintendent's office they found Spainhower, Brawley, and Ora Blessingame, the sheriff, seated around the table. Blessingame, a big fellow who wore a silver badge pinned to the front of his tan jacket, sat back comfortably against the wall, drawing a small pocket comb through his walrus moustache. Spainhower looked cowed, but Brawley, resplendent in a blue suit and jeweled cuff links, sat in a cold defiant fury, his black eyes darting searchingly over each of them in turn.

"Will you please explain," he demanded of Sam Stooky, "why it is necessary to send the sheriff for me? After all, I donated the land on which this school stands, and I've served on its Board of Education for the last twenty years."

"Nobody sent the sheriff for you, Gus," Sam Stooky rasped gently. "The sheriff merely called on you to serve you with a peremptory writ of mandamus signed by the district judge. He also served one on Superintendent Spainhower."

Anger flared in Brawley's craggy face. "Why?"

"The writ tells why. You were probably too upset to read your copy." The lawyer patted the old alligator-skin briefcase so vigorously that Lee feared its contents might spill out the rent in one corner. "It's all here," Stooky soothed. "We'll talk about it when Jack Sides gets here. He's still the attorney for the Board of Education, isn't he?"

Brawley bristled. "Why do we need him? I didn't call him."

"I called him," said Stooky. "Thought it might save time. He should be here any minute."

Brawley's dimpled chin began to lift and his bushy eyebrows to knit together. "Sir, you take too much on yourself. We've never needed an attorney before."

Stooky's blue eyes twinkled. "You need one now, Gus."

A timid knock disclosed Miss Rogers, tense and fearful, holding the door only three inches ajar. "Mr. Sides is here."

Mr. Sides, bald as a billiard ball, walked in and glanced around. Surprised and confused, he sat down in the steam-heated room without taking off his gray-checked topcoat.

Stooky stood. "Jack, I think you know everybody here." He looked around the table, "Except maybe Mr. Driskill, the girls basketball coach?"

Sides scrambled to his feet with a look of pleasure. He shook hands warmly with Lee. "It's nice to meet you, Mr. Driskill. Our daughter Margaret is going out for basketball this spring. Mrs. Sides and I are looking forward to having you coach her."

"Thank you," Lee replied quietly. The compliment couldn't have come at a more appropriate time.

"That's why we're here," Stooky's gravelly voice

intoned. "If Mr. Brawley has his way, Mr. Driskill won't be coaching Margaret next year or any of our other high school girls."

Sides looked more puzzled than ever. "Oh?"

Brawley scowled, peering at his watch. "Let's get on with it, gentlemen. I have a meeting at five o'clock with our church vestry board."

"Very well." Sam Stooky clicked open his shabby briefcase and distributed tissue copies of something to everyone. "This peremptory writ of mandamus, signed by District Judge Harper, prohibits Mr. Brawley, the Middleton Board of Education, Superintendent Spainhower, or anybody in their administration from forfeiting the state championship in girls basketball just won by Middleton High School for the reason that Frances Ice, one of the Middleton players, was ineligible, or for any other reason."

Stooky paused and looked meaningfully around the table. "It also enjoins the said Mr. Brawley, the school board, Superintendent Spainhower, or anybody in their school administration from demoting in any way Mr. Driskill, the coach of Middleton High School, because he played Frances Ice in the state tournament or for any other reason. I believe this has already been served on both Mr. Brawley and Mr. Spainhower. Is that correct, Mr. Blessingame?" The sheriff nodded elaborately, then gazed modestly at the floor and again began combing his moustache.

Stooky picked up another sheaf of copies and began distributing them. Punching his own copy with a pudgy forefinger, he looked around perceptively. "Here are two separate opinions from the state attorney general, one dated 1958, the other 1960, both dealing with the right of a married child of school age to attend school and enjoy the same privileges as other students attending said school, including the right to participate in extracurricular activities, such as band, vocal music not offered for credit." He paused, gazing meaningfully this time at Sides instead of at Brawley although the latter was listening, his black eyes cold and alert.

" . . . athletics, class parties, class plays, etc., etc. In both cases the attorney general ruled that school boards cannot place restrictions on the activities of married students of either sex under this authority." This time he looked straight at Brawley. "Gentlemen, the opinion of the attorney general is the law in this state until overruled by the courts."

Brawley looked blank. For once, he had nothing to say. Jack Sides had removed his topcoat and was reading everything closely and thoughtfully.

Sides faced Sam Stooky. "Could Mr. Brawley, Mr. Spainhower, and myself be excused while we confer in the superintendent's private office?"

Stooky nodded. "Of course."

The three men retired to the other office, Sides carrying all the papers Stooky had given him. Lee sat back, marveling at the power of lawyers and how everybody listened to them. Stooky and Sides were pulling the strings, running the show.

In five minutes, the men returned and resumed their seats around the table. Spainhower's face was ashen, Brawley's sullen and withdrawn. Sides looked around politely.

"Both Mr. Brawley and Mr. Spainhower accept Mr. Stooky's disclosure and interpretation of the attorney general's ruling," he announced. "Mr. Brawley has assured me that the Board of Education will not demote Mr. Driskill in any way or forfeit the state championship won by his team."

A thrill of triumph ran wildly through Lee. They had won!

Stooky's head bobbed agreeably up and down. "Very well. I'll file a dismissal in the morning."

Brawley stood, drawing himself up into a posture of self-righteousness. "Gentlemen," he began in his soft, contemptuous tones, "I see I've come to that point in my life where I must take the garbage as well as the garlands. The time comes when a man who has devoted the best years of his life to courageous public school service finds himself ruthlessly cast aside because he dares to stand for principles he knows to be right. This has happened to me and to Middleton." His black eyes swept haughtily, left to right. "But, gentlemen, I do not apologize for my position. Good day."

Saul Myerson's scornful chuckle intruded. "My heart bleeds for you, Gus," he said. "I've been checking up on you with the editor of your hometown paper back in Calico, Texas. Editors know the people in their towns the way they know every key in their typewriters. Your editor tells me that at Calico you were the high school basketball coach. He says you failed as a coach because you couldn't get along with young men and young women. Then you became a superintendent, and you failed in that for the same reason. Now I'm going to tell you why you've given our coach here so much trouble. You resent a successful coach because you could never be one yourself. You'll tolerate and protect a poor coach or a poor superintendent"—he motioned toward Spainhower—"because you can't stand to have a good one around. Take a tumble to yourself, fella, and try to straighten up."

Brawley reached casually for his topcoat. He draped it over one arm and walked slowly around the table. Lee blinked, admiring the man's self-possession. He's still warm and snug in his own ego, Lee thought. He still lives by himself in a tree.

In the doorway, Brawley faced them, his black eyes flicking disdainfully from face to face. "Garbage as well as garlands. Good day, gentlemen."

"Nuts!" Saul Myerson snickered. Brawley walked out.

Sam Stooky stood, stuffing papers into his briefcase. He turned to Lee. "Well, young man. Feel better?"

Lee shook his head incredulously. "How can I thank you? That's the first time I've ever seen him back down."

Old Sam chuckled modestly. "Gus is a power man. He understands power. He uses power to gain his ends. But he also respects power when it's used against him."

Lee said, "What's the bill? Whatever it is, I'm going to enjoy paying it."

Stooky snapped the old briefcase shut. "It's all taken care of. All I expect is to be paid for my time. Saul Myerson raised so much money downtown that I had to give some of it back. Your team and their papas and mamas wanted to help, too. They've been having meetings all over the place."

Lee held his coat for him; then they all walked outside. The number of students still waiting had grown to fifty, Lee's players among them. When Myerson told them, "Everything is jake. You keep the championship and the coach keeps his job," their cheering shook the halls.

Lee got into his own car and looked at his watch—almost five o'clock. He just had time to meet Jean and tell her they were staying in Middleton after all.

Next morning the school had its victory celebration in assembly, which Dale Spainhower presided over gracefully enough. When it ended and eleven o'clock classes convened, Pat Thompson waited for Lee at his desk in the gymnasium. Her rust-brown hair tumbled almost to the shoulders of her red woolen coat, which had gold buckles sewn to each pocket. The coat was open, disclosing her white blouse and beige corduroy skirt.

"Mr. Driskill, may I talk to you a minute?" she said.

Lee stood. "Sure, Pat." She seemed depressed.

"Mom just telephoned that my scholarship offer from the Quinlan Queens arrived special delivery this morning. Dad came home from the post office, proudly carrying it."

Lee beamed. "That's fine, Pat. Congratulations."

Pat looked miserable. "Mr. Driskill, I don't want to go."

Lee stared at her, puzzled. "Don't you want to play more basketball?"

She shook her head and looked him in the eye. "No. I want to go to teachers college and be a lady."

Lee liked her decision. Pat was growing up. He

nodded understandingly. "Fine, Pat. I think that's sensible."

To his astonishment, her face puckered up, and she looked as if she were about to cry. "Daddy won't think so. He's set his heart on my playing with the Queens. He's home now waiting for me to sign that scholarship so he can mail it back to Mr. Schulte and then brag about it all over town."

Lee stroked his chin reflectively. He liked having his players bring their personal problems to him, liked his close relationship with them. He thought, this is the best thing of all about coaching—better even than the excitement and the winning. It's a knitting together, like a father and his daughters. If I ever stop coaching I'll miss this most of all. To Pat he said, "All you can do is to tell him how you feel."

She looked at him imploringly. "Mr. Driskill, will you go with me?"

Lee drove her to the Thompson farm at noon. He did so reluctantly, feeling that he was intruding in a family matter. He had heard that the big auctioneer had a nasty temper, but he went because Pat had asked him. Frank Thompson's green pickup stood parked near the barn.

They walked into the living room. Dorothy Thompson, Pat's mother, sat in a rocking chair, shelling peas. She glanced up, surprised. Pat looked at her gravely and sniffed once. A black cocker, stub tail blurring, flashed down a stairway and danced around Pat affectionately, but the girl was too choked with emotion to notice him.

Lee licked his upper lip. "Mrs. Thompson, Pat's got

a problem that she can't talk to her dad about. She asked me to come home with her while she tells him. It's about that scholarship offer from the Quinlan Queens. She doesn't want to go."

Pat hung her head. Surprised, Lee looked from one to the other. Pat hadn't even talked to her mother about it.

The back door slammed. Lee looked nervously over his shoulder and told himself, here's where I get punched. Mrs. Thompson got up and set the kettle of peas on the cabinet. "Mr. Driskill, here comes Frank. He'll blow his top when he first hears about this. But he cools off quick."

Frank Thompson, wearing his big hat and carrying an armload of blackjack logs for the fireplace, came into the kitchen. When he saw Lee, he halted. "Hello, Coach. What in God's world is going on?"

Pat faced her father. She sniffed a couple of times, then found her voice. "Daddy, I'm not going to school at Quinlan College. I don't want to play more basketball. I want to go to teachers college and learn to be an elementary school teacher. I want to teach children."

Frank Thompson stared at Pat, his face stiff with shock. Then his neck reddened with rage, and he hurled the armful of logs onto the rug with a fearful crash. The black cocker dropped its ears and darted under a nearby table.

Slack-jawed, the auctioneer took two steps toward his daughter. His lips twitched, and his eyes went flint hard. He breathed through his open mouth in gasping inhalations.

"Well then," he told Pat, "don't come home no more."

Lee's jaw dropped, and he stood with his mouth open. Had he heard the man correctly? Dorothy Thompson stood, quiet and unruffled, waiting.

Pat's response was perfect. She knew her father's moods as she knew every pass and route in the Middleton basketball offense. She ran to him, clasping him around the neck and hiding her auburn head against his big chest. "Oh, Daddy," she sobbed, "I'm so sorry for you. I know how badly you wanted me to play with the Queens."

A strange confusion came into Frank Thompson's moon face. His big arms came up around Pat. With one hand he stroked her hair fondly. "There, there," he comforted her gently. "You don't have to go with the Queens if you don't want to. We'll be glad to send you to teachers college." Lee blinked and felt almost like crying himself. Frank added, "You know I'm crazy about you, honey. I didn't mean what I said about your not coming home no more."

Dorothy Thompson looked at him coolly. "Of course, you didn't. Or I'd have gone with her."

Frank began picking up the logs. Lee helped him. The black cocker thrust its head from beneath the white fringed tablecloth, its bright eyes investigating the scene.

After a minute, Pat blew her nose and looked at Lee. "Thank you for coming home with me, Mr. Driskill," she said, red-eyed and smiling.

Lee moved off toward the door. "See you tomorrow."

Pat stood there, trim and straight, her head held slightly on one side. "Tomorrow," she said simply, "is the first day of the rest of my life."

For a moment, Lee stood there. Again that haunting line from the A. E. Housman poem ran through his mind. Brief garland. He wondered how coaching at Middleton would be without a girl like Pat Thompson.

Frank Thompson walked with Lee to the car. He said, "You've been through it, haven't you?"

Lee dropped his eyes and toed the Bermuda grass. "I've probably been through something that wasn't any of my business."

"Hoo haw!" scoffed Frank Thompson softly. "Anything that's Pat's business is your business and my business both."

As Lee drove back to town to pick up Jean, he thought that he had just witnessed Pat Thompson's finest hour. Knowing when to quit was a rare quality, a quality possessed only by champions.

And so passed the month of March in Lee Driskill's fourth year at Middleton. Looking back on it later, he thought it the most eventful month of his life. Not only had his team won the state championship but it was in March that Doctor York was persuaded to be a candidate for the Board of Education and defeated George Brand handily, wresting the balance of power away from Gus Brawley's clique.

The new board quickly elected Saul Myerson president and began holding regular meetings in various ward schools, encouraging parents and teachers to attend. A course in family living, preparing young people for marriage, was introduced, and a specialist brought in to teach it. Dale Spainhower and Horace Hawkins resigned. Hugh Morgan left his post as principal at Crockett to become superintendent at Middleton. Lee received a solid raise.

And that wasn't all. At six o'clock in the morning of the last day of March, a muffled buzzing cut insistently through the darkness at the Driskill home. Awakening, Lee raised his head. It was the telephone, and its strident summons, pealing at regular intervals, alarmed him with its possibility of accident or disaster.

He walked barefoot into the living room to answer it. "Hullo," he mumbled sleepily.

"Lee Driskill? This is Judge Rutherford. Do you and Mrs. Driskill still want to adopt a baby? There's one available at the Baptist Hospital in Seymour City. Third floor. Born yesterday. It's not a boy. Everybody wants a boy, and we're fresh out. This one's a girl. The adoption people say she's yours right now, if you want her."

Wild with excitement, Lee tried to swallow but couldn't. "You bet we want her, Judge. We'll dress quickly and jump in the car. It's only a hundred and fifteen miles. The road through this old shortgrass country is flat and easy."

His hand shook as he hung up the telephone. Three years ago he would have insisted on a son.

But not anymore. He hurried into the bedroom to waken Jean.

About the Author

Harold Keith writes with sympathy and understanding about the world of sports. Not only did he play and coach high school basketball in Oklahoma, but for thirty-nine years he has been Director of Sports Information at the University of Oklahoma. Although he attended Northwestern State Teachers' College in Alva, Oklahoma, Mr. Keith has been an observer of girls' high school basketball in the shortgrass country of southwestern Oklahoma where *Brief Garland* is set.

He was graduated from the University of Oklahoma at Norman, where he also earned a master's degree in history. Mr. Keith's first story was published when he was fourteen years old, in a magazine called *Lone Scout*. For years he wrote sports stories for the *American Boy*. He has also published a number of books, among them *Rifles for Watie,* winner of the 1958 Newbery Medal, *Komantcia,* and *Sports and Games*.